Familienunternehmen und KMU

Sowohl Familienunternehmen als auch kleine und mittlere Unternehmen (KMU) zeichnen sich durch eine Reihe spezifischer Besonderheiten aus, die ihnen im Marktumfeld einen klaren Wettbewerbsvorteil bieten aber auch zu besonderen Risiken führen können. Die vorliegende Schriftenreihe präsentiert wissenschaftliche Arbeiten, die einen empirischen und theoretischen Beitrag zur Erkundung dieser Besonderheiten und deren Auswirkungen auf die betriebswirtschaftliche Praxis leisten. Übergeordnetes Ziel ist es, die Theorieentwicklung des Managements von Familienunternehmen und KMU voranzutreiben. Both Family Firms and Small and Medium Sized Enterprises (SME) feature a number of distinct behaviors and characteristics which could provide them with a competitive advantage in the market but could also lead to certain risks. The scientific series at hand presents research which provides an empirical and theoretical contribution to the investigation on these specific characteristics and their impact on business practice. The overall aim of this series is to advance the development of theory in the areas of family firm and SME management.

Kirsten Stotmeister

Publicly Traded Family Businesses

A Long-Term Study on Family Involvement and Company Longevity

Springer Gabler

Kirsten Stotmeister
Waldshut-Tiengen, Germany

Dissertation Zeppelin University, 2023
Supervisors: Prof. Dr. Hermut Kormann, Prof. Dr. Torsten M. Pieper, Prof. Dr. Jörn Hendrich Block
Date of Oral Examination: May 31st, 2023

ISSN 2520-1174 ISSN 2520-1182 (electronic)
Familienunternehmen und KMU
ISBN 978-3-658-44302-3 ISBN 978-3-658-44303-0 (eBook)
https://doi.org/10.1007/978-3-658-44303-0

This Springer Gabler imprint is published by the registered company Springer Fachmedien Wiesbaden GmbH, part of Springer Nature.
The registered company address is: Abraham-Lincoln-Str. 46, 65189 Wiesbaden, Germany

… to my Family.

Foreword

Dr. Stotmeister's research project is embedded in a larger, comprehensive research program to understand the longevity of family businesses. The analysis of the longevity of family-owned companies that are listed on the stock exchange should reveal particularly important prerequisites and constraints. Listed family businesses either enjoy superior qualifications for achieving longevity, as they combine the advantages stemming from family influence with the additional options available to listed companies, or they suffer from reduced performance in the longevity test, which would reveal specific risks for longevity in general.

The dissertation examines several issues of critical importance, such as drivers of longevity, growth and survival (or demise) of publicly listed family businesses, and the family-specific attributes behind these drivers. To explore these relationships, Dr. Stotmeister created a unique dataset of family-owned enterprises that launched their IPOs between 1950 and 1988. She further enhanced her database by extending the observation period to 2018 and including more recent narrative evidence. Given the importance of family businesses to the German economy (and to pretty much any economy in the world), the importance and relevance of the research are apparent. Moreover, with many family businesses and family-sponsored ventures entering the stock market, it is vital to understand what makes these businesses last over the long run.

Other researchers have looked at the phenomenon before. However, Dr. Stotmeister's work takes the research to the next level by analyzing changes over an extended period of time and taking into account a host of explanatory variables not previously considered. Moreover, Dr. Stotmeister supplements her quantitative findings with a narrative analysis that adds rich and vivid insights. With her research, Dr. Stotmeister is able to shed light on a persistent conundrum that prior studies on the topic were unable to resolve to this point. That is, how do growth aspirations and family involvement interact when organizations enter the stock market through an IPO, how do they develop over time, and how do surviving organizations differ in these characteristics from their unsuccessful (early failed) counterparts. Clearly, Dr. Stotmeister is well positioned to inform these questions through her groundbreaking work, and thereby change the current state of affairs and advance the field and business practice in significant ways.

Dr. Stotmeister's work is important in several respects. Her review of the literature is comprehensive. The identification of a persistent gap in current knowledge is precise and apt. Based on this gap, she identifies an integrated line of inquiry that she effectively answers with her study. In particular, her focus on family-specific factors of influence is to be commended since the literature still lacks widespread acknowledgement of the family side of family business, and scholars have been calling for this type of research for quite some time.

Dr. Stotmeister's research is highly relevant to family business owners and their advisors. Going public is a momentous decision for a family business and its many stakeholders. There is hardly any trial and error, and reversing the decision by delisting is only possible in rare cases. Therefore, it is of utmost importance to analyze the experience of previous IPOs in order to provide the stakeholders with a balanced view of the pros and cons. The conclusion based on this research is that family shareholders need to think twice before going public. If they do not want to see the family's influence disappear within a generation or two, they need to take at least some of the steps outlined in this study.

Prof. Dr. Hermut Kormann
Zeppelin University
Friedrichshafen, Germany

Prof. Dr. Torsten M. Pieper
The University of North Carolina at Charlotte
Charlotte, USA

Acknowledgements

Many people have accompanied me on the path to this dissertation, without whom I wouldn´t have achieved the goal in the way I have. As a working mother, I was struggling to find the right way to approach this journey—uncertain about whether it was even possible to combine the given circumstances into a construct that would allow for the necessary time and effort for this dissertation.

In the very beginning, my dear friend, Laura Seibold, had introduced me to the idea of asking Apl. Prof. Dr. Hermut Kormann to be my first supervisor. The first introductory meeting was the beginning of a wonderful and inspiring adventure together. For a while, it was the three of us conquering the topic of *stock-listed family businesses*. I am grateful to Laura for sharing her experience and advice with me.

Apl. Prof. Dr. Hermut Kormann not only embodied a supervisor, but he was also a mentor. I have enjoyed the long discussions and value his experience, his wealth of knowledge and his infinite passion for family business and business family research. He not only offered helpful advice regarding my research, but also regarding my own shareholding family issues, and therefore helped shape my work as a family officer.

Shortly after beginning my journey, I met Prof. Dr. Torsten M. Pieper, who guided me as second supervisor. He welcomed me into the international world of family business research in a very motivating, yet challenging manner. He always had a tickling comment at the right time, which inspired new thoughts and ensured an open mind. I am very grateful for the honest and open collaboration. His mentoring enabled personal growth.

Prof. Dr. Jörn Hendrich Block joined my journey along the way. He provided me with supportive honesty and guidance through his large store of knowledge and experience. I very much appreciate his support and his immediate availability for discussions.

I would like to thank Prof. Dr. Reinhard Prügl for always being available for advice and intellectual exchange. I look forward to future get-togethers at ZU.

A big thank you goes to the team of the ZU Graduate School. They assisted me in any possible way. The support I experienced on behalf of ZUGS was flawless and immediate.

Moving on to the most valuable people, without whom I never would have been able to achieve this. First of all, my children—even though they were still very small, they accepted the circumstances and supported me the only way little children can. My husband Kim played a key role by taking care of our children when I was busy once again. He took the night shifts when the children were sick or took them on excursions when I needed time to work. He was a very good listener with whom I could discuss my thoughts. We are a wonderful team and I thank you for everything.

Another key role was played by my mother, Ulrike. She jumped in for childcare whenever necessary. She always had an open ear for the upsides and downsides of my journey, and she gave me motivation when I needed it. I am grateful that I can trust you completely.

I would like to thank my father, Jochen, for putting so much trust into me. He has offered me so many opportunities. I have been accompanying him for many years in our family business and have learned so much from him on so many different levels. His achievements are incredible, and I am proud to be able to learn from him.

My sister, Katja, and my brother, Carlo, have been part of my life, not only as close siblings, but also as fellow shareholders. They have showed me how siblings can successfully combine two relationships—the emotional familial ties and the rational shareholder responsibilities. I am very grateful for our close and trustful relationship, in the past, the present and in future.

Finally, I would like to mention my grandfather, Fritz Stotmeister, the founder of our family business. He recognized the importance of nourishing family bonds at a very early stage, also for the benefit of the company. We miss him dearly and value his life work.

Habt's nett mitänand.

Abstract

Many international scholars have tackled the field of family business research in recent years, studying the phenomena accompanying this special form of business from various angles and thereby uncovering fascinating observations. Our pool of knowledge has grown considerably larger. However, there is a research gap regarding stock-listed family businesses, waiting to be filled. This is where this study latches on, with a research focus on German stock-listed family firm longevity and family involvement. With an observation period comprising 68 years, German family businesses with an IPO launch between 1950 and 1988 have been screened for changes regarding family shareholding and involvement along the timeline until the end of observation in 2018. The study comprises two parts. Initially, a survival analysis has been conducted by applying Cox PH models and Kaplan-Meier Estimators. Secondly, a more qualitative analysis has been conducted in order to complement the empirical findings. The analyses have revealed insightful findings, which have been combined into a model describing success factors supporting stock-listed family firm longevity and, in the end, have allowed for deriving practical advice for future family firm decision makers.

Contents

Abbreviations

AFT	Accelerated Failure Time
AktG	Aktiengesetz
AO	Active Ownership
DM	Deutsche Mark
EB	Executive board
FC	Family control
FO	Family ownership
HR	Hazard ratio
IPO	Initial Public Offering
KM	Kaplan-Meier
M	Mean
M&A	Merger and acquisition
Max	Maximum value
Min	Minimum value
MorA	Merger or acquisition
MorA/A	Acquisition
N	Absolute number
NS Regime	National Socialist Regime
PH	Proportional Hazards
PIE	Public Interest Entity
P-value	Probability value
WW II	World War II
SD	Standard deviation
SEW	Socioemotional Wealth
ST	Survival time
TF	Time frame
TO	Turnover

List of Figures

List of Tables

1 Introduction

Nur wer die Vergangenheit kennt, hat eine Zukunft.

Only those who know the past have a future.

by Wilhelm von Humboldt, 1789

Some decisions have a life-altering impact on our futures. But what do we base our decisions on? We follow a feeling, we weigh advantages and disadvantages, we consider the consequences, and we factor in prior experiences. In the business world, corporate leaders face decisions that may impact the wellbeing of many stakeholders. One example of a high-stakes decision that corporate leaders often make is whether or not to publicly list a privately owned company on the stock market. This can be especially complex for family businesses, where this decision bears great uncertainties and risks. Can a family business remain a *family* business when the firm goes public? This thesis aims at analyzing the post-IPO development of German family businesses with regard to family involvement and firm longevity.

1.1 Chapter Overview

The following chapter provides the reader with background information that provides context for this study on stock-listed family business longevity, beginning with a brief discussion of the family enterprise as such, and followed by an overview of possible reasons for stock market flotations—both for classic

K. Stotmeister, *Publicly Traded Family Businesses*, Familienunternehmen und KMU, https://doi.org/10.1007/978-3-658-44303-0_1

IPO firms as well for reasons connected specifically with family businesses. The chapter will also include discussion of the possible risks of family firm flotation, and will conclude with an introduction of the dissertation's structure, methodology, and analytical framework.

1.2 The Family Enterprise

Family enterprises account for a very large proportion of the economy. In Germany, 90% of all active enterprises are family controlled, generating 52% of all revenue and providing 58% of all employment that is relevant to social insurance (Stiftung Familienunternehmen, 2019, p. 7). Furthermore, the most recent study conducted by the *Stiftung Familienunternehmen* has identified a strong increase in employment and revenue development among the Top 500 family enterprises, not only in Germany but worldwide (Stiftung Familienunternehmen, 2019, p. 38).

Among German stock-listed companies, approximately 40% are family-owned (Achleitner et al., 2019, p. 57).[1] The equity ratios of family-owned businesses are significantly higher than those of publicly owned firms. They have also been identified with a larger growth of employment and revenue (Achleitner et al., 2019, p. 51).

Family businesses are not only of great economic significance to the German economy—they also offer stability to the population in the region through their local roots (Block, 2010, p. 113; Block & Spiegel, 2013, p. 271). Furthermore, stakeholders benefit from these firms' long-term orientation (Le Breton-Miller & Miller, 2006, p. 732; Lumpkin et al., 2010, p. 242; Gambatese & Hallowell, 2011, p. 553; Andres, 2008, p. 433). Therefore, the family enterprise offers a structure of stability for present and future generations.

Family-controlled companies bring non-financial benefits to the German economy, as well as a sincere interest in the communal and national economy. The decision to go public can give rise to various consequences and uncertainties: Can the family maintain its family specific orientation? Can it maintain the status of a family business? Which conditions make the decision favorable for the endeavor, and can be viewed as success factors? These are some of the questions that this dissertation will explore.

[1] Achleitner et al. (2019) base their study on the "Founding Family" definition. This signifies a blocking minority of minimum 25% voting rights in family ownership and/or founding family member/s on the Executive Board and/or founding family member/s on the Supervisory Board.

1.2.1 The Family in Family Enterprises

It is the *family* that gives each family-controlled public company its important extra dimension. Each family is a unique and highly dynamic structure, with emotional relationships, tensions and ideologies that influence the corresponding company's operation. Of the wide variety of family enterprises, the connected shareholding family or families may range from young (only a few generations and a few shareholders) to the very old (multiple family branches and over a hundred shareholders). Hence, there is no single "by the book" guideline for handling these complex structures—which is exactly what makes the shareholding family and its impact on the firm so interesting.

With every generation added to the family, the structure of the shareholder group grows more complex and intrinsically challenging. Emotional ties to the firm and to the life's work created by ancestors may weaken over time. The burden of responsibilities as shareholder may outweigh shareholder benefits, and at some point, one or more individuals among the shareholding group may ask, "Why am I doing this?".

The emotional factor in the family is critical to the firm's success. On the positive side, emotions in families shape family culture and *tie* the family together. Family traditions and gatherings nourish these emotional ties. The values and responsibilities passed on from elders to their children shape the personalities of future generations. These factors are what shape the foundation of family businesses and what make the difference, as they are lived within the firm. On the other hand, emotions can drive discord and conflict. As most people know from personal experience, pain received from a loved and trusted one burns far more than in more hierarchical and objective environments. Hurt feelings or envy can even impact a healthy family under normal circumstances, so extra measures must be taken to maintain a healthy and trusting environment among the shareholders. Actions and decisions, whether private or business-related, within the shareholding family must always be communicated well and weighed for their impact on and potential aggravation of existing tensions. Pieper (2010) draws attention specifically to the psychological aspect that accompanies family firms and how an interdisciplinary approach would bring value to family firm research.

1.2.2 The Combination of Family and Enterprise

When adding the family to the business, a unique structure is created. The family defines the family business through their lived culture and dynamics. Given the intrinsic diversity of each family, no family business resembles another.[2]

On one side there is the family, with its emotional ties and low hierarchical structures. On the other side is the business, in which rationality tends to

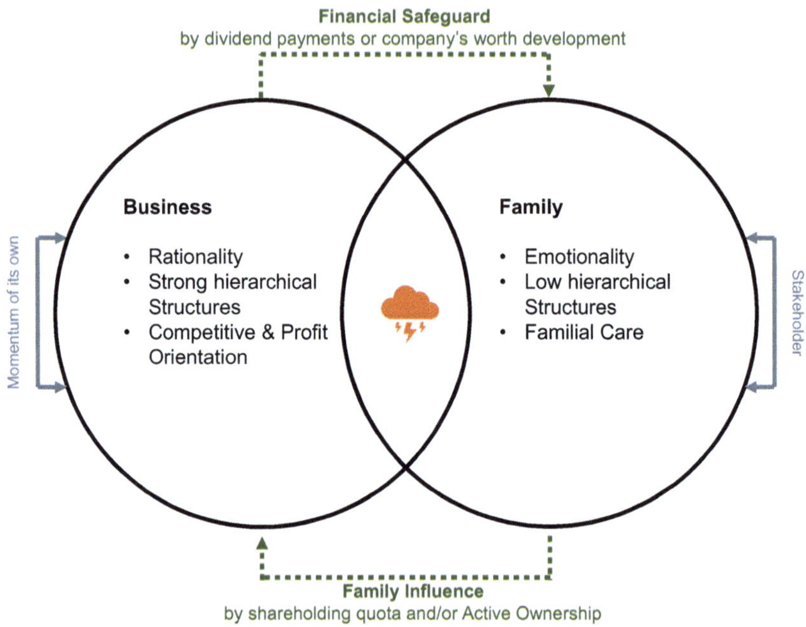

Figure 1.1 The Point of Friction. (Source: Author´s own figure, adapted from Scholes & Wilson (2014, pp. 1286) and Baus (2013, p. 26))

[2] The Institute of Family Business (WIFU) of the University of Witten/Herdecke have addressed the peculiarities of the intertwinement of family and business in various studies. Representative researchers are Arist von Schlippe, Professor at the Witten Institute of Family Business (WIFU) of the University Witten/Herdecke, and Tom A. Rüsen, Professor at and Director of the Witten Institute of Family Business (WIFU) of the University of Witten/Herdecke. Among other literary works by these authors, see Schlippe et al. (2018) and Rüsen et al. (2021).

drive decision-making, and in which stronger hierarchical structures apply. Furthermore, the nature of businesses is competitive and strongly profit-oriented. These traits are necessary for long-term survival in a world full of competitors.[3] Figure 1.1 illustrates the contrasts between both institutions and their resulting points of friction. It also illustrates the cycle of benefit, since the family serves the firm beyond the mere expectation of profit and in exchange the firm sustains the family.

In order to keep tensions low, the family and firm must learn to work together. On the family side, there will always be business-related decisions or developments that are not approved of by all shareholders. Family shareholders must learn to separate personal interests and feelings from their business decisions, especially in critical times. Nevertheless, the social bond is what makes the family influence so valuable to the firm and stakeholders. There is therefore the need to establish a very fine balance between emotionality and objectivity. Often that balance dictates that the interests of the firm must come before family emotions, since in many cases it is the firm that provides the family with financial security, and for that the firm itself needs to be healthy.

On the other hand, the business side must allow for family shareholders as a complementing institution. Family businesses may have different goals from non-family firms, for example long-term profit maximization. Furthermore, the family as the company's main shareholding group is intrinsically heterogeneous regarding professional background, life experience, and understanding. Hence, a certain degree of sensitivity helps keep tensions low.

> "Die Betroffenen beteiligen und nicht die Beteiligten betroffen machen."
>
> "Integrating the connected ones and not disconnecting the integrated ones."
>
> by Rolf Wöhrle (CFO of a stock-listed family firm)

While the point of friction may bear risks for firm and family, the family influence on the firm is generally likely to be beneficial and give the firm its unique character. To achieve optimal outcomes for all stakeholders, both institutions must find a balance to create one healthy family business.[4] For instance, family firm goals have been found to reflect and unite both aspects—the family and the business (Basu, 2004; Gagné et al., 2014; Williams Jr et al., 2018).

---

[3] Also see Scholes & Wilson (2014) and Baus (2013).

[4] Also see Schlippe et al. (2011), Pieper et al. (2013), Ruiz Jiménez et al. (2015) & Vallejo (2008).

1.3 Family Enterprises entering the Public Market—how much Tension can a Family Enterprise take?

The family firm constitutes a structure of potential tension. The regulations and consequences of a stock market flotation may add significantly to that tension.

Firms seeking a stock market flotation are confronted with a number of challenges. First, the preparation process and the actual IPO launch are a tedious and costly endeavor. Second, since public firms are subject to corporate law,[5] they are legally bound to fulfill a number of publicity requirements, which in turn state recurring costs and efforts. Compliance with these regulatory requirements is annually audited, and so the corporation is required by law to fulfill these responsibilities towards their shareholders.

Because of the high degree of publicity, the firm becomes more transparent, and interested acquirers have easy access to data in order to establish a firm value. This development may result in attractive acquisition offers for family shareholders, which in turn may diminish the family´s bond with the firm and persuade them to sell their stake.

Furthermore, corporate law strictly defines and prohibits certain actions. For instance, family shareholders holding voting rights (Stammaktien) are to be treated equally as the external shareholders holding preferred shares (Vorzugsaktien). After IPO, the family shareholders are then simply shareholders in a legal sense. They are strictly prohibited from gaining benefits from the firm, besides those that are legally defined. This may lead to a distancing process among family shareholders, because suddenly becoming a simple shareholder instead of a connected family shareholder may lead to estrangement.

In general, access to new liquidity is the most common reason why firms consider stock market flotations. The decision is strategic, often in order to finance growth and larger investments.[6] Although for family businesses considering an IPO, there are a number of relevant other reasons. There are two orientations that might ignite the urge to access the public market—firstly, families seeking an *exit* and secondly, families seeking *long-term involvement and development*. The reasons for stock market flotations are diverse and therefore just being touched for the purpose of this particular study, but there is comprehensive investigation

[5] In this context, corporate law is synonymous with the German *Aktienrecht* in the *Aktiengesetz (AktG) v. 6. September 1965*.

[6] Also see Frericks et al. (in print, 2023), Schürmann (1980), Schürmann & Körfgen (1987, 1997) and Koch & Wegmann (2000).

on the topic being carried out by other researchers as part of the superordinate research project.[7]

In conclusion, the family firm as such is already challenged with potential tensions. When adding the regulatory requirements and legal restrictions that come with being a public interest entity (PIE), the challenges of controlling these tensions grow. Kormann & Schlippe (2017) tackle the paradox given between family and firm and discuss the additional paradoxical effects of IPO´s on these firms in detail.

1.4 Introducing the Structure of the Dissertation

Hermut Kormann[8] launched the research project "Das börsennotierte Familienunternehmen" in the year 2018 in cooperation with Torsten Pieper[9] and Jörn Block.[10] The project has been generously supported by the EQUA Foundation.[11] Kormann has gathered together a group of young researchers with different university affiliations to cover the field of stock-listed family firm research in their dissertations, focusing on the German market. Research topics vary widely and cover topics such as growth, corporate development, and ownership issues.

This study, however, concerns itself specifically with stock-listed family firm longevity, survival, and family involvement, using historical data of post-WWII family-owned PIEs that launched their IPOs between 1950 and 1988, with an observation period that extends to 2018. The value of the superordinate research project lies in the intertwined and overlapping points, as they complement one another and thereby cover a large field of research concerning German stock-listed family businesses.

This dissertation approaches the subject of stock-listed family businesses from an exploratory angle and utilizes historical data to analyze both the longevity of German stock-listed family businesses and the influence of family involvement. The extraordinarily long time frame of observation (nearly seventy years) allows

[7] For further information, see Section 1.4. "Introducing the Structure of the Dissertation".

[8] Hermut Kormann, Professor at Friedrichshafener Institute for Family Enterprises, Zeppelin University and the University of Leipzig, both in Germany.

[9] Torsten Pieper, Associate Professor of Management at Belk College, University of North Carolina, USA.

[10] Jörn Block, Professor of Management at the University of Trier, Germany.

[11] The EQUA Foundation, based in Munich, Germany, supports family firm research in various disciplines with the goal to enable practical implications through research for family businesses.

for meaningful and conclusive observations. This long-term orientation is, in fact, unique among stock-listed family firm research so far. The study follows a mixed methods approach, and therefore includes both a quantitative and a qualitative analysis.

1.4.1 Part I—Focus on the Quantitative Analysis

The first part of the comprehensive examination of stock-listed family firm longevity comprises the quantitative analysis. A survival analysis has been conducted, applying the Cox PH model and measuring survival spells of family-owned PIE´s from the IPO launch until any form of crucial change[12] has occurred, resulting in the end of the life of the family business as it was at the time of IPO (*death*). By conducting the Cox PH model, independent variables that have a significant effect on the risk of failure (*death*) have been identified. For a detailed description of the procedure, see Section 3.5.2., "The Quantitative Approach—Survival Analysis".

1.4.2 Part II—Focus on the Narrative Analysis

The lean empirical quantitative analysis is followed by a more qualitative and narrative approach. The aim of this mixed methods approach was to add a sense of life and dynamic to the firms and their life expectancies by introducing conspicuous family businesses and their attributes. By juggling and cross-checking the data, observations and findings were made visible in graphs and figures. Soft features such as clusters, patterns, and success factors have also been identified. Furthermore, significant findings that have been identified by the quantitative methods of data analysis have been supported by the narrative analysis.[13]

---

[12] For further information, see Section 2.5.2. "The Concept of Crucial Change".

[13] For a detailed description of this approach, see Section 3.5.3. "The Narrative Approach—Clusters, Patterns and Success Factors".

References

Achleitner, A.-K., Braun, R., Kaserer, C., Jarchow, S., Keppler, H. & Szewcyk, J. (2019). *Börsennotierte Familienunternehmen in Deutschland—Bedeutung, Merkmale, Performance.* München: Stiftung Familienunternehmen.

Andres, C. (2008). Large shareholders and firm performance—An empirical examination of founding-family ownership. *Journal of Corporate Finance*, 14, 431–445.

Baus, K. (2013). *Die Familienstrategie—Wie Familien ihr Unternehmen über Generationen sichern (4. ed).* Wiesbaden: Springer-Gabler.

Basu, A. (2004). Entrepreneurial aspirations among family business owners: an analysis of ethnic business owners in the UK. *International Journal of Entrepreneurial Behavior and Research*, 10,12–33.

Block, J. (2010). Family management, family ownership, and downsizing: Evidence from S&P 500 firms. *Family Business Review*, 23(2), 109–130.

Block, J.H. & Spiegel, F. (2013). Family firm density and regional innovation output: An exploratory analysis. *Journal of Family Business Strategy*, 4, 270–280.

Frericks, S., Stotmeister, K. & Kormann, H. (in print, 2023). Extant Research and other Literature on Listed Family Enterprises. Fleischer, H. & Prigge, S. (Eds)., Listed family Companies. Hamburg Conference 2021: Law and Management of Family Firms.

Gambatese, J.A. & Hallowell, M. (2011). Enabling and measuring innovation in the construction industry. *Construction Management and Economics*, 29, 553–567.

Gagné, M., Sharma, P. & De Massis, A. (2014). The study of organizational behavior in family business. *European Journal of Work and Organizational Psychology*, 23, 643–656.

Koch, W. & Wegmann, J. (2000). *Praktiker-Handbuch Börseneinführung—Ablauf des Börsengangs mittelständischer Unternehmen—mit Erfahrungsberichten vom Neuen Markt (3. ed.).* Stuttgart: Schäffer-Poeschel.

Kormann, H. & Schlippe, A.v. (2017). Börsennotierung des Familienunternehmens—Ein Ansatz zur Überbrückung von Paradoxien und seine Erfolgsaussichten. *Zeitschrift für Familienunternehmen und Strategie*, 06, 200–205.

Le Breton-Miller, I. & Miller, D. (2006). Why do some family businesses out-compete? Governance, long-term orientation, and sustainable capability. *Entrepreneurship Theory and Practice*, 30(6), 731–746.

Lumpkin, G.T., Brigham, K.H. & Moss, T.W. (2010). Long-term orientation: implications for the entrepreneurial orientation and performance of family businesses. *Entrepreneurship & Regional Development*, 22(3–4), 241–264.

Pieper, T.M. (2010). Non solus: Toward a psychology of family business. *Journal of family Business Strategy*, 1, 26–39.

Pieper, T.M., Astrachan, J.H. & Manners, G.E. (2013). Conflict in Family Business: Common Metaphors and Suggestions for Intervention. *Family Relations*, 62, 490–500.

Ruiz Jiménez, M.C., Vallejo Martos, M.C. & Martínez Jiménez, R. (2015). Organisational Harmony as a Value in Family Business and Its Influence on Performance. *Journal of Business Ethics*, 126, 259–272.

Rüsen, T.A., Kleve, H. & Schlippe, A.v. (2021). *Management der dynastischen Unternehmerfamilie—Zwischen Familie, Organisation und Netzwerk.* Heidelberg: Springer.

Schlippe, A.v., Nischak, A. & El Hachimi, M. (2011). *Familienunternehmen verstehen—Gründer, Gesellschafter und Generationen* (2. ed.). Göttingen: Vandenhoeck & Ruprecht.
Schlippe, A.v., Groth, T. & Rüsen, T. (2018). *Die beiden Seiten der Unternehmerfamilie: Familienstrategie über Generationen* (2. ed.). Göttingen: V&R Verlag.
Scholes, L. & Wilson, N. (2014). The Importance of Family Trust in Family Firm Governance. *Entrepreneurship Theory and Practice*, 38(6), 1285–1293.
Schürmann, W. (1980). *Familienunternehmen und Börse—Emittieren, warum und wie?* Wiesbaden: Gabler.
Schürmann, W. & Körfgen, K. (1987). *Familienunternehmen auf dem Weg zur Börse—Ein Leitfaden für potenzielle Börsenkandidaten mit Beispielen aus der Praxis (2. ed.).* München: C.H. Beck.
Schürmann, W. & Körfgen, K. (1997). *Familienunternehmen auf dem Weg zur Börse—Ein Leitfaden für potenzielle Börsenkandidaten (3. ed.).* München: C.H. Beck.
Stiftung Familienunternehmen (2019). *Die volkswirtschaftliche Bedeutung der Familienunternehmen (5. ed.).* München: Stiftung Familienunternehmen.
Vallejo, M.C. (2008). Is the Culture of Family Firms Really Different? A Value-based Model for Its Survival through Generations. *Journal of Business Ethics*, 81, 261–279.
Williams Jr, R.I., Pieper, T.M., Kellermanns, F.W. & Astrachan, J.H. (2018). Family Firm Goals and their Effects on Strategy, Family and Organization Behavior: A Review and Research Agenda. *International Journal of management Reviews*, 20, 63–82.

From the Literature Review to the Research Question and the Relevant Definitions

2

What do we know about stock-listed family businesses and longevity? How much has research revealed so far? What are the key points of connection for this study? This chapter leads the reader through the current field of research on survival for both family firms that are stock-listed and those that are not. It also introduces the starting point of the present study. The current standard of knowledge based on previous investigation ignites the spark of curiosity and inspires deeper research.

2.1 Chapter Overview

The reader will first be presented with an overview of the current state of research in the field. This requires an extensive analysis of the literature, as it serves as the foundation for this study. This analysis will be followed by an account of the process by which the research gap was identified, which in turn will lead to formulation of the research questions. Furthermore, crucial terminology and concepts will be defined, as these stretch through the entire analysis.

2.2 Status Quo on Current Research

Family firm research has gained considerable importance over the last decades. Today, research fields vary greatly, bringing different interesting attributes of family firms to light. These stretch from organizational and cultural benefits by family

K. Stotmeister, *Publicly Traded Family Businesses*, Familienunternehmen und KMU, https://doi.org/10.1007/978-3-658-44303-0_2

influence[1] to consumer behavior towards family firm branding, as well as to family firm innovation,[2] growth,[3] and family firm longevity.

Longevity is a key concept for this study. Family firms have been identified in prior research with various beneficial attributes. Andres (2008), for instance, has identified the "founder effect" (p. 439) as a phenomenon unique to family firms. He found that family businesses achieve superior financial performance and market valuation when the firm is still founder-managed. This can be traced back to the incentive of reducing agency costs while also increasing firm value, in order to secure financial stability for future generations. Hence, long-term orientation has been found to be one of the most prominent features among the family firm benefits, next to a strong corporate culture, which is influenced by family values.[4]

Kormann & Wimmer (2018) wrote an essay tracing the history of family firm research from its beginning up to the current day. They identified the first research approaching the topic in works by Hengstmann (1935) and Knur (1941), showing that even the early German literature of the times of World War II have tackled the phenomenon of family enterprises.

To narrow down the wide field of family firm research, this literature review will focus mainly on the current state of research on family firm longevity and *stock-listed* family firm longevity. Longevity refers to the survival duration of a family business under certain specified circumstances. The specifications vary as does the definition of longevity. For instance, longevity may be measured until insolvency of the firm or to the family business as such (dilution of family influence). This review serves as a funnel to demonstrate the status quo on both topics separately, and thereby carve out the research gap by identifying overlaps (or a lack thereof). The review aims at mapping out the current state of the field, which, in turn, may add to the identification of further research questions. It may also offer context and background for this study's findings and discoveries (Figure 2.1).

---

[1] Also see Le Breton-Miller & Miller (2006), Lindow et al. (2010), Lumpkin et al. (2010), Lumpkin & Dess (1996), Naldi et al. (2007), Villalonga & Amit (2006), Beck et al. (2020) and Rauschendorfer et al. (2021).

[2] Also see Block (2012), Block & Spiegel (2013), Craig et al. (2014) and Kraiczy et al. (2014).

[3] Also see Seibold (2019), Lantelme et al. (2021) and Lantelme (2017).

[4] Also see Le Breton-Miller & Miller (2006), James (1999), Anderson & Reeb (2003), Block & Spiegel (2013, p. 271), Baus (2013, p. 82) and Tellis et al. (2009, p. 7).

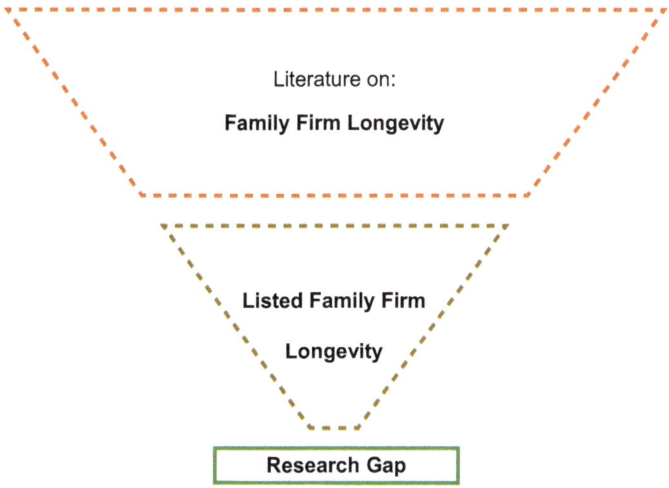

Figure 2.1 Literature Funnel. (Source: Author's own figure)

2.2.1 Status Quo on Family Enterprise Longevity

Family firm longevity is a widely researched field and reaches back many decades (Löhde et al. 2020, p. 132). International research has tackled the topic from various angles—longevity and the question of successful succession, longevity and the question of innovativeness, longevity and the question of external influence factors, and many more.

Table 2.1 displays an overview of the latest scholarly literature in the field of family firm longevity. The extensive research analysis has identified four major fields of impact factors, which have been analyzed for effects on family business longevity and survival.

Impact of family control, family governance and family ties: Most prominently, the impact of the family—in the sense of family control, family governance and family ties—has been screened by scholars such as Santarelli & Lotti (2005) and Kim & Gao (2012). Very recent studies in this field have been taken up by Chirico et al. (2020), Löhde et al. (2020) and Ahmad et al. (2020). The studies cover a diverse range of target firms. While they are all family firms, the age and survival time up to examination vary significantly. For instance, Santarelli & Lotti (2005) examined family start-up firms in Italy from 1950 until 1965, with a survival duration of at least 25 years and one next-generation family member in a higher management position. Hence, these firms had at the time of examination already been confronted with succession, or were about to. They argue that a higher age of >30 years of entrepreneurial firms has a negative effect on survival. Furthermore, they find that the founders see an emotional value, in addition to the calculable value of the firm, which makes them reluctant to sell to outsiders. Hence, if a family successor is not available, the founders would rather dissolve the firm than pass it on to non-family parties. This development has been found to be a "failure of an entrepreneurial system based on the strength of family ties." (p. 190).

Chirico et al. (2020) compare Swedish privately-held family and non-family enterprises with regards to the exit strategies in connection with SEW. They find that in times of deteriorating performance, family businesses hold on to the firm. Non-family firms, on the other hand, have been found to be more likely to exit. Hence, Chirico et al. (2020) argue that the families are more focused on non-financial features and rather strive for continuation. Furthermore, they argue that as family firms are more focused on "extracting SEW from the firm for future generations." (p. 28) and on merging, rather than dissolving, to affect a liquidity event. Meanwhile, non-family businesses tend to be more willing to sell the firm outright, dissolving the firm as a last resort rather than merge with another company.

Very old family businesses in founding family ownership are targeted by Löhde et al. (2020). They tackle the topic of successful succession as the basis of family firm longevity—does the family learn from earlier experiences in order to improve future transgenerational shifts to secure firm survival?

Ahmad et al. (2020) have screened family businesses in Pakistan, second generation and older, and they focus on innovation capability and the family's involvement. As innovation has been closely linked to firm longevity by prior literature, Ahmad et al. (2020) find that family involvement in the business and innovation capability has a significant positive impact on family business longevity.

Chinese family firm longevity has been analyzed with respect to family involvement in management by Kim & Gao (2012), who examined a total number of 158 Chinese family businesses. According to their findings, family involvement in management does not by itself have an impact on firm performance, but a firm's orientation towards the family goals may have a positive impact on the family managers' behavior, which in turn may have a positive effect on firm performance. Hence, they argue that if the firm supports the family goals, this may have a positive influence on longevity.

Impact of overlapping family and business demands: Moving on to the next field of interest by international scholars regarding family enterprise longevity, Niehm et al. (2009) focus on the impact of overlapping family and business demands on family firm longevity. They screened data of small family businesses in family management over a timeline of four years. They found differences in several aspects between single-role managers (only firm management) and dual-role managers (firm and family management). Hence, both types of managers have been identified with different coping strategies to meet all needs and to ensure firm survival.

Impact of the interplay between family and organization: The impact of the interplay between family and organization has been tackled by Stafford et al. (2010) and Zellweger et al. (2012). Stafford et al. (2010) screened data from 1997–2007. They identified beneficial influence factors for family enterprise longevity, such as community characteristics, familial achievements, and processes during periods of change, as well as business and owner characteristics. Zellweger et al. (2012) applied a new approach by focusing on the family itself as a key factor. They believe that by integrating the family into family firm longevity research, a new set of values can be derived for the business and the family. This allows for a shift away from classic succession planning, opening minds to new understandings of the family and future leadership roles.

Impact of external influence factors: Stafford et al. (2013) and Moya et al. (2020) focus on how external factors influence family business longevity. In their work on long-term family business survival under circumstances of natural disasters, Stafford et al. (2013) analyze small family businesses within a time frame of ten years, ranging from 1997 until 2007, and examine how the family's adaptive capacity affects firm survival under such circumstances. Moya et al. (2020) have established an extensive study on family firm longevity by comparing two intrinsically different contexts which nonetheless share a strong presence of family firms: Germany and Spain. They follow an economic-historical approach to observing a time frame of around fifty years, namely the second half of the 20th century. They use data on the 100 largest family businesses in Germany and Spain from the year 2005. In a short summary, they find that survival times differ considerably between both countries: German family businesses are on average twice as old. They conclude that these differences are a result of specific differences in the political, social, and economic histories of the two countries.

Overall, international scholars have thus found that family influence tends to be beneficial for family firm longevity. The family's close link to the firm generally has a positive effect on the firm's current and future well-being.

Table 2.1 Scholarly Literature on Family Enterprise Longevity

Family Firm Longevity	Scholarly Literature	Core Statements/Findings
Impact of family control, family governance and family ties (e.g. succession)	Santarelli & Lotti (2005); Chirico et al. (2020); Löhde et al. (2020); Ahmad et al. (2020); Kim & Gao (2012)	Santarelli & Lotti (2005) Target: small entrepreneurial firms, Italy Time frame of interest: current, firms at least 25 years in the market Findings: age (>30 years) has an effect on survival; firm is a "value" which should be passed on to familial heirs (or possibly a loyal employee). In case of lack of heirs, it is perceived as failure. Chirico et al. (2020) Target: family-controlled and non-family-controlled private firms Time frame of interest: current Findings: Family firms seek continuation of SEW, hence they choose merger over dissolution and lastly sale. Non-family firms seek higher financial returns, hence they choose sale over dissolution and lastly merger. Löhde et al. (2020) Target: 300-year old family businesses in founding-family hand Time frame of interest: current Findings: family members take past experiences into consideration and apply these to future visions. They exert "transgenerational control" (succession process). Hence, family members go through learning processes in order to optimize family succession and control strategies. Ahmad et al. (2020) Target: family firms in the second generation and up Time frame of interest: current Findings: family involvement in business and innovation capability has a significant impact on sustainable firm longevity. Kim & Gao (2012) Target: 158 Chinese family firms Time frame of interest: current Findings: family involvement in management doesn't relate to firm performance. Furthermore, a firms' family goals can influence the behavior of family managers that may affect firm performance in a positive way.

(continued)

Table 2.1 (continued)

Family Firm Longevity	Scholarly Literature	Core Statements/Findings
Impact of overlapping family and business demands (personal vs. organizational)	Niehm et al. (2009);	Niehm et al: (2009) Target: small family firms with family management (household manager and business manager equally) Time frame of interest: data from 1997–2000 of the National Family Business Survey Findings: Survival rate from 1997–2000 of 82%. For surviving family firms in 2000 the single-role managers have been found to have a higher gross income, mostly managed by a male, fewer underaged children, came from larger communities and were predominantly active in sectors such as agriculture, retail and service. The dual-role managers were predominantly female, had slightly more underaged children, were from small to larger communities and active in retail and service sectors. Of these, both surviving and non-surviving family businesses, the dual-role managers tended to take household work to business in hectic times, and vice versa. Hence, overlapping fields of family and business.

(continued)

Table 2.1 (continued)

Family Firm Longevity	Scholarly Literature	Core Statements/Findings
Impact of the interplay between family and organization	Stafford et al. (2010); Zellweger et al. (2012)	Stafford et al. (2010) Target: data from the National Family Business Panel and Spatial Hazard Events and Losses Database, etc. Time frame of interest: data from 1997–2007 Findings: beneficial influence factors for long-term survival have been identified as community characteristics, familial achievements and process during periods of change as well as business and owner characteristics, etc. Attributes such as home-based family firms with female owners and costumer focus have been found to have a decreasing effect on the survival time. Zellweger et al. (2012) Target: data from the members of the Family Firm Institute, Boston and students/alumni form Babson College Time frame of interest: current Findings: Include the factor family in family firm longevity research. The shift allows a creation of new values and a new self-understanding of the family, also with respect to succession and next generation leadership roles.

(continued)

Table 2.1 (continued)

Family Firm Longevity	Scholarly Literature	Core Statements/Findings
Impact of external influence factors	Stafford et al. (2013); Moya et al. (2020)	Stafford et al. (2013) Target: small family business owners; data from the National Family Business Panel and data on federal disaster assistance by the Public Entity Risk institute Time frame of interest: 10 years; with data from 1997–2007 Findings: some types of family processes or and/or capital have positive, some have negative effects on long-term survival. Hence, a lower count of negative stressors on behalf of the family improves the chance of ten-year survival and revenue growth. A lack of family adaptive capacity decreased the chance of ten-year survival. Moya et al. (2020) Target: 100 largest family businesses in Germany and Spain Time frame of interest: data for 2005, economic-historical approach of the second part of the 20th century Findings: Comparison of two countries with differences in business structures and economic history, but both with a large number of family firms. Considerable differences regarding family business longevity due to political and social-economic occurrences.

2.2.2 Status Quo on Stock-Listed Family Enterprise Longevity

While family firm longevity is widely researched, the field of *stock-listed* family firm longevity has received less scholarly attention. Nevertheless, two studies provide insight into the survival durations of stock-listed family businesses: Franks et al. (2015) and Klasa (2007).

Impact of Family involvement, control and ownership: Cho et al. (2018) and Casillas et al. (2019) studied the impact of family involvement, control and ownership on stock-listed family firm longevity. Cho et al. (2018) analyzed 280 Korean stock-listed family SME's which were active in IT-close industries with a time frame of interest ranging from 1997 until 2014. Their analysis suggests that a balance between family and public ownership is beneficial for long-term survival. Equally, a balance regarding the family's involvement in management can also affect longevity in a positive way.

Casillas et al. (2019) laid their focus on 126 Spanish stock-listed family enterprises with a time frame ranging from 2008 until 2012, covering the World Financial Crisis. They studied the effect the families have on retrenchment strategies in situations of crises, and found that families have an effect on retrenchment strategies *when firm performance is weakening*, even if firm survival is not threatened. The family takes even greater effect when survival is in jeopardy. Hence, they argue that the family seeks to maintain SEW whether or not there is a perceived or actual threat to firm survival.

Acquisition and Survival: Steen & Welch (2006) conducted a single case study on acquisition behavior in the Australian wine industry, pinpointed to the year 2003. Based on their case analysis, they argue that merger or acquisition can be used as a tool to prolong firm survival and can allow future family involvement. They find that certain guidelines are beneficial for firm survival regarding the acquiring firm. The acquiring firm must keep the family firm heritage in mind when approaching the family firm for acquisition and after, such as future family involvement, maintaining the enterprises name and brand, and cultivating quality and relationship matters.

Survival Durations: Franks et al. (2015) address the ownership landscape of stock-listed companies. They gathered ownership data on the largest German stock-listed businesses, with the intention of replicating an earlier analysis, in order to examine whether the ownership landscape among German stock-listed enterprises has changed. They find a reduction in intercorporate and bank-holding ownership, which has been found to be consistent with international research findings. Nevertheless, they also uncover an observation which runs against international findings: There has been "no sign of a reduction in the importance of family holdings in German corporate ownership." (p. 27).

Klasa (2007) has analyzed 84 stock-listed American family enterprises which were family-controlled and managed at the time they sold their family stake, with an observation time frame from 1984 to 1998. Her study focuses on the reason why the family sells their stake. She differentiates between a sale to an acquirer who acquires all equity of the firm or just to the family's controlling shares (p. 340). In order to be able to identify the reasons, she compares her sample to an equivalent number of stock-listed family firms that haven't sold their stake. Klasa (2007) finds that most families decide to sell in favor of a bidder who acquires the entire equity, i.e. the whole firm. She argues for several possible reasons, for instance the fact that the sales process to such an acquirer is easier than in other cases, due to scattered family ownership. Furthermore, synergy reasons may influence the family's decision on whom to sell to. (A side note: Most research on U.S. family enterprises is conducted on stock-listed family firms. According to Frericks et al. (in print, 2023), this is due to problems of accessibility to data on privately-held family businesses. Publicity is a requirement for going to market, which in turn allows easier firm evaluation for potential acquirers, which in turn again may lead to attractive acquisition offers.) Her findings demonstrate a contradiction to Franks et al. (2015). According to Klasa (2007), majority block sales among stock-listed family businesses are detectable, whereas according to Franks et al. (2015), there is no sign of reductions in the ownership landscape of stock-listed family enterprises. Klasa examines the US-American market, while Franks et al. examine the German market. Klasa's findings are supported by the findings of this study (Table 2.2).[5]

[5] For further information, see Section 5.3.2.1. "Does the Age at IPO influence Longevity?".

Table 2.2 Scholarly Literature on Stock-Listed Family Enterprise Longevity

Listed Family Firm Longevity	Scholarly Literature	Core Statements/Findings
Impact of Family involvement, control and ownership	Cho et al. (2018); Casillas et al. (2019)	Cho et al. (2018) Target: 280 Korean listed family SME's in IT-close industries Time frame of interest: 1997–2014 Findings: appropriate balance between family and public ownership as well as regarding management involvement is beneficial for longevity. Casillas et al. (2019) Target: 126 Spanish stock-listed family businesses Time frame of interest: 2008–2012, during World Financial Crisis Findings: family members have been found to have an effect on retrenchment strategies, when performance results are declining, even when survival is not threatened, even more so when survival is threatened. Families try to maintain SEW, no matter whether actual or a perceived threat to survival is given.
Acquisition and Survival	Steen & Welch (2006)	Steen & Welch (2006) Target: single case study Time frame of interest: 2003 Finding: Merger or acquisition can allow further family involvement, and therefore can serve as a survival strategy. Acquiring firms must approach family firms with a certain understanding for family firm issues, such as future family involvement, maintaining the company's name and brand and cultivating quality and relationship matters.
Survival Duration	Franks et al. (2015); Klasa (2007)	Franks et al. (2015) Target: largest 171 listed German companies in 1990, focus on families, banks and other companies as blockholders Time frame of interest: 20 years Findings: a decline in intercorporate- and bank-holdings in Germany has been identified, although no decrease in the relevance of family holdings. Klasa (2007) Target: 84 public American family businesses, controlled and managed by family/-ies who sold their stake between 1984–1998 Time frame of interest: 1984–1998 Findings: Optimal risk bearing, separation of ownership and management and CEO succession, among others, have been found to explain sales decisions by the family. Furthermore, families tend to sell their stake to acquirers who acquire the entire firm, firstly because scattered family ownership, secondly because such an entire sale would turn out better for both parties.

In conclusion, there is a side note which must be emphasized. When analyzing financial markets or stock corporations, the country allocation plays an important role. This is due to the fact that every country has differences in stock corporation law and tax law. Berghoff & Köhler (2020), for instance, tackle the question of very old family businesses and compare the U.S. to Germany. They find that tax legislation plays an important role in family firm longevity and that an IPO in this regard may be indispensable.

Hence, these differences make comparability of international studies difficult and may lead to false conclusions.

2.3 Identifying the Research Gap and Formulating the Research Question

As previously demonstrated, international scholars have approached the topic of family firm longevity in depth. Even the field of stock-listed companies as such, without family connection, has been tackled in a variety of studies.[6] Nevertheless, scholars have merely scraped the surface of *stock-listed* family firm longevity. In general, the current literature on family firm IPOs takes a positive view. Kormann & Schlippe (2017) state this exactly in their essay "Börsennotierung des Familienunternehmens" They tackle the paradoxes that come with stock market flotation and point out gaps in research, emphasizing the potential need for a critical approach. Most literature within this field is advisory literature on when and how to approach an IPO, such as by Schürmann & Körfgen (1987, 1997), Schürmann (1980), Sander (2008), to mention a few German works.

Narrowing down the relevant literature, reveals a significant research gap (see Table 2.3). By combining three of the scholars who were presented in the previous subchapters, relevant features have been identified, and these relevant features—in combination with one another—raise the simple question:

How long do family firms survive after IPO?

Scholarly literature so far in the field of stock-listed family business longevity has always tackled longevity through the prism of a specific theory, or detailed question. For family businesses considering an IPO, more information and data

[6] Also see Daepp et al. (2015), Chancharat et al. (2012), Khurshed (2000), Jain & Kini (2000), Jain & Kini (2008), Carpentier et al. (2008), Carpentier & Suret (2011) and Wilbon (2002).

around the question of how long the firms survive afterwards may help families who are trying to decide whether or not to go public.

Table 2.3 Identifying the Research Gap

Schlolarly Literature	Target	Time Frame	Method. Approach	Stock-listed FF	Relevant Features
Cho et al (2018)	280 Korean listed family SME's in IT-close industries	1997–2014	Survival Analysis using Cox PH Model	Yes	**Survival analysis using Cox PH Model**
Klasa (2007)	84 public American family businesses, controlled and managed by family/-ies which sold their stake between 1984–1998	1984–1998	Treatment-Control Approach	Yes	**Dilution process of family stake**
Moya et al. (2020)	100 largest family businesses in Germany and Spain	ca. 1950–2000	Economic-Historical Approach, Comparative Approach	No	**Historical approach with an extended time frame of analysis**
GAP	**How long do family firms survive after IPO?** – **dilution process** of family influence and control after IPO – explorative approach to identify **reasons, clusters and patterns** – **extended time frame** of observation with a long developmental phase ➔ **Is failure as a stock-listed family business a given fate or can we influence the outcome?**				

Cho et al. (2018) have conducted a survival analysis by means of applying a Cox PH model. They have examined the survival durations of stock-listed family enterprises, with the precondition of IT-close industry and with a rather short time frame of observation of seventeen years. Klasa (2007) has tackled the topic of family exits of stock-listed family enterprises through sale of stake (dilution of family influence). She aims at identifying reasons for sale, rather than survival durations. In this case the time frame of interest comprises fourteen years. Moya et al. (2020) have conducted an economic-historical approach with an extensive time frame of analysis of approximately fifty years, yet they don't make a distinction between whether or not a family firm was stock-listed.

Hence, an extensive analysis of historical data on the actual survival times within a long time frame of observation including a long developmental period would be of great significance, for both future research and for real-world application. By applying an exploratory approach without preconditions, clusters and patterns may be identified, that may explain survival durations and in further application, may allow the development of practical implications and advice.

Resulting from the literature review and the further processing of relevant literature to pinpoint the research gap, the defined features of interest in the research gap (see Table 2.3) have been combined into a specific line of inquiry:

How did German stock-listed family firms develop after IPO, especially with regards to longevity and family involvement?—Development of a model based on the long-term analysis of historical data ranging from 1950–2018

- *How long do families of publicly traded family firms maintain their influence through shares after IPO?*
- *How does family influence (shareholding quota) develop after IPO?*
- *Which forms of crucial change lead to failure (sale/family exit, delisting, bankruptcy, etc.)?*
- *Are there beneficial/success factors for family firm survival (industry, number of families involved, age of firm, etc.)?*

2.4 Definition of the Stock-Listed Family Enterprise

In family firm research, the definition of requirements for eligible family businesses differs according to focus. In some cases, the operationally active family members are a requirement. Not so for this study. The research question clearly puts firm longevity of stock-listed family businesses at the center, and therefore a wider range of family businesses is of interest, with or without active family members in the organization. By allowing a wider range of eligible family businesses, the range of possible influence factors on longevity widens, and the degree of activity of family members becomes an independent variable in the equation of stock-listed family firm longevity. Additionally, due to the fact that this study is based on historical data, details on certain data are not always available. Adding more requirements to the definition of the family enterprise would decrease the number of firms eligible for the study. Hence, the definition for this study has purposefully been kept to a minimum of requirements with a wide scope:

A German stock-listed firm is an eligible stock-listed family firm

- *when at least 25% of shares are*
- *held directly or indirectly*
- *by one or more founder/s*
- *of German origin*
- *or their descendant family/-ies.*

2.5 Development of Fundamental Assessment Criteria

In the course of the study, the researcher was faced with numerous situations in which the evaluation, interpretation, and specification of certain phenomena were hard to combine and describe. Hence, the researcher implemented concepts and processes in order to grasp and capture the complexity and significance of these observations. These concepts and processes are a further development of well-known topics covering shareholder structure of family enterprises or family involvement in the firm, but they have been developed to fit this study and to describe the observation and impact at hand.

2.5.1 The Dilution Process

Family businesses intrinsically suffer from tension between the family with all its socio-emotional ties on the one side and the business with its clear hierarchical and operational structures on the other. Despite this, the two-sided business structure has demonstrated its value.[7] Among stock-listed family businesses, the family can maintain influence by holding on to a major block of controlling shares—mostly by holding on to the ordinary shares that are connected to voting rights. But what happens when, for any reason, the family/-ies start selling shares? With reference to the definition of family enterprises described in Section 2.4., the stock-listed family firms are required to be family-owned by a minimum of 25%.

---

[7] For further information, see Section 1.2. "The Family Enterprise".

One point of focus within this study is the *Dilution Process* of family influence, i.e. the process by which family influence dilutes when the family sells blocks of shares through MorA and thereby crosses critical thresholds. As displayed in Figure 2.2, the safest field of strong family influence is given by a family shareholding quota of between >50% and 100%, inclusive. These family firms are categorized as *family-controlled.* Hence, the family holds a solid majority of stake in the company and ensures familial control and influence.

By selling shares to outside acquirers and thereby reducing the family shareholding quota to below 50.1%, the family business becomes categorized as merely *family-owned.* This reduction affects the level of family influence to a critical, yet nevertheless, sufficient level. The family has limited control. They no longer have the power of sole decision-making, but they can hinder certain decisions through a blocking minority. These businesses are still eligible family businesses, according to the definition.[8]

When the family shareholding quota falls below 25% as a result of the family selling shares to outside acquirers, the family business loses the family firm status and consequently counts as a non-family enterprise. By crossing this critical threshold, this step counts as *death* of the family-owned business in the survival analysis and results in failure with regards to longevity.

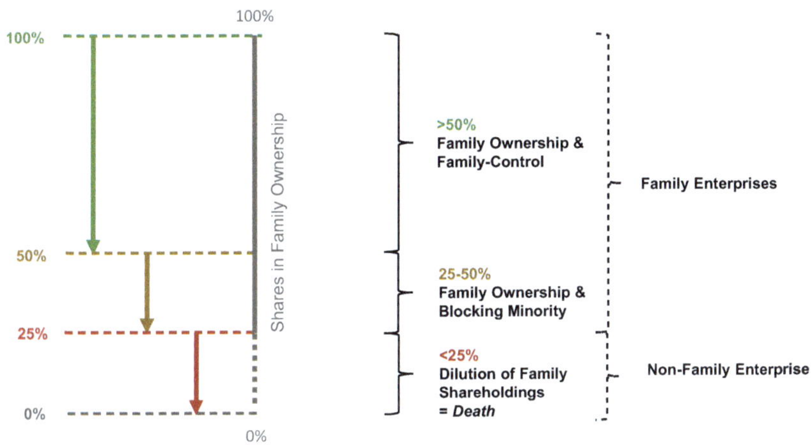

Figure 2.2 The Dilution Process of Family Influence. (Source: Author's own figure)

[8] For further information, see Section 2.4. "Definition of the Stock-Listed Family Enterprise".

Hence, pre-IPO family firms that have lost their family firm status, either through extensive dilution beforehand or through stock market flotation, are categorized as non-family businesses and are assigned to the control sample. Family businesses that have maintained >25% until the end of the observation period have been categorized as survivors. Nevertheless, in the course of the analyses, another distinction has been identified among this group: the weak and strong survivors.[9] The family businesses that have maintained family ownership with a shareholding quota between 25 and 50% are defined as *weak survivors*. The *strong survivors*, on the other hand, have maintained family control with a quota of >50%.

2.5.2 The Concept of Crucial Change

Two concepts have been developed in the course of the study, one of which is the concept of *crucial change*—the form of failure or *death* that the firm experiences, which leads to the falling out of observation. The research question aims at illuminating longevity of post-IPO family businesses, as they remain in their original state. Hence, crucial change constitutes a severe incisive development that changes the original structure of the firm as it was at the time of the IPO launch, either on the side of the firm itself or on the side of the family.

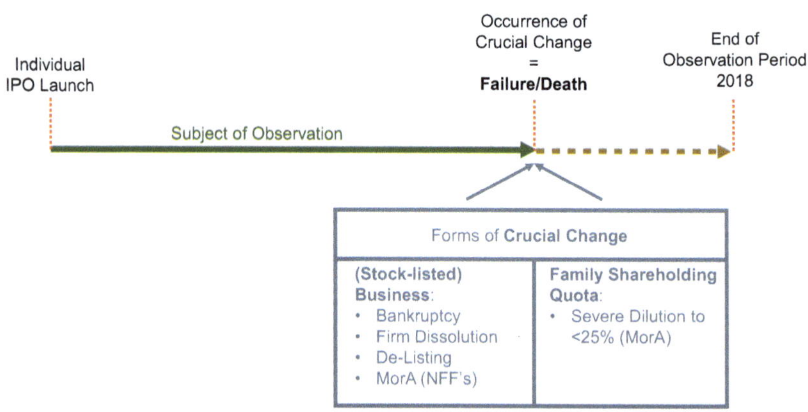

Figure 2.3 The Concept of Crucial Change. (Source: Author's own figure)

[9] See Section 6.3.2. "Success Factors—Weak vs. Strong Survivors".

The occurrences of crucial change vary between both samples. Among the family businesses, the most important form of crucial change for the purpose of this study is *merger or acquisition* (MorA). This form of crucial change is directly connected to the dilution process of family influence by shareholding quota. Other forms of crucial change that have occurred among the family business sample are bankruptcy, firm dissolution, and de-listing.

Among the non-family businesses, all forms of crucial change concern only the firm itself, either with respect to survival as a stock-listed firm (de-listing) or to survival as a firm (MorA, bankruptcy or firm dissolution). Furthermore, especially in the early decades of the observed timeline, many firms were state-owned at the time of their IPO launch. Over the years, these experienced a privatization run. Privatization of the firm is not considered a form of crucial change, since this development is not applicable to family businesses or non-family businesses that were not owned by the State at the time. Hence, in order to maintain comparability among all firms, the forms of crucial change displayed in Figure 2.3 constitute the entirety for both samples.

2.5.3 The Concept of Active Ownership

The second concept that follows throughout the study is the concept of *Active Ownership* (AO). It measures the degree of family influence on the firm's strategic and operational development.

Family members have two ways of exerting influence on the firm and its development (see Figure 2.4). Firstly, direct influence is possible through active directory as an executive board member. Secondly, one or more family members can exert indirect influence by obtaining a supervisory board mandate. In this case, the family member or members are not directly involved in operational decision making, but the board of directors has a reporting obligation to the supervisory board. The supervisory board, in turn, appoints the Executive Board members.

The degree of AO plays an important role in determining clusters and success factors for post-IPO family firm longevity. The concept distinguishes between three stages of AO.

The highest level is the *continuous AO*, which means at least one family member has taken on a role either as an executive director or through a supervisory mandate at the time of the IPO launch and at the time of crucial change/observation end. Hence, active family involvement and influence is exercised continuously throughout the firm's survival time.

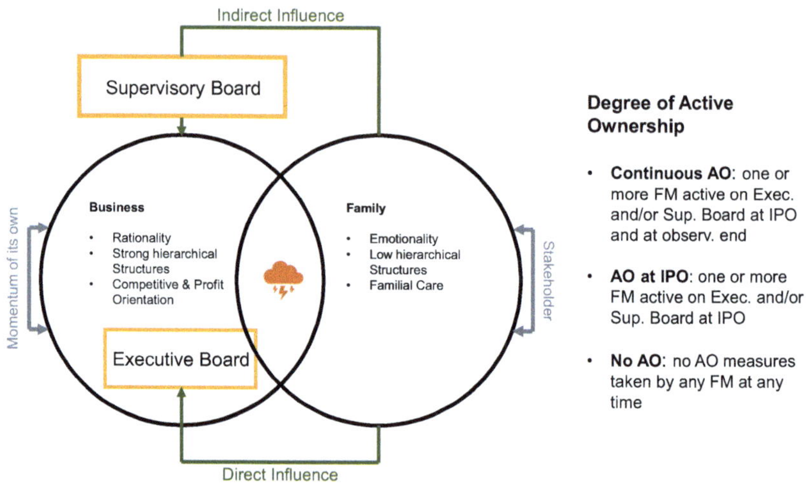

Figure 2.4 The Concept of Active Ownership. (Source: Author's own figure (further development of Figure 1.1))

The second level of AO comprises all firms, of which at least one member of the shareholding family/-ies exercised a supervisory mandate or operated on the Executive Board at the time of the IPO launch (*AO at IPO*). The level of active family involvement and influence has diluted over time, until finally no family member applies AO measures at the end of the observed timeline.

A complete lack of AO measures executed by the shareholding family at any point along the observed timeline has been defined as the lowest level (*no AO*). These firms had external directors and supervisory board members from the beginning. It may well be assumed that the level of family interest in the firms' strategic and operational development was lower in comparison to the firms of another categorization. Possible reasons for the lack of AO measures are that the family members lacked professional qualifications, executed jobs in other fields, or simply had no interest in exerting AO measures.

References

Ahmad, S., Omar, R. & Quoquab, F. (2020). Family firms' sustainable longevity: the role of family involvement in business and innovation capability. *Journal of Family Business Management*, 11(1), 86–106.

Anderson, R.C. & Reeb, D.R. (2003). Founding family ownership and firm performance: evidence from the S&P 500. *The Journal of Finance*, 58(3), 1301–1328.

Andres, C. (2008). Large shareholders and firm performance—An empirical examination of founding-family ownership. *Journal of Corporate Finance*, 14, 431–445.

Baus, K. (2013). *Die Familienstrategie—Wie Familien ihr Unternehmen über Generationen sichern* (4. ed.). Wiesbaden: Springer-Gabler.

Beck, S., Prügl, R. & Walter, K. (2020). Communicating the family firm brand: Antecedents and performance effects. *European Management Journal*, 38, 95–107.

Berghoff, H. & Köhler, I. (2020). *Verdienst und Vermächtnis—Familienunternehmen in Deutschland und den USA seit 1800*. Frankfurt: Campus.

Block, J.H. (2012). R&D investments in family and founder firms: An agency perspective. *Journal of Business Venturing*, 27, 248–265.

Block, J.H. & Spiegel, F. (2013). Family firm density and regional innovation output: An exploratory analysis. *Journal of Family Business Strategy*, 4, 270–280.

Carpentier, C., L'Her, J.-F. & Suret, J.-M. (2008). Competition and Survival of Stock Exchanges: Lessons from Canada. *Review of Pacific Basin Financial Markets and Policies*, 11(2), 255–286.

Carpentier, C. & Suret, J.-M. (2011). The survival and success of Canadian penny stock IPOs. *Small Business Economics*, 36, 1010–121.

Chancharat, N., Krishnamurti, C. & Tian, G. (2012). Board Structure and Survival of New Economy IPO Firms. *Corporate Governance: An International Review*, 20(2), 144–163.

Casillas, J.C., Moreno-Menéndez, A.M., Barbero, J.L. & Clinton, E. (2019). Retrenchment Strategies and Family Involvement: The Role of Survival Risk. *Family Business Review*, 32(1), 58–75.

Chirico, F., Gómez-Mejia, L.R., Hellerstedt, K., Withers, M. & Nordqvist, M. (2020). To Merge, Sell, or Liquidate? Socioemotional Wealth, Family Control, and the Choice of Business Exit. *Journal of Management*, 46(8), 1342–1379.

Cho, J., Miller, D. & Lee, J. (2018). Too much of a good thing: Family involvement and the survival of listed Korean firms. *Journal of Family Business Strategy*, 9, 223–237.

Craig, J.B., Dibrell, C. & Garrett, R. (2014). Examining relationships among family influence, family culture, flexible planning systems, innovativeness and firm performance. *Journal of Family Business Strategy*, 5, 229–238.

Daepp, M.I.G., Hamilton, M.J., West, G.B. & Bettencourt, L.M.A. (2015). The mortality of companies. *The Royal Society Publishing*, 12, 1–8.

Franks, J., Mayer, C. & Wagner, H.F. (2015). The Survival of the Weakest: Flourishing Family Firms in Germany. *Journal of Applied Corporate Finance*, 27(4), 27–35.

Frericks, S., Stotmeister, K. & Kormann, H. (in print, 2023). Extant Research and other Literature on Listed Family Enterprises. Fleischer, H. & Prigge, S. (Eds)., Listed family Companies. Hamburg Conference 2021: Law and Management of Family Firms.

Hengstmann, W. (1935). *Die Familiengesellschaft. Dissertation der Rechts- und Staatswissenschaftliche Fakultät der Martin-Luther-Universität Halle-Wittenberg.* Berlin: Triltsch & Huther.

Jain, B.A. & Kini, O. (2000). Does the Presence of Venture Capitalists Improve the Survival Profile of IPO Firms? *Journal of Business & Accounting*, 27(9), 1139–1176.

Jain, B.A. & Kini, O. (2008). The Impact of Strategic Investment Choices on Post-Issue Operating Performance and Survival of US IPO Firms. *Journal of Business Finance & Accounting*, 35(3), 259–490.

James, H.S. (1999). Owner as manager, extended horizons and the family firm. *International Journal of the Economics of Business*, 6(1), 41–55.

Khurshed, A. (2000). *Discussion of* Does the Presence of Venture Capitalists Improve the Survival Profile of IPO Firms? *Journal of Business Finance & Accounting*, 27(9), 1177–1183.

Kim, Y. & Gao, F.Y. (2012). Does family involvement increase business performance? Family-longevity goals' moderating role in Chinese family firms. *Journal of Business Research*, 66, 265–274.

Klasa, S. (2007). Why Do Controlling Families of Public Firms Sell Their Remaining Ownership Stake? *Journal of Financial and Quantitative Analysis*, 42(2), 339–368.

Knur, A. (1941). *Die Familiengesellschaft. Eine vergleichende Untersuchung der Unternehmensformen.* München: Franz Vahlen.

Kormann, H. & Wimmer, R. (2018). Vom Ursprung der Forschung zu Familienunternehmen. *Zeitschrift für Familienunternehmen und Strategie*, 05, 148–153.

Kormann, H. & Schlippe, A.v. (2017). Börsennotierung des Familienunternehmens—Ein Ansatz zur Überbrückung von Paradoxien und seine Erfolgsaussichten. *Zeitschrift für Familienunternehmen und Strategie*, 06, 200–205.

Kraiczy, N.D., Hack, A. & Kellermanns, F.W. (2014). New product portfolio performance in family firms. *Journal of Business Research*, 67, 1065–1073.

Lantelme, M. (2017). *The Rise and Downfall of Germany's Largest Family and Non-Family Businesses—A Historical Study and Strategic Analysis from 1971 to 2011.* Wiesbaden: Springer Gabler.

Lantelme, M., Seibold, L.K.C. & Kormann, H. (2021). *German Family Enterprises—A Sourcebook of Structure, Growth, Downfall and Corporate Longevity* (2. ed.). Cham: Springer Nature.

Le Breton-Miller, I. & Miller, D. (2006). Why do some family businesses out-compete? Governance, long-term orientation, and sustainable capability. *Entrepreneurship Theory and Practice*, 30(6), 731–746.

Lindow. C.M., Stubner, S. & Wulf, T. (2010). Strategic fit within family firms: The role of family influence and the effect on performance. *Journal of Family Business Strategy*, 1, 167–178.

Löhde, A.S.K., Calabrò, A. & Torchia, M. (2020). Understanding the main drivers of family firm longevity: the role of business family learning. *International Studies of Management & Organization*, 50(2), 130–152.

Lumpkin, G.T. & Dess, G.G. (1996). Clarifying the entrepreneurial orientation construct and linking it to performance. *Academy of Management Review*, 21 (1), 135–172.

Lumpkin, G.T., Brigham, K.H. & Moss, T.W. (2010). Long-term orientation: implications for the entrepreneurial orientation and performance of family businesses. *Entrepreneurship & Regional Development*, 22(3-4), 241–264.

Moya, M.F., Pérez, P.F. & Lubinski, C. (2020). Standing the test of time: External factors influencing family firm longevity in Germany and Spain during the twentieth century. *Journal of Evolutionary Studies in Business*, 5(1), 221–264.

Naldi, L., Nordquist, M., Sjöberg, K. & Wiklund, J. (2007). Entrepreneurial Orientation, Risk Taking, and Performance in Family Firms. *Family Business Review*, 20(1), 33–47.

Niehm, L.S., Miller, N.J., Shelley II, M.C. & Fitzgerald, M.A. (2009). Small Family Business Survival: Strategies For Coping With Overlapping Family And Business Demands. *Journal of Developmental Entrepreneurship*, 14(3), 209–232.

Rauschendorfer, N., Prügl, R. & Lude, M. (2021). Love is in the air. Consumers' perception of products from firms signaling their family nature. *Psychology & Marketing*, 39, 239–249.

Sander, B. (2008). *Börsenerfolg Familienunternehmen—Höhere Rendite mit GEX-Werten.* München: FinanzBuch Verlag.

Santarelli, E. & Lotti, F. (2005). The Survival of Family Firms: The Importance of Control and Family Ties. *International Journal of the Economics of Business*, 12(2), 183–192.

Schürmann, W. (1980). *Familienunternehmen und Börse—Emittieren, warum und wie?.* Wiesbaden: Gabler.

Schürmann, W. & Körfgen, K. (1987). *Familienunternehmen auf dem Weg zur Börse* (2. ed.). München: Beck.

Schürmann, W. & Körfgen, K. (1997). *Familienunternehmen auf dem Weg zur Börse* (3. ed.). München: Beck.

Seibold, L.K.C. (2019). *Family Businesses' Growth—Unpacking the Black Box.* Wiesbaden: Springer Gabler.

Stafford, K., Bhargava, V., Danes, S.M., Haynes, G. & Brewton, K.E. (2010). Factors Associated with Long-Term Survival of Family Businesses: Duration Analysis. *Journal offamily and Economic Issues*, 31, 442–457.

Stafford, K., Danes, S.M. & Haynes, G.W. (2013). Long-term firm survival and growth considering owning family adaptive capacity and federal disaster assistance receipt. *Journal of Family Business Strategy*, 4, 188–200.

Steen, A. & Welch, L.S. (2006). Dancing With Giants: Acquisition and Survival of the Family Firm. *Family Business Review*, 19(4), 289–300.

Tellis, G.J., Prabhu, J.C. & Chandy, R.K. (2009). Radical Innovation across Nations: The Preeminence of Corporate Culture. *Journal of Marketing*, 73, 3–23.

Villalonga, B. & Amit, R. (2006). How do family ownership, control and management affect firm value? *Journal of Financial Economics*, 80, 385–417.

Wilbon, A.D. (2002). Predicting survival of high-technology initial public offering firms. *Journal of High Technology Management Research*, 13, 127–141.

Zellweger, T.M., Nason, R.S. & Nordquist, M. (2012). From longevity of Firms to Transgenerational Entrepreneurship of Families: Introducing Family Entrepreneurial Orientation. *Family Business Review*, 25(2), 136–155.

Methodology 3

This chapter introduces the methodological background of the study, allowing for a deeper introduction into the research approach and design, the data collection process, the data set, the variables, and finally the applied methods of data analysis. It thereby provides the necessary foundation for the reader to comprehend the structure of the analysis and to construe the findings appropriately.

3.1 Chapter Overview

Initially, the chapter introduces the reader to the research approach, design of the dissertation, and the research objective. The data collection process is also described in great detail, offering the reader an insight into the challenges of the process in connection with the hurdles of working with historic data. It demonstrates what kind of data was available and how lack of data has been dealt with. The data collection process leads to the set of requirements and subsequently to the compilation of the main sample of stock-listed family enterprises, as well as the comparison sample of classic IPO firms without family involvement. After the introduction of the samples, the corresponding variables are presented for each sample. In the end, the reader is provided with an overview of the methods of data analysis.

K. Stotmeister, *Publicly Traded Family Businesses*, Familienunternehmen und KMU, https://doi.org/10.1007/978-3-658-44303-0_3

3.2 The Research Approach and Design of the Dissertation

The present study is part of a large research project named "Das börsennotierte Familienunternehmen," under the guidance of Hermut Kormann, Torsten Pieper and Jörn Block.[1] The research focus of the superordinate project lays on *German Stock-Listed Family Enterprises.* It supports studies concerning research topics from historical and current issues and developments. It is a comprehensive project covering the diversity of topics regarding German stock-listed family businesses. The current study, as part of the research project, concerns itself with the historical development of German stock-listed family businesses, with a focus on longevity and family involvement.

This study attempts to reveal the developments of publicly traded family businesses from both perspectives—both failures and survivors as an original founding-family business at the German Stock Exchange. It is the first of its kind in examining the long-term development of the target population, being German publicly traded family businesses, with an observation period ranging from the mid 20th century to 2018 inclusive. There is little research focusing on the downside of family firm characteristics and development (Stafford et al, 2010, pp. 445).[2] Most literature, particularly in family business research, is written about success factors, growth, succession and longevity,[3] mainly highlighting positive traits of family enterprises.

A data set has been constructed with data all around firm characteristics at the time of the stock market flotation as well as developmental data of German family businesses in the main sample, and German non-family businesses in a comparison sample. The comparison group has explicitly been defined as the one mentioned, since the effect of stock market flotations on the firms in general is of interest to whether family enterprises develop differently from non-family enterprises.[4] The observation period comprises 68 years, which allows an observation of firm development over two to three generations in familial life cycles, giving this study an exceptional standing regarding long-term observation in comparison to others in the field. Klasa (2007), for instance, examined 84 U.S. publicly traded family businesses, of which the invested family sold either their controlling shares or all shares within the timeline between 1984 and 1998. For

---

[1] For further information, see Section 1.4. "Introducing the Structure of the Dissertation".

[2] For an example, see Rau (2013).

[3] See Klein (2000).

[4] For further information, see Section 6.2. "Limits of the Study".

comparison, Klasa examined 84 publicly traded family businesses that remained in family ownership in order to derive reasons why the selling families sold their controlling shares. So far, this is the most extended long-term study on publicly traded family businesses.[5]

As a starting point, it was necessary to define the appropriate research approach. The initial questions were: What are the goals of this study? How can the underlying research question be answered in a way that allows for a complete and extensive understanding of the phenomenon? An inductive approach was decided upon, as a means through which to keep an open mind and reduce bias. There is no prior research in this particular field with such an extensive data set and time frame, which offers already existent theories. Therefore, the investigative path has been exploratory.

It was important to the researcher to allow the data to tell the story. Hence, there are no hypotheses to direct the research into predefined directions. Simply, the goal of the examination is to find out *how* German family firms developed after IPO, in order to derive conspicuous features of long-term development of stock-listed German family enterprises.

3.2.1 The Inductive Research Approach

In deductive research, theory and hypotheses are at the beginning of the project. Therefore, assumptions based upon already existent theories are tested for their validity. Inductive research, on the other hand, aims at creating new theories by analyzing data without prior assumptions or hypotheses (Sreejesh et al., 2014, p. 31; Hair Jr. et al., 2016, p. 156). In these cases, theory building is positioned at the end of the research process (Churchill & Brown, 2007, p. 81; Glaser & Strauss, 2010, p. 32; Fredebeul-Krein, 2012, p. 65). Rost (2003, p. 29) describes the difference between deduction and induction as an "interplay" between theory and empiricism. The circular demonstration of the "interplay" between deductive and inductive research in Figure 1.1 complements the statements by Hair Jr. et al. (2016), Glaser & Strauss (2010) and colleagues.

Figure 3.1 demonstrates how induction is applied for this study: beginning with empiricism and leading to new theory.

[5] For more detail on Klasa (2007) and further research in this field, see Section 2.2.2. "Status quo on Stock-listed Family Enterprise Longevity".

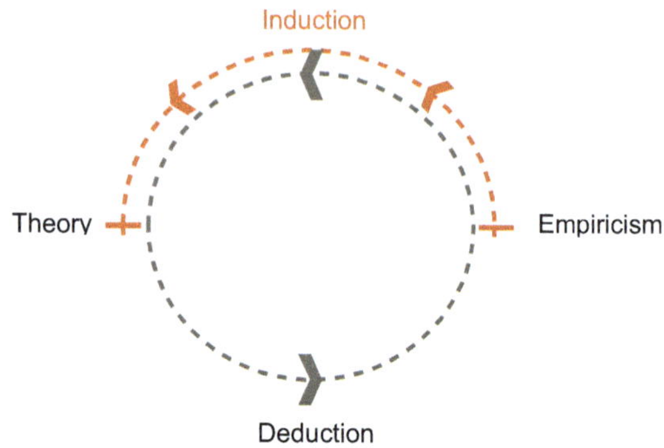

Figure 3.1 The Cycle of Empiricism and Theory. (Source: Author´s own figure, adapted from Rost (2003, p. 29))

3.2.2 Particularities of an Exploratory Research Design

Inductive approaches in research are of exploratory nature. The confirmatory approach, as its name suggests, seeks a confirmation of hypotheses based on preexistent theory (Fredebeul-Krein, 2012, p. 65). From a historical perspective, exploratory research design has usually been applied in qualitative research. It has found less use in quantitative data analysis (Glaser & Strauss, 2010, p. 32). Even today, the confirmatory research design is more common in business research practice.

According to Glaser and Strauss (2010, pp. 32), exploratory research was generally applied when a field was bare of prior research. Exploratory studies were conducted in order to generate a preliminary understanding of the field (Hair Jr. et al., 2016, p. 155). From this point on, with use of confirmatory research methods, the verification of hypotheses was conducted (Sreejesh et al., 2014, p. 31). Typical exploratory research methods comprise case study analyses, interviews, observations, and/or field experiments (Seibold, 2019, p. 177).

3.2.2.1 Exploratory Research Applied to this Study

This study investigates the development of German publicly traded family enterprises, with exclusively quantitative data. It is the first study of its kind, with a data set covering nearly seventy years of development of German stock-listed founding-family firms and non-family firms for comparison. More precisely, the development of family businesses regarding dilution of family influence after their stock market flotation has never been investigated in such detail and to such an extent. Despite the fact that this study is based on purely quantitative data, there are certain overlaps with the characteristics of exploratory research. For instance, the gross research field of publicly traded family firms has already been tackled in prior research, yet the field of IPO-firms´ survival as listed firms is not yet widely examined, mostly with no particular focus on family enterprises and only with a limited observation time frame.[6] Therefore, this work enters new territory. No prior research offers already existent theories on which to base assumptions or hypotheses, hence the current study lays the groundwork. This is a good precondition for an exploratory approach.

The data set comprises historical data for both family and non-family businesses on how each individual business developed after IPO regarding shareholder structure and survival. The samples comprise 77 stock-listed founding-family corporations and 39 stock-listed non-family corporations, giving a total of 116 individual cases on development and survival of German public corporations.

Hence, an exploratory approach allows for getting the most out of the given data without restrictions or predisposition.

3.2.2.2 Exploratory Research and the Present Research Question

Conducting exploration aims at investigating a given development or problem (Hair Jr. et al., 2016, p. 155), rather than seeking solutions or deriving practical advice. Hence, this study doesn't primarily aim at creating solutions, but rather at clarifying how family firms, in particular, have developed as public firms, with the final objective of creating a model based on clusters, patterns, and observations that have been derived from the data. With exploration, the researcher lays the foundation for explanations, hence enabling the later creation of solutions and advice.

As the term implies, exploratory research is conducted in order to *explore* unknown grounds—respectively, to explore the research question[7]:

How did German stock-listed family firms develop after IPO, with a main focus on longevity and family involvement?—Development of a model based on the long-term analysis of historical data ranging from 1950-2018

- *How long do families of publicly traded family firms maintain their influence through shares (>25%) after IPO?*
- *How does family influence (shareholding quota) develop after IPO?*

[6] Compare to Brown (1970), Jain & Kini (2000), Khurshed (2000), Wilbon (2002), Jain & Kini (2008) and Klasa (2007).

[7] For further information, see Section 2.3. "Identifying Research Gaps and Formulating the Research Question".

- *In cases of dissolution or dilution, what were the reasons (sale/family exit, delisting, bankruptcy, etc.)?*
- *Are there beneficial factors/success factors for family firm survival (industry, number of families involved, age of firm, etc.)?*

3.2.3 The Research Objective of the Dissertation

This research aims at investigating the long-term development of *publicly traded founding-family businesses* and *publicly traded non-family businesses* after their IPO, with particular focus on *longevity* and *survival.* This leads to the next focus, which is on *family influence through shareholder structure* (dilution) on the family businesses, based on *exploratory quantitative analysis.*

While companies go public for a number of reasons, the most common is to gain access to new capital from the capital market for business development and growth. A stock market flotation may have further benefits for the company, such as improving the public image or offering reassurance for external stakeholders, such as for customers or suppliers. For family businesses, entering the public market may have additional reasons. Some IPOs may be considered due to lack of familial succession, other reasons may be creating a corporate valuation in order to realize a partial or total family exit. The family may also be seeking the stability and governance which comes with the regulatory demands of a public firm. Finally, the family corporation may simply need new capital to finance growth.[8]

The reasons or goals may differ from one company to another, but the common denominator is that this decision is connected with uncertainty and risk (for some more than for others). The decision to go public is a high stakes bet, and there is only one chance at a successful stock market flotation. This point is where the present study latches on.

[8] For further information, see Section 1.3. "Family Enterprises Entering the Public Market—How Much Tension Can a Family Enterprise take? ".

3.3 Data Collection Process

In the following subchapter, the data collection process will be described to provide for a full understanding of how the final samples have been collected and analyzed, and a full reconstruction of the train of thought behind the research construct.

This subchapter begins with the definition of the time frame for eligible company flotations relevant for this research and how the timeline for development was determined. From there, the data collection process will be explained, beginning at the top of the inverted pyramid presented in Figure 3.3, sorting through the entirety of available data sources, until the final sample comes together at the end. Especially regarding the challenges in connection with historical data, this subchapter is important. First it lays open where the data for the final samples of publicly traded family firms, as well as the comparison group of publicly traded non-family firms, comes from. Second, it shows how they differ.

3.3.1 Defining the Time Frame

In order to define the appropriate time frame, the political, economic and social aspects of post-WWII in Germany must be taken into consideration. On May 8th, 1945, World War II ended in Europe. It left the German people, landmarks, and economy shattered—the entire country was buried under ashes. The German Stock Market remained in business for the near entirety of the war under NS-Regime, and was instrumental to financing the war economy (Deutsche Börse AG, 2010).

Shortly before the end of the war, the German Stock Exchange had to close the Official Market (*Amtlicher Handel*) on April 18th, 1945 (Bremer, 1969, p. 44). Two months after the war ended, Hamburg opened its stock market on July 9th, 1945, as the first of all German stock markets, to the Regulated Market (*Regulierter Markt*) (Bremer, 1969, p. 44). The main stock exchange in Germany, the *Frankfurter Börse*, which was also an internationally renowned stock market prior to the war, opened for unofficial trading in September 1945 (Deutsche Börse AG, 2010). Only through the monetary reform in 1948 and a stabilizing German economy, did the *Frankfurter Börse* regain importance and reliability. As a result, the Official Market was opened in Frankfurt in 1949 (Deutsche Börse AG, 2010). Furthermore, on October 1st, 1949, the *Wertpapierbereinigungsgesetz* came into effect, declaring bonds and securities from West German companies invalid and reevaluating the eligible securities to the new West German currency (Rudolph, 1992, p. 39; Bundesgesetzblatt, 1955).

Taking the historical development of the German economy and the German Stock Exchange of post-World War II under consideration, and connecting these findings with the goal of this research work and the defined research questions, the lower cutoff has been set at the year of 1950. This pre-1950s cutoff was chosen to minimize the risk of extraordinary war- and post-war-related bias, due to war- and post-war-related disparities.

Regarding the upper cutoff, one historical event is crucial: the German Reunification (*Deutsche Wiedervereinigung*). The years 1989 and 1990 were of particular historical value to Germany. On November 9th, 1989, the Berlin Wall fell (Presse- und Informationsamt der Bundesregierung, 2015, p. 2). Nearly a year later, on October 3rd, 1990, East and West Germany were officially unified as the *Bundesrepublik Deutschland* (Presse- und Informationsamt der Bundesregierung, 2015, p. 92). These events marked a radical change for the German economy. In order to ensure a high degree of comparative reliability and to reduce bias caused by severe political and economic changes, the upper cutoff for case selection has been set at the year of 1988.

The upper cutoff for the developmental phase has been defined as 2018, in order to exclude the effects of the Covid-19 Global Crisis, which sent the entire globe into a state of emergency and ultimately set an immense strain on the global economy. Hence, adding these additional thirty years, the general observation period ranges from 1950 to 2018. This allows for the most recently floated firms in the late 1980's to develop for at least thirty years before being subjected to evaluation in this research work (Figure 3.2).

In addition to the political, economic, and social aspects relevant to the definition of the timeline, there is another main factor which is characteristic of family enterprises, and plays an equally significant role: longevity.

Family companies have been identified with numerous features, some of beneficial and some of more disadvantageous nature. One of the positive characteristics is a long-term orientation in company strategy and goal development (Le Breton-Miller & Miller, 2006, p. 732; Lumpkin et al., 2010, p. 242; Gambatese & Hallowell, 2011, p. 553; Andres, 2008, p. 433), which can ensure survival and success for generations to come. Therefore, in order to capture a most realistic rendering of the development of family firms after the realization of their decision to enter the public market, an extended period of observation is necessary. Only by ensuring this wide range for company development can the research question be answered thoroughly and in good conscience.

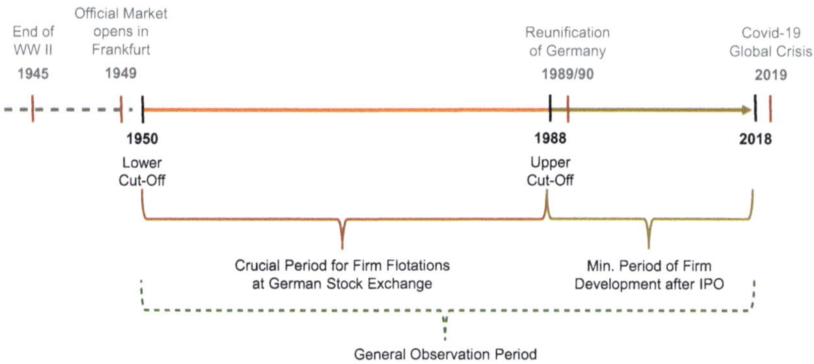

Figure 3.2 Timeline. (Source: Author's own figure)

3.3.2 Screening Multiple Data Sources

3.3.2.1 The Compilation of Stock Market Flotations 1950–1988

The database was generated through a multi-channel approach. Since the timeline reaches back to pre-digital 1950, the data collection process required a variety of sources in order to generate a database as complete as possible, such as early-year stock market reports, newspaper articles, earlier research literature and, for more recent data, internet research. All of these also required different evaluation practices. When working with historical data, the most prominent challenge is coping with fragmentary information. In general, one must assume that contemporary witnesses are very rare to non-existent. Even if witnesses are available, the reliability of long-term cognitive recollection decreases as time passes and therefore must be taken with some reservation. The farther back the data reaches, the only reliable sources are on video-, audio-, photography- or paper-based media. Increasing difficulties in tracking the media down also apply to the timeline of interest. Many documents are rare, possibly even unique, leading to geographical challenges and time issues. Hence, historical data is rarely without gaps.

In a first step, various state, university and newspaper archives were consulted, and department heads for economic history, research institutes and the Stock Exchange in Stuttgart were all contacted and systematically screened for useful information regarding IPOs at the German Stock Exchange[9] within the defined timeline from 1950 to 1988. This initial research phase was necessary for sounding out the general existence and availability of useful documentation.

The initiation of the actual process of data generation followed the primary data-source screening. In a multi-tracking approach, a list of IPOs registered at the German Stock Exchange was compiled, reaching from 1950 to 1988. As shown in Table 3.1, the list incorporates the year of the initial public offering, the company's name at the time of IPO, and the branch of economic activity.[10]

The data was fragmentally composed through multi-tracking. Components were gathered in stock market reports reaching from 1950 until 1981, found in the *Wirtschaftsarchiv Baden-Württemberg—Universität Hohenheim*, and previous research literature.[11] Putting the fragments together led to an overall number of 154 companies launching their initial public offering at the German Stock Exchange within the previously defined time frame.[12]

In retrospect, it is surprising that the process of gathering and retrieving such official information regarding firm flotations at the German Stock Exchange is as cumbersome as it is. On the other hand, the collection period begins in 1950, only five years after the war ended. The repercussions of the Second World War were far-reaching and most certainly still had an influence on the initial years of the time frame.

[9] The terms *German Stock Market* or *German Stock Exchange* are generally with reference to West-Germany for the time between 1945 and 1988.

[10] The categorization of industries in Table 3.1 has been adapted from the official *Klassifikation der Wirtschaftszweige* by the *Statistische Ämter des Bundes und der Länder* (2008b).

[11] See Koch & Wegmann (2000), Schürmann & Körfgen (1987, 1997) and Schürmann (1980).

[12] Please note that completeness is not guaranteed.

Table 3.1 Total IPOs at German Stock Exchange between 1950 and 1988

Year of IPO	Company at IPO	Industry
1951	Kienzle Uhrenfabrik AG	Manufacture of computer, electronic and optical products
1959	Erdölwerke Frisia AG	Extraction of crude petroleum and natural gas
1959	Preussische Bergwerks- und Hütten-AG	Mining of coal and lignite
1960	G.M. Pfaff AG	Manufacture of machinery and equipment n.e.c.
1961	WOLKO Schuhfabrik AG	Manufacture of leather and related products
1961	Volkswagenwerk AG	Manufacture of motor vehicles, trailers and semi-trailers
1961	Westag & Getalit AG	Manufacture of rubber and plastic products
1961	Pschorrbräu AG	Manufacture of beverages
1963	Neckermann Versand KGaA	Retail trade, except of motor vehicles and motorcycles
1964	Pegulan-Werke AG	Manufacture of rubber and plastic products
1964	Braun AG	Manufacture of electrical equipment
1965	Vereinigte Elektrizitäts- und Bergwerks AG	Electricity, gas, steam and air conditioning supply
1966	Deutsche Lufthansa AG	Air transport
1966	Vereinigte Elektrizitätswerke Westfalen AG	Electricity, gas, steam and air conditioning supply
1966	Rudolf Hussel AG	Manufacture of food products
1967	Deutsche Klinik für Diagnostik AG	Human health activities
1968	Schwab AG	N/A
1969	Horten AG	Retail trade, except of motor vehicles and motorcycles
1972	Dyckerhoff & Widmann AG	Construction of buildings
1973	Badenwerk AG	Electricity, gas, steam and air conditioning supply
1976	Mercedes-Automobil-Holding AG	Manufacture of motor vehicles, trailers and semi-trailers
1977	Standard Elektrik Lorenz AG	N/A
1977	ALTANA Industrie-Aktien und Anlagen AG	Manufacture of chemicals and chemical products

(continued)

Table 3.1 (continued)

1977	CEAG Industrie-Aktien und Anlagen AG	N/A
1977	BayWa AG	Wholesale trade, except of motor vehicles and motorcycles
1977	ASKO Deutsche Kaufhaus AG	Retail trade, except of motor vehicles and motorcycles
1977	Herlitz AG	Retail trade, except of motor vehicles and motorcycles
1977	Leffers AG	Retail trade, except of motor vehicles and motorcycles
1978	Progress-Werk Oberkirch AG	Manufacture of motor vehicles, trailers and semi-trailers
1978	Norddt. Hypotheken- und Wechselbank AG	Financial service activities, except insurance and pension funding
1979	Drägerwerk AG	Manufacture of computer, electronic and optical products
1979	C.J. Vogel Draht- und Kabelwerke AG	N/A
1979	Aachener & Münchner Versicherung AG	Insurance, reinsurance and pension funding, except compulsory social security
1979	Mauser Waldeck AG	Manufacture of fabricated metal products, except machinery and equipment
1980	Vogtländische Baumwollspinnerei AG	Manufacture of textiles
1980	Joh. Friedrich Behrens AG	Manufacture of fabricated metal products, except machinery and equipment
1980	AGAB AG für Anlagen und Beteiligungen	Activities auxiliary to financial services and insurance activities
1981	Knürr Mechanik für die Elektronik AG	Manufacture of fabricated metal products, except machinery and equipment
1981	Friedrich Deckel AG	Manufacture of machinery and equipment n.e.c.
1982	Electronic 2000 Vertriebs-AG	Computer programming, consultancy and related activities
1982	Main-Gaswerke AG	Electricity, gas, steam and air conditioning supply
1982	Monachia Grundstücks-AG	Real estate activities
1982	Ferd. Rückforth Nachfolger AG	Manufacture of beverages
1983	Kerkerbachbahn AG	Land transport and transport via pipelines

(continued)

Table 3.1 (continued)

1983	SM Software AG	Computer programming, consultancy and related activities
1983	Joseph Vögele AG	Manufacture of machinery and equipment n.e.c.
1983	TEWIDATA AG	Computer programming, consultancy and related activities
1983	Wella AG	Manufacture of basic pharmaceutical products and pharmaceutical preparations
1983	Gestra AG	Manufacture of motor vehicles, trailers and semi-trailers
1983	GfC AG für Computersysteme in der Medizin	Computer programming, consultancy and related activities
1983	Hagen Batterie AG	Manufacture of electrical equipment
1983	Treuwo Verwaltunsg-AG	Real estate activities
1983	Etienne Aigner AG	Manufacture of wearing apparel
1984	Konrad Hornschuch AG	Manufacture of rubber and plastic products
1984	Zanders Feinpapiere AG	Manufacture of paper and paper products
1984	BCT Computer AG	Computer programming, consultancy and related activities
1984	MCS Modulare Comp. Und Software Syst. AG	Computer programming, consultancy and related activities
1984	Kolbenschmidt AG	Manufacture of motor vehicles, trailers and semi-trailers
1984	Dr. Ing. h.c.F. Porsche AG	Manufacture of motor vehicles, trailers and semi-trailers
1984	YMOS AG Industrieprodukte	Manufacture of motor vehicles, trailers and semi-trailers
1984	Carl Schenck AG	Manufacture of machinery and equipment n.e.c.
1984	Hegener + Glaser AG	Computer programming, consultancy and related activities
1984	Markt & Technik Verlag AG	Publishing activities
1984	Nixdorf Computer AG	Manufacture of computer, electronic and optical products
1984	Berliner Bank AG	Financial service activities, except insurance and pension funding
1984	Garny AG	Manufacture of fabricated metal products, except machinery and equipment

(continued)

Table 3.1 (continued)

1984	Leifheit AG	Other manufacturing
1984	Schmalbach-Lubeca AG	Other manufacturing
1984	Berliner Elektro-Beteiligungen AG	N/A
1984	Krones AG Hermann Kronseder Masch.fabrik	Manufacture of machinery and equipment n.e.c.
1984	Scheu & Wirth AG	Specialised construction activities
1984	Nino AG	Manufacture of textiles
1984	Sinn AG	Retail trade, except of motor vehicles and motorcycles
1984	MotoMeter AG	Manufacture of computer, electronic and optical products
1984	ADV/ORGA F.A. Meyer AG	Computer programming, consultancy and related activities
1985	Fuchs Petrolub AG Oel & Chemie	Manufacture of coke and refined petroleum products
1985	Brilliantenleuchten AG	Manufacture of electrical equipment
1985	Schumag AG	Manufacture of machinery and equipment n.e.c.
1985	Koenig & Bauer AG	Manufacture of machinery and equipment n.e.c.
1985	Nürnberger Lebensversicherung AG	Insurance, reinsurance and pension funding, except compulsory social security
1985	Henkel KGaA	Other manufacturing
1985	Trinkhaus & Burkhardt KGaA	N/A
1985	FAG Kugelfischer Georg Schäfer KGaA	Manufacture of machinery and equipment n.e.c.
1985	Axel Springer Verlag AG	Publishing activities
1985	Peter Temming AG	Manufacture of paper and paper products
1985	Euro-Kai KGaA	Warehousing and support activities for transportation
1985	Deutsche Beteiligungs AG	Activities auxiliary to financial services and insurance activities
1985	Hugo Boss AG	Manufacture of wearing apparel
1986	Vogt Electronic AG	Manufacture of computer, electronic and optical products
1986	VDO Adolf Schindling AG	Manufacture of computer, electronic and optical products

(continued)

Table 3.1 (continued)

1986	Feldmühle Nobel AG	Manufacture of paper and paper products
1986	Massa AG	Construction of buildings
1986	Traub AG	Manufacture of machinery and equipment n.e.c.
1986	Escada AG	Manufacture of wearing apparel
1986	Oberland Glas AG	Manufacture of other non-metallic mineral products
1986	Antriebstechnik G. Bauknecht AG	Manufacture of electrical equipment
1986	Kampa-Haus AG	Construction of buildings
1986	VIAG AG	Electricity, gas, steam and air conditioning supply
1986	aqua signal AG	N/A
1986	Technocell AG München	Manufacture of paper and paper products
1986	Piper Generalvertretung Deutschland AG	N/A
1986	PUMA AG Rudolf Dassler Sport	Manufacture of wearing apparel
1986	Sixt AG	Land transport and transport via pipelines
1986	AVA Allg. Handelsges. Der Verbraucher AG	Wholesale trade, except of motor vehicles and motorcycles
1986	Felten & Guilleaume Energietechnik AG	Other manufacturing
1986	Ferdinand Hoffstätter AG	N/A
1986	Industrieverwaltungsgesellschaft AG	Real estate activities
1986	Schneider Rundfunkwerke AG	Manufacture of computer, electronic and optical products
1986	Edding AG	Other manufacturing
1986	Mineralbrunnen Überkingen-Teinach AG	Manufacture of beverages
1986	Riedel-Haus AG	N/A
1986	G. Bluthardt AG	N/A
1986	Nucletron Electronic AG	Manufacture of electrical equipment
1986	Irmen & Richter Textil AG	Manufacture of textiles

(continued)

Table 3.1 (continued)

1986	Fresenius AG	Manufacture of basic pharmaceutical products and pharmaceutical preparations
1986	Maho AG	Manufacture of machinery and equipment n.e.c.
1986	Greiffenberger AG	Manufacture of machinery and equipment n.e.c.
1986	Leonberger Bausparkasse AG	Financial service activities, except insurance and pension funding
1987	Pegasus Beteiligungen AG	Activities auxiliary to financial services and insurance activities
1987	SABO-Maschinenfabrik AG	Manufacture of machinery and equipment n.e.c.
1987	BBS Kraftfahrzeugtechnik AG	Manufacture of motor vehicles, trailers and semi-trailers
1987	Adolf Ahlers AG	Manufacture of wearing apparel
1987	Hertel AG Werkzeuge & Hartstoffe	Other manufacturing
1987	INFO Gesellschaft für Informationssyst. AG	Computer programming, consultancy and related activities
1987	Schwabengarage AG	Wholesale and retail trade and repair of motor vehicles and motorcycles
1987	Hornbach AG	Retail trade, except of motor vehicles and motorcycles
1987	Jagenberg AG	N/A
1987	GMN Georg Müller Nürnberg AG	Manufacture of fabricated metal products, except machinery and equipment
1987	Stelcon AG	Civil engineering
1987	Hans Einhell AG	Other manufacturing
1987	Rheinisch-Westf. Kreditgarantiebank AG	Financial service activities, except insurance and pension funding
1987	Boge AG	Manufacture of machinery and equipment n.e.c.
1987	Glunz AG	Manufacture of wood and of products of wood and cork, except furniture; manufacture of articles of straw and plaiting materials
1987	Stixi AG	Manufacture of food products
1987	Biotest AG	Manufacture of basic pharmaceutical products and pharmaceutical preparations
1987	Linotype AG	Computer programming, consultancy and related activities

(continued)

Table 3.1 (continued)

1987	co op AG	Retail trade, except of motor vehicles and motorcycles
1987	A. Moksel AG	Manufacture of food products
1988	Deutsche Verkehrs-Kredit-Bank AG	Financial service activities, except insurance and pension funding
1988	Deutscher Lloyd Versicherungs-AG	Insurance, reinsurance and pension funding, except compulsory social security
1988	Landshuter Kunstmühle AG	Manufacture of food products
1988	Bijou Brigitte modische Accessoires AG	Retail trade, except of motor vehicles and motorcycles
1988	Fernheizwerk Neukölln AG	Electricity, gas, steam and air conditioning supply
1988	Pietzsch AG	Manufacture of machinery and equipment n.e.c.
1988	Marschollek, Lautenschläger und Partner AG	Financial service activities, except insurance and pension funding
1988	Computer 2000 AG	Computer programming, consultancy and related activities
1988	Kunert AG	Manufacture of wearing apparel
1988	Macrotron AG für Datenerfassungssysteme	Computer programming, consultancy and related activities
1988	Compudent AG	Computer programming, consultancy and related activities
1988	Schwälbchen Molkerei Jakob Bertz AG	Manufacture of food products
1988	Oppermann Versand AG	Retail trade, except of motor vehicles and motorcycles
1988	SAP AG	Computer programming, consultancy and related activities
1988	SPAR Handel-AG	Retail trade, except of motor vehicles and motorcycles
1988	MVG AG für Internationale Mode	Retail trade, except of motor vehicles and motorcycles

3.3.2.2 The Initial Filtering Process

The next step was a revision of the initial compilation of stock market flotations. Banks and insurance companies were eliminated to clean up the data. They were removed from the sample, due to their fundamentally different business model compared with industrial companies. Firms without fully reliable data were also removed from the sample.[13]

3.3.2.3 Developing the Shareholder Structure at the Time of IPO—Firm Allocation

After the initial rough filtering process, the eligible firms were subjected to one of the most crucial examinations of this work: the identification and allocation of the firms to the samples. By defining the shareholder structure at the time of IPO, the companies were either assigned to the sample of family firms at IPO or to the sample of non-family firms at IPO as the control group (see Figure 3.3).

This step marks the point of departure for the entirety of the research. In order to establish a reliable data foundation, three significant sources were used: one publication series by Hoppenstedt/Saling, another by the Commerzbank Berlin, and previous research literature. These sources will be introduced on the following pages.

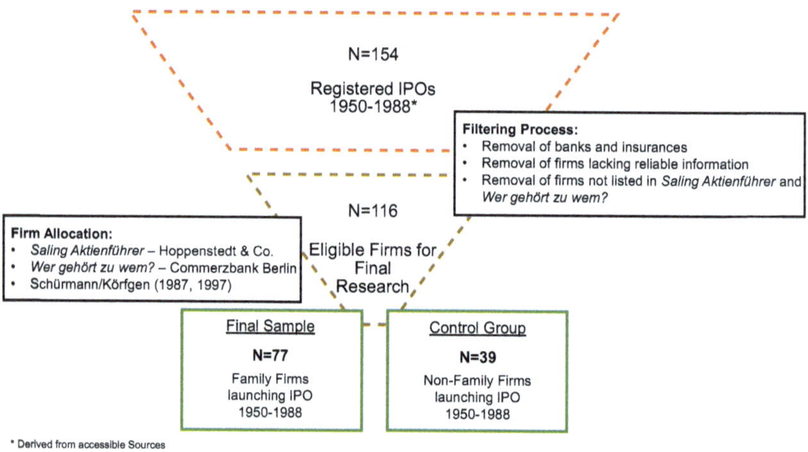

Figure 3.3 The Data Filtering Process. (Source: Author's own figure)

[13] Several firms in Table 3.1 have been marked with N/A in the *Industry* column, due to a lack of reliable information.

3.3.2.3.1 Definition of the Primary Source for the In-Depth Data Collection

The *Saling Aktienführer* by Hoppenstedt & Co. Publishing and the *Wer gehört zu wem?* publication series by the German *Commerzbank Berlin* serve as the basis for further data sorting and collection. These are reference series, listing the larger German businesses with their corresponding shareholder structures and governance. In particular, the *Saling Aktienführer* is an annual composition of stock-related shareholder and governance data for firms listed at the German Stock Exchange. The first publication goes back to 1870 and appeared annually as the *Saling´s Börsenpapiere* until 1942. After WWII, the publication series appeared annually starting 1953 as *Saling Aktienführer*. This work offers a striking regularity and comprehensiveness, therefore serving as a reliable source for firm allocation and further data collection.

The first volume of the publication series *Wer gehört zu wem?* was published in 1954, with subsequent updated volumes every two to four years. The last volume was published in the year 2010. This series focuses on the shareholder structure of the firms in detail. It lists all firms that offer a decent degree of publicity of their shareholder structure and record a minimum capital of 500,000 *DM* (*Deutsche Mark*).

Both publication series together offer the most detailed information available and allow for reliable firm allocation and data collection, making the development of changes in the shareholder structure retrievable over decades. Still, it must be mentioned that the degree of detail of the information provided may vary, which leaves some space for inaccuracy in the data.

3.3.2.3.2 Definition of Complementary Sources

Schürmann & Körfgen (1987, 1997), Koch & Wegmann (2000) and Schürmann (1980) offer detailed information on the shareholder quotas at the exact time of firm flotation. These works serve as complementary sources for the critical part of defining the initial structure in the year of IPO, as well as defining whether the firm is categorized as a family or non-family firm (see Figure 3.3).

In the end, the final firm allocation results in the group of family enterprises, comprising 77 firms, and the group of non-family enterprises, comprising 39 firms.

3.3.3 Derivation of Final Sample Groups

3.3.3.1 Selection Criteria for the Sample of Family Enterprises

The sample of family enterprises comprises all companies—family and founder firms[14]—that meet the selection criteria, defined in Section 2.4., "Definition of the stock-listed Family Enterprise". Building upon the list presented in Table 3.1 and following the initial cleansing process demonstrated in Figure 3.3, the enterprises have been identified with their initial shareholder structure at the time of their IPO launch at the German Stock Exchange. Next, the separation process takes place.

First, a reminder of the definition of family firms[15] that serves as a foundation for this research work.

A firm, meeting the following criteria, is, per definition by this work, a German family firm:

| *when at least 25% of stock are*
| *held directly or indirectly*
| *by one or more founder/s*
| *of German origin*
| *or their descendant families.*

Table 3.2 presents the results for the sample of family enterprises. The table includes the year of IPO and the corresponding company name, as well as the detailed shareholder quotas at the time of IPO, which have been extracted from *Saling Aktienführer*, the *Wer gehört zu Wem?* series, and the complementary literature.

A total of 77 enterprises has been assigned to this sample.

[14] Due to the very small number of founder firms and the rather small sample size of family enterprises, no distinction was made between the two. Family and founder firms are treated equally.

[15] For further information, see Section 2.4. "Definition of the Stock-Listed Family Enterprise".

Table 3.2 IPOs between 1950 and 1988—Sample of Family Enterprises

Year of IPO	Company	Shareholder Structure at Time of IPO
1951	Kienzle Uhrenfabrik AG	>80% in Family Ownershhip
1960	G.M. Pfaff AG	Karl Pfaff Heirs 70.4%, Georg Michael Pfaff Gedächtnisstiftung 8.7%
1961	WOLKO Schuhfabrik AG	Major Shareholder: Sigmund Irell, Rose Israel, Lilian& Gerard Wolfe
1961	Westag & Getalit AG	100% in Family Ownership
1961	Pschorrbräu AG	Family Pschorr >80%
1963	Neckerrmann Versand KGaA	Josef Neckarmann and Family 51.8%, Rest: Free Float
1964	Pegulan-Werke AG	Family Konsul Dr. jur. Fritz Ries including Vermögensverwaltungs GmbH 57.4%, Fabrikant Rudolf Strunz 14.3%, Direktor G.R. Zentner (Zürich) 6.66%
1964	Braun AG	Dipl.-Kfm. Erwin Braun & Ingenieur Arthur Braun >95%
1972	Dyckerhoff & Widmann AG	Family Ownership ca. 37%, ALOKA Allgemeine Organisations- und Kapitalbeteiligungs-Aktien-Gesellschaft 9%, VBB Gesellschaft für die Verwaltung von Bau-Beteiligungen mbH 26%
1977	ALTANA Industrie-Aktien und Anlagen AG	Major Shareholder: Family Members, Rest: Free Float
1977	Herlitz AG	95% in Family Ownership

(continued)

Table 3.2 (continued)

1977	Leffers AG	Dr. Ernst Leffers, Georg Leffers, Gerhard Leffers, Werner Leffers 100%
1978	Progress-Werk Oberkirch AG	Community of Heirs Josef Frisch 50%, Free Float 50%
1979	Drägerwerk AG	Major Shareholder: Family Dräger, Rest: Free Float
1979	Mauser Waldeck AG	Family Mauser > 25%, Rest: Free Float
1981	Knürr Mechanik für die Elektronik AG	Ordinary Shares mainly held by Family Knürr, 100% Prefence Shares in Free Float
1983	Joseph Vögele AG	Major Shareholder: Family Vögele, Rest: Free Float
1983	Wella AG	Family Ownership 67% Ordinary Shares, Free Float 33% Prefence Shares
1983	Gestra AG	45% in Family Ownership, Rest: Free Float
1983	GfC AG für Computersysteme in der Medizin	Major Shareholder: Dr. Jürgen Knipps, Hans-Ullrich Knipps & Dr. Franz Otte
1983	Hagen Batterie AG	Family Hagen 75%, Rest: Free Float
1983	Treuwo Verwaltungs-AG	Dr. L. Schuhmann, Dr. G. Ahrens, R. Burmeister, H.-H. Didt & B. Ehrlich 66.7%
1984	Zanders Feinpapiere AG	J.W. Zanders KG >50%
1984	BCT Computer AG	Wolfgang Böhmer 43.4% Ordinary Shares, Marita Böhmer 24.1% Ordinary Shares, Dr. Rolf Türk 8.9% Ordinary Shares, F+T Finanzierungsvermittlung und Treuhandgesellschaft mbH 11.8% Ordinary Shares, Rheinisch-Westfälische Verwaltungsgesellschaft für Kapitalbeteiligungen mbH & Co. KG

(continued)

Table 3.2 (continued)

1984	MCS Modulare Comp. Und Software Syst. AG	Manfred B. Lepiorz 87.7%
1984	Dr. Ing. h.c.F. Porsche AG	Families Porsche & Piech ca. 70%, Free Float 30%
1984	YMOS AG Industrieprodukte	100% Ordinary Shares in Family Ownership, Rest: Free Float
1984	Hegener + Glaser AG	Manfred Hegener & Florian Glaser 75%, Rest: Free Float
1984	Nixdorf Computer AG	Family Nixdorf 70%, Rest: Free Float
1984	Garny AG	50% in Family Ownership, Rest: Free Float
1984	Krones AG Hermann Kronseder Masch.fabrik	100% Ordinary Shares in Family Ownership, Preference Shares in Free Float
1984	Scheu & Wirth AG	Heriberth Wirth 100% Ordinary Shares & 20% Preference Shares, Rest: Free Float
1984	Nino AG	Major Shareholder: Community of Heirs Bernhard Niehues
1984	Sinn AG	Members of the Families Sinn, Becker & Cordes 75%
1984	ADV/ORGA F.A. Meyer AG	Friedrich A. Meyer 77.7% Ordinary Shares, Standard Elektrik Lorenz AG 12.7 % Ordinary Shares, Preference Shares in Free Float
1985	König & Bauer AG	Bolza Group 51% Ordinary Shares, Thomas de la Rue AG 12.5% Ordinary Shares, Giori Group 12.5% Ordinary Shares, Rest: Free Float
1985	Fuchs Petrolub AG	Family Fuchs 54% Ordinary Shares, Westdeutsche Landesbank Girozentrale & Dresdner Bank AG & Südwest LB 20% Ordinary Shares, Deutsche Bank AG 10% Ordinary Shares & Prefence Shares, Rest: Free Float

(continued)

Table 3.2 (continued)

1985	Henkel KGaA	Limited Partners: Family Henkel 100% Ordinary Shares
1985	FAG Kugelfischer Georg Schäfer KGaA	Family Schäfer 51.5% Ordinary Shares
1985	Axel Springer Verlag AG	Axel Springer Gesellschaft für Publizistik GmbH & Co. KG 26.1%, F&F Burda Gesellschaft für Beteiligungen mbH & Co. KG >25%, Rest: Free Float
1985	Peter Temming AG	Family Temming >25%, Steinbeis & Consorten GmbH <50%
1985	Euro-Kai KGaA	Family Eckelmann 100% Ordinary Shares, Preference Shares in Free Float
1985	Hugo Boss AG	Uwe Holy & Jochen Holy each >50% Ordinary Shares, Preference Shares in Free Float
1986	Vogt Electronic AG	Vogt GmbH 100% (Vogt GMBH: Hans Vogt 33.17%, Johanna Hecht geb. Vogt 26.53%, Gerda von der Meden geb. Vogt 33.17%, Walter Hecht 6.63%), Preference Shares in Free Float
1986	VDO Adolf Schindling AG	Liselott Schindling-Rheinberger 100% Ordinary Shares
1986	Traub AG	Simon van Kempen, Simone van Kempen-Bader, Hermann van Kempen, Martin van Kempen, Lore van Kempen >50%, Rest: Free Float
1986	Escada AG	Major Shareholder: Margaretha Ley & Wolfgang Ley
1986	Oberland Glas AG	Family Wiegand indirectly via Oberland-Glas Holding-GmbH 60%, Free Float 40%
1986	Kampa-Haus AG	Wilfried Kampa & Eugen Kampa 75%, Rest: Free Float
1986	Technocell AG München	MD Verwaltungsgesellschaft Nicolaus GmbH & Co. KG (Family Nicolaus 60%) 51%, Rest: Free Float

(continued)

Table 3.2 (continued)

1986	PUMA AG Rudolf Dassler Sport AG	Families Armin & Gerd Dassler 100% Ordinary Shares, Preference Shares in Free Float
1986	Sixt AG	Erich Sixt 73.3% with 100% Ordinary Shares, Rest: Free Float
1986	Schneider Rundfunkwerke AG	Albert & Bernhard Schneider indirectly via Gebr. Schneider GmbH & Co. KG 75.07%
1986	Edding AG	Family Edding & Family Ledermann 99.7% Ordinary Shares, Prefence Shares in Free Float
1986	Irmen & Richter Textil AG	Daun & Cie AG (directly & indirectly) 63.3%, Rest: Free Float
1986	Fresenius AG	Family Kröner 100% Ordinary Shares
1986	Greiffenberger AG	Heinz Greiffenberger 60%, Dr. Karl Gerhard Schmidt 15%, Rest: Free Float
1987	Pegasus Beteiligungen AG	Family Diechtierow 40% Ordinary Shares, Bayerische Beamten Lebensversicherung a.G. 40% Preference Shares, Members of Supervisory Board 34.65% Ordinary Shares & 1.5% Preference Shares, Rest: Free Float
1987	BBS Kraftfahrzeugtechnik AG	Major Shareholder: Heinrich Baumgartner, Klaus Brand & Martin Braungart 100% Ordinary Shares, Preference Shares in Free Float
1987	Adolf Ahlers AG	Kommanditgesellschaft Westfälisches Textilwerk Adolf Ahlers 76.67%, Jan A. Ahlers 5.93%, Jan Ahlers Textil-Verwaltungsgesellschaft mbH 0.66%, Ahlers Beteiligungsgesellschaft mbH 0.07%, Rest: Free Float
1987	Hertel AG Werkzeuge & Hartstoffe	Günther Hertel 50% Ordinary Shares, Karl G. Hertel 50% Ordinary Shares, Günther & Karl G. Hertel 18.4% Preference Shares, Rest: Free Float

(continued)

Table 3.2 (continued)

1987	Hornbach AG	Major Shareholder: Family Hornbach
1987	GMN Georg Müller Nürnberg AG	Paul Müller, Margarete Karl & Babette Wortner 66.77%, Nürnberger Lebensversicherung AG 10.32%, Rest: Free Float
1987	Hans Einhell AG	Josef Thannhuber 90% Ordinary Shares, Gisela Thannhuber 10% Ordinary Shares, Preference Shares in Free Float
1987	Glunz AG	Family Glunz (directly & indirectly) 85%, Preference Shares in Free Float
1987	Biotest AG	Dr. Hans Schleussner 72% Ordinary Shares, Renate Schleussner, nee Krumm 3% Ordinary Shares, AGAB AG für Anlagen und Beteiligungen 25% Ordinary Shares
1987	A. Moksel AG	Zentralverwaltung Alexander Moksel KG 40.1%, Rodo Schneider 10%, Rest: Free Float
1988	Landshuter Kunstmühle AG	100% in Family Ownership
1988	Bijou Brigitte modische Accessoires AG	Friedrich Wilhelm Werner 50.1%, Rest: Free Float
1988	Pietzsch AG	Dr.-Ing. Ludwig Pietzsch 50% Ordinary Shares, Litton International S.A. 50% Ordinary Shares, Karlsruher Lebensversicherung 10% Preference Shares, Rest: Free Float
1988	Marschollek, Lautenschläger und Partner AG	Manfred Lautenschläger Lautenschläger 74.995% Ordinary Shares, Angelika Lautenschläger 25.005% Ordinary Shares, Preference Shares in Free Float
1988	Computer 2000 AG	WFG Deutsche Gesellschaft für Wagniskapital mbH & Co. KG 33%, Family Tschunke 29.5%, Family Lichtenecker 29.5%

(continued)

Table 3.2 (continued)

1988	Kunert AG	Julius Kunert Holding KG 51.5% Julius Kunert 1%, Rest: Free Float
1988	Macrotron AG für Datenerfassungssysteme	Richard Bladowski 61%, WFG Deutsche Gesellschaft für Wagniskapital mbH & Co. KG 5%, Rest: Free Float
1988	Schwälbchen Molkerei Jakob Berz AG	Elfriede Berz 37.5%, Dr. G. Berz-List 31.66%, Leo Weimann 5.84%, Rest: Free Float
1988	Oppermann Versand AG	100% in Family Ownership
1988	SAP AG	Dietmar Hopp & Sons 22.9%, Dr. h.c. Hasso Plattner 19.6%, Klaus Tschira 17.9%, Hans-Werner Hector 14.6%

3.3.3.2 Selection Criteria for the Sample of Non-Family Enterprises

As previously stated, the original compilation of companies was already filtered in prior steps. Hence, the enterprises which are not eligible for the sample of family enterprises have been assigned to the comparison sample of non-family businesses. The sample comprises private as well as state-owned enterprises, at the time of the initial public offering. Furthermore, several of the non-family businesses within the sample were formerly family-controlled or family-owned. But as defined in Section 2.4., only family firms of which at least 25% of stake is held by the founder/s or their descendant family/-ies are eligible family firms. The original family influence may have been given up or lost before the company entered the public market or is <25% and therefore too small. The 25% share ownership marks the line between family-owned (25% and up) and non-family business (<25%).[16] Even if another family firm takes over the majority in shares, it does not qualify as an *original* family company. Furthermore, previous family companies in which the original family utilized the firm flotation to sell the entire

[16] For further information, see Section 2.5.1. "The Dilution Process".

stock or the majority of stock, have been assigned to this sample, since they begin their public existence as non-family businesses. Table 3.3 presents the list of 39

Table 3.3 IPOs between 1950 and 1988—Sample of Non-Family Enterprises

Year of IPO	Company at IPO	Shareholder Structure at Time of IPO
1961	Volkswagenwerk AG	Land Niedersachsen 20%, Bundesrepublik Deutschland 20%, Rest: Free Float
1965	Vereinigte Elektrizitäts- und Bergwerks AG	Bundesrepublik Deutschland 36%, Rest: Free Float
1966	Deutsche Lufthansa AG	Bundesrepublik Deutschland 74.38%, Kreditanstalt für Wiederaufbau 3%, Land Nordrhein-Westfalen 2.25%, Deutsche Bundespost 1.75%, Deutsche Bundesbahn 0.85%, Free Float 17.77%
1966	Vereinigte Elektrizitätswerke Westfalen AG	Energie-Verwaltungs-Gesellschaft mbH 25.31%, Stadt Dortmund 16.90%, Stadt Bochum 4.40%, Other Municipalities 31.26%, Free Float 22.13%
1967	Deutsche Klinik für Diagnostik AG	Siemens AG >25%, ALLIANZ Lebensversicherungs AG 5%, Frankfurter Versicherungs AG 5%
1969	Horten AG	Helmut Horten 25%, contractually tied to Degav 25%
1973	Badenwerk AG	Land Baden-Württemberg >75%, Rest: Free Float
1977	Joh. Friedrich Behrens AG	Free Float
1977	BayWa AG	Bayerische Raiffeisen-Zentralbank AG >25%
1977	ASKO Deutsche Kaufhaus AG	Free Float

(continued)

Table 3.3 (continued)

1980	AGAB AG für Anlagen und Beteiligungen	LR Beteiligungsgesellschaft mbH 25%, DSV Silo- und Verwaltungsgesellschaft mbH 25%
1982	Electronic 2000 Vertriebs-AG	20% in Family Ownership, Rest: Free Float
1982	Main-Gaswerke AG	Stadt Frankfurt >50%, Land Hessen 15.06%, Thüringer Gas AG 10%
1982	Monachia Grundstücks-AG	ALLIANZ Versicherungs AG 45%, HOCHTIEF AG 45%
1983	Etienne Aigner AG	Major Shareholder: Rauball Group
1984	Konrad Hornschuch AG	Kunz Holding GmbH & Co. KG 51%
1984	Kolbenschmidt AG	Metallgesellschaft AG 62.5%, Rest: Free Float
1984	Carl Schenck AG	Aktiengesellschaft für Industrie und Verkehrswesen >50%, INDA Verwaltungsgesellschaft mbH & Co. KG >25%
1984	Leifheit AG	Free Float 65%, Institutional Investors 35%
1984	Schmalbach-Lubeca AG	Continental Europe Holding Co. Inc. 39.3%, Thomassen & Drijver-Verblifa N.V. 24.9%, Rest: Free Float
1984	MotoMeter AG	"Thesaurus" Continentale Effekten-Gesellschaft >25%, Atlas-Vermögensverwaltungs-Gesellschaft mbH <25%
1985	Schumag AG	Philias Finance B.V. 52.3%, Rest: Free Float
1985	Deutsche Beteiligungs AG	Deutsche Bank AG 92.5%, Karl Schmidt Bankgeschäft KG 7.5%
1986	Feldmühle Nobel AG	Major Shareholder: Deutsche Bank AG
1986	Antriebstechnik G. Bauknecht AG	Bank Syndicate

(continued)

Table 3.3 (continued)

1986	VIAG AG	Bundesrepublik Deutschland 47.44%, Kreditanstalt für Wiederaufbau 12.56%, Rest: Free Float
1986	AVA Allg. Handelsges. Der Verbraucher AG	EDEKA Zentrale AG >25%, ASKO Deutsche Kaufhaus AG 15%
1986	Felten & Guilleaume Energietechnik AG	Gas-, Elektrizitäts- und Wasserwerke Köln AG 20%, Rest: Free Float
1986	Industrieverwaltungsgesellschaft AG	Bundesrepublik Deutschland 55%, Rest: Free Float
1986	Mineralbrunnen Überkingen-Teinach AG	Versorgungshilfe e.V. der Mineralbrunnen Überkingen-Teinach AG 24%, Wohlfahrtsverein des Württem.-Hohenz. Gaststättengewerbes e.V. Stuttgart 20%
1987	SABO-Maschinenfabrik AG	70% Free Float, Family Wolf 10%
1987	Schwabengarage AG	Gothaer Versicherungsbank VVaG 25.9%, Stuttgarter Strassenbahnen AG 26%, Suevia Verwaltungsgesellschaft mbH 25.1%
1987	Stelcon AG	B.V. DE METEOOR 25.02%, 74.98% Free Float
1987	Boge AG	Commerzbank AG 10%, VDO Adolf Schindling AG 10%, Rest: Free Float
1987	Stixi AG	n/a
1987	Linotype AG	Frega Vermögensverwaltungsgesllschaft mbH >25%, Rest: Free Float
1987	co op AG	Major Shareholders: co op Gesellschaft für Handelsbeteiligungen 23.2%, Beteiligungsgesellschaft für Gemeinwirtschaft AG 39%, 10% Free Float
1988	Fernheizwerk Neukölln AG	Land Berlin 50%
1988	SPAR Handel-AG	Free Float

non-family enterprises and is identical in format and categorization to Table 3.2, which describes the sample of family enterprises.

3.3.4 Developments along the Timeline

The definition of the initial shareholder quotas as a starting point and the firm allocation into either category have been conducted by means of *Saling Aktienführer, Wer gehört zu wem?,* and complementary literature. From this point on, changes in the shareholder structures of each company along the timeline have been identified and noted. Furthermore, any significant alterations within the company's development have also been researched, in order to complement the changes in shareholder quotas and provide a full understanding of the company's development.

Due to varying detail in information provided by *Saling Aktienführer* and *Wer gehört zu wem?*, gaps in information and uncertainties may have arisen. In order to reduce information asymmetries, supplementary information has been derived from various sources, such as previous research literature, archived newspaper articles, or company history files. This was necessary to establish a reliable understanding of each individual firm and to establish a database that is as reliable as possible through cross-referencing.

This approach was practiced along the entire development of the shareholder structure for each firm until the point of either a significant shareholder change (dilution), or a change in company fate, such as de-listing or bankruptcy. These changes have been defined as *crucial changes.*[17] For example, it was occasionally the case that a company would drop out of the publication series from one edition to the other. In these cases the alternative research aimed at finding out whether significant changes had occurred and why the firm had been removed from the publication series. By only relying on the data given in the series, it is not possible to assess the type of change, such as de-listing, dissolution, bankruptcy, etc. By integrating complementary sources, the encountered uncertainties could be eliminated.

[17] For further information, see Section 2.5.2. "The Concept of Crucial Change".

3.4 Data and Variables

This subchapter focuses on explaining the data set in detail, i.e. how the data was compiled. It also offers an overview over the variables derived for each sample group. In due course the individual variables will be explained in detail, in order to allow the reader to gain full insight into the backgrounds and development of the set of variables.

3.4.1 The Research Samples of the Present Study

With respect to the underlying research questions, the main focus of this study is on the sample of public founding family enterprises that launched their initial public offering at the German Stock Exchange between 1950 and 1988. The second sample is the comparison group and comprises public non-family enterprises with equal preconditions regarding the IPO-time frame. The general observation period for the individual firm's development extends to and includes the year 2018. Adding the IPO-relevant period from 1950 until 1988 inclusive with the developmental period from 1989 until 2018 inclusive, the overall time frame of interest to this study covers up to 68 years.[18]

After the data collection and data filtering process, the final samples comprise 77 family businesses, as well as 39 non-family businesses, both of which include firms compliant with the time frame[19] and shareholder requirements.[20] This leads to a total of 116 firms across both sample groups.

Furthermore, as the publication series *Saling Aktienführer* and *Wer gehört zu wem?* by the German *Commerzbank Berlin* were defined as the main source of data for shareholder development, a crucial criterion for the firms being eligible for the samples is that the firm be listed in the publication series.[21]

Figure 3.4 shows the overall distribution of IPOs by decade, based on the data collected by accessible sources prior to the data cleansing process. Furthermore, the pillars represent the distribution of IPO's before and after the filtering process.

---

[18] For further information, see Section 3.3.1. "Defining the Time Frame".

[19] For further information, see Section 3.3.1. "Defining the Time Frame".

[20] For further information, see Section 2.4. "Definition of the Stock-listed Family Enterprise".

[21] For further information, see Section 3.3.2.3.1. "Definition of the Primary Source for the In-Depth Data Collection".

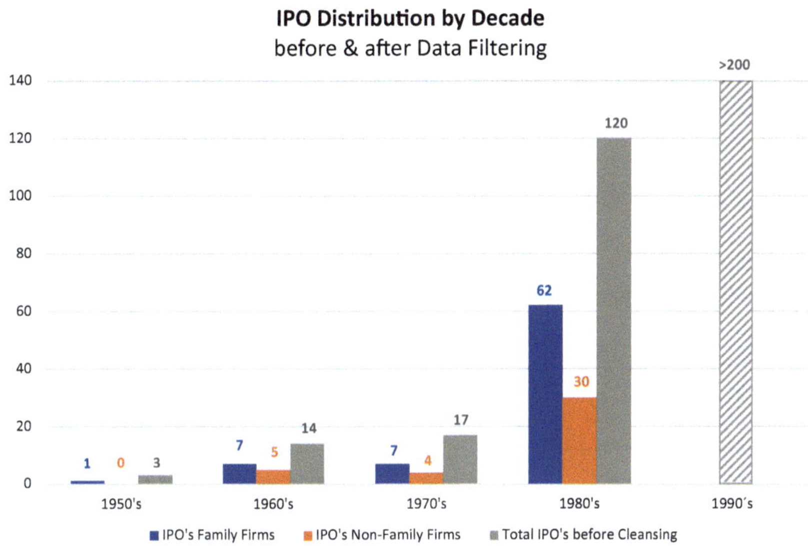

Figure 3.4 IPO Distribution by Decade—before & after Data Filtering. (Source: Author's own figure)

It is important to mention that the sample of the group of non-family firms contains firms that used to be family enterprises or in which the founding family is still invested, yet with a shareholding quota below the critical value of 25% of stake in family hands, which is a prerequisite per definition to count as a family business.[22] Some former family businesses in this sample are in family hands, although the controlling family has no familial connection to the founding family. These are cases in which the original family firm was taken over by another independent family corporation, but are no longer under founding family ownership.[23]

Figure 3.5 offers a compacted overview of the crucial attributes of both samples. It advances and builds upon Figure 3.3, *Derivation of Final Sample and Control Group.*[24]

---

[22] For further information, see Section 2.4. "Definition of the Stock-Listed Family Enterprise".

[23] See Section 2.4. "Definition of the stock-listed family Enterprise".

[24] See Section 3.3.2.3.2. "Definition of Complementary Sources".

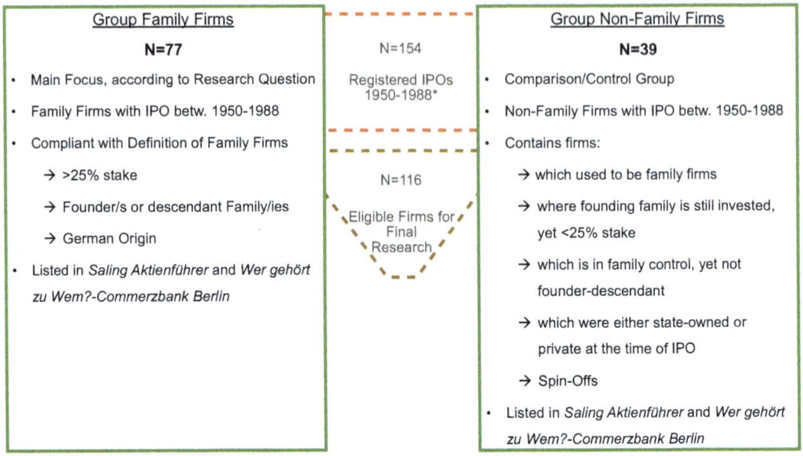

* Derived from accessible Sources

Figure 3.5 The Research Samples. (Source: Author's own figure)

At this point, the role as a *stock-listed firm* must be emphasized. This means that the firm becomes the object of interest for research starting with the date of its IPO and falls out of interest as soon as the firm experiences any form of crucial change.[25] For instance, examples include cases of de-listing, dissolution, bankruptcy or, highly relevant for the sample of family enterprises, a loss of family influence regarding ownership as in the case of merger or acquisition (MorA). These final states are considered *failures* or *deaths* of the firms in regard to the underlying survival analysis.[26]

3.4.2 In-Depth Data Introduction

The goal of the present study is to establish as accurately as possible a picture of the development of family corporations in their role as a PIE. This is why an inductive approach was applied. The researcher constructed a data set by extracting various measures of firms from the point on of their stock market flotation. Starting from the individual IPO date, changes were noted annually, until the

[25] For further information, see Section 2.5.2. "The Concept of Crucial Change".

[26] For further information, see Section 2.5.2. "The Concept of Crucial Change".

firm experienced a crucial change that ended the life[27] of the firm as it was when it entered the public market, such as bankruptcy, delisting, dissolution or severe dilution in shares in cases of family enterprises, which ends in a loss of family influence and therefore results in a loss of the family firm status, or according to survival analysis, in the company's death.

As a result, the observation time for each firm varies. Some companies fall out of observation shortly after their initial public offering, due to early life-changing events. Others remain in observation throughout the designated observation period,[28] because they have remained steady and have survived at the stock market without experiencing any form of crucial change. These cases in particular are known as *right-censored observations* (Kiefer, 1988, p. 658; Oakes, 2000, p. 282; Carpentier & Suret, 2011, p. 111), because their ending is open at the time the observation ends. This form of data is defined as *survival data* and lays the foundation for survival analysis.

The publication series *Saling Aktienführer* and *Wer gehört zu wem?*, published by the German *Commerzbank Berlin*, are defined as the main sources for the relevant data.[29] This is due to the beneficial attributes of the series for this study. The series both focus in great detail on shareholder structure, which is very important, particularly regarding the development of the shareholder quotas for the sample group of family enterprises. The samples are therefore limited to firms listed in the series, in order to enable and maintain steady and reliable reporting on the shareholder quotas, which are the most crucial data for the survival analyses, and consequently for the entire study.

According to Hair Jr. et al., secondary data is "(...) *data used for research that was not gathered directly and purposefully for the project (...)*" (2016, p. 116). Hence, in order to determine the kind of data used for the present study, one must reflect the data collection process, described in detail in Section 3.3.2.

There was also an assessment of various sources which contained data on firm-specific information, such as founding years, dates of stock market flotation, incisive changes after IPO, and more. Furthermore, shareholder quotas were

---

[27] When conducting survival analysis, *death* states the end of the examination span. For more detail, see Section 2.5.3. "The Concept of Crucial Change".

In this research case, the survival analysis focuses on survival of family enterprises as publicly traded entities. Hence the *life* of the company ends as soon as the enterprise experiences any relevant changes which have an effect on the original state of the enterprise as it was when it entered the public market.

[28] See Section 3.3.1. "Defining the Time Frame".

[29] For further information, see Section 3.3.2.3.1. "Definition of the Primary Source for the In-Depth Data Collection".

derived from the previously introduced main sources. As a result, one can define the used data as secondary, already existent raw data, extracted and compiled from various sources, which were processed to develop a full bouquet of information for this study. The secondary data collected in the process has primary data quality for this study, since the information collected by the accessed sources is much more comprehensive than if the researcher had attempted to collect the data herself.

Secondary business data is used most commonly by economists, especially with respect to stock market statistics (Hair Jr. et al., 2016, p. 116). As the study investigates historical developments, primary data is difficult or impossible to access, as contemporary witnesses are rare and nearly unreachable for interviews. Accordingly, the case studies are restricted to quantitative data, which has certain advantages over qualitative data, gathered by interview-based case studies. For example, there is no risk of bias on the part of the interviewer or interviewee. According to Hair Jr. et al. (2016), a further advantage of using secondary data sources is the avoidance of "*respondent fatigue*" (p. 125). This also poses a risk, when questionnaires are used for data collection. The return rate may be very low to begin with and may decrease when several rounds of questioning are necessary. Furthermore, secondary data is well suitable for comparative analysis. This attribute is especially crucial for the current study, with respect to identifying clusters or trends when comparing the development of family businesses and non-family businesses.

The compilation process of the secondary data presented some challenges, the most prominent of which is "*quality concern*" (Hair Jr. et al., 2016, p. 125). First of all, since the data is of a historical nature, the degree of accuracy is difficult to establish. Furthermore, in cases of uncertainty or complete lack of information, there is barely a possibility of gaining access to the information, since contemporary witnesses are nearly impossible to find. If the sources don't offer the data, then there is none. Hence, missing values eliminate potential cases from the sample, or the cases are not fully enclosed.[30] With respect to the data collection process, Hair Jr. et al. (2016) describe "*access complications*" (p. 125) as a dominant disadvantage, which was occasionally experienced within this research. The main challenge in the beginning of the data collection process was finding reliable sources which offered the necessary data. In the end, the relevant data for this study had to be fragmentally composed through various sources, a time-consuming and meticulous procedure. In the end, the challenges did not pose a risk or have any negative effect on the study. On the contrary, the stumbling

[30] For further information, see Section 6.2. "Limits of the Study".

blocks and dead ends the researcher encountered led her to new sources and ultimately to more completeness of the data and more diversity in interesting aspects to be examined in connection to the research questions. This diversity translates into a wide range of examinable variables.[31]

3.4.3 Definition of Variables for the Present Study

With a thorough observation of the data set, the variables assigned to both samples were defined. Overall, the variables are similar for both sample groups. Nevertheless, differences result from the main focus on the shareholder structure of family enterprises regarding family firm longevity, as defined in the research questions, and mainly with respect to family firm characteristics.

3.4.3.1 Variables Describing the Sample of Family Enterprises

In general, the variables were defined in order to capture all information provided by the accessible data, with the goal of deriving observations as accurately as possible. An overview of the variables describing the sample group of family enterprises is presented in Table 3.4. The first column shows the variables as used in the analysis, and the second column shows the extended variable description.

A total of 32 variables are divided into descriptive and survival variables. The descriptive variables, as the term suggests, describe the firm's characteristics. These are then divided into categorical, numerical, and binary variables. Among the binary variables are variables describing the highly critical data concerning active ownership and crucial changes. The variables describing the dilution process fall into the descriptive numerical variables.[32]

The survival variables are relevant for the survival analysis and describe the durations of each firm's survival. All in all, seven survival variables have been established in order to capture different angles of survival. The most crucial survival variables regarding publicly traded family firm longevity are ST2, ST3, and ST6, which measure the ST until any form of crucial change sets in, the ST until observation ends for the survivors, and the ST until death as family firm occurs in the form of MorA regarding dilution of family shareholding influence below the critical threshold of 25%.

---

[31] For further information, see Section 3.4.3. "Definition of Variables for the Present Study".

[32] For more information, see Sections 2.5.1. "The Dilution Process", 2.5.2. "The Concept of Crucial Change" and 2.5.3. "The Concept of Active Ownership".

Table 3.4 Variables describing the Sample of Family Enterprises

Variable	Description
Descriptive categorical variables	
Year of IPO	Categorized by decade (1950´s, 1960´s, 1970´s, 1980´s)
Turnover at IPO	Categorized by size of turnover (<50mio DM, 50-99mio DM, 100-499mio DM, 500-999mio DM, >1bn DM)
Sharehold. str. at IPO	Categorized by shareholding quota (>25%-50%, >50%-75%, >75%)
Industry	Categorized by *Klassifikation der Wirtschaftszweige des Statistischen Bundesamts* (2008)
Descriptive metrical variables	
Age at IPO	Indicator for the age of the firm at IPO
Families involved	Indicator of the number of founding families that were invested in the firm at the time of IPO
Dilution Process:	
Reductions total	Approx. indicator for the number of reduction steps of family held shares
Time frame of reductions	Approx. Indicator of the time frame the family reduced their stake in
Descriptive binary variables	
Active Ownership:	
Fam.memb. Exec. Board at IPO	Indicator whether one or more family member/s was/were operationally active on the Executive Board at the time of IPO
Fam.memb. Sup. Board at IPO	Indicator whether one or more family member/s was/were active on the Supervisory Board at the time of IPO
Fam.memb. both Board at IPO	Indicator whether family members were active on the Executive as well as the Supervisory Board at the time of IPO
Fam.memb. Exec. Board at cr. change/obs. end	Indicator whether one or more family member/s was/were operationally active on the Executive Board at the time of crucial change (failures) or observation end (survivors)

(continued)

Table 3.4 (continued)

Variable	Description
Fam.memb. Sup. Board at cr. change/obs. end	Indicator whether one or more family member/s was/were active on the Supervisory Board at the time of crucial change (failures) or observation end (survivors)
Fam.memb. both Boards at cr. change/obs. end	Indicator whether family members were active on the Executive as well as the Supervisory Board at the time of crucial change (failures) or observation end (survivors)
Descriptive binary variables	
Crucial Changes/Final States:	
Survival	All surviving family firms with the founding family holding >25% of shares
Survival fam.cont.	All surviving family firms with the founding family holding >50% of shares
Survival fam.owned	All surviving family firms with the founding family holding >25%-50% of shares
MorA	All family firms experiencing merger or acquisition as form of crucial change (failure)
Merger	Share of MorA-family firms experiencing merger as form of crucial change (failure)
Acquisition	Share of MorA-family firms experiencing acquisition as form of crucial change (failure)
MorA by foreign firm	Share of MorA-family firms experiencing merger or acquisition by a foreign firm as form of crucial change (failure)
MorA by family firm	Share of MorA-family firms experiencing merger or acquisition by another family firm as form of crucial change (failure)
De-listing	All family firms experiencing de-listing as form of crucial change (failure)
Bankruptcy	All family firms experiencing bankruptcy as form of crucial change (failure)
Dissolution	All family firms experiencing dissolution as form of crucial change (failure)

(continued)

Table 3.4 (continued)

Variable	Description
Survival variables	
ST1	Survival time until 1. reduction of family held shares was recorded
ST2	Survival time until crucial change occured (all failures)
ST3	Survival time until observation end (all survivors)
ST4	Survival times until death as listed firm (dissolutions, bankruptcies and de-listings)
ST5	Survival times until death as firm (dissolutions and bankruptcies)
ST6	Survival times until death as family firm (all merger or acquisitions)
ST7	Survival times after 1. reduction until MorA (ad-hoc exits or long-term exits?)

3.4.3.2 Variables Describing the Sample of Non-Family Enterprises

The derivation of the variables for the comparison sample group of non-family enterprises follows the same approach as for the group of family enterprises. The goal is to adopt all possible variables that fully describe the data, in order to enable a full understanding of the company's public history. Table 3.5 is equivalent in its structure to Table 3.4 and reveals the total number of 16 variables for the non-family businesses with the according descriptions.

The structure of the set of variables is equivalent to the structure in connection to the family businesses. The descriptive variables are divided into categorical, numerical, and binary variables. The binary variables describe the forms of crucial change or the final states that apply to the firms in the sample. These are mostly equivalent to the forms of crucial change applying to the family businesses.

Variables describing AO are not applicable to this sample, hence they provide no meaning in the variable set. Furthermore, the dilution process only refers to family influence,[33] so again these variables are not applicable to this sample.

[33] For further information, see Section 2.5.1. "The Dilution Process".

To a certain extent, the variables are equivalent to the variables describing the family businesses. Apart from the categorical variable describing the family shareholding quota of the family firms, the categorical variables describing the year of IPO, the turnover at IPO and the specific industry equally apply to the sample of non-family firms. On the other hand, only one numerical variable applies to both samples—the age at IPO.

The variable set describing the firms within the sample of non-family businesses has one additional variable which is not applicable to the sample of family businesses. That is the variable indicating a non-family firm once being a family-owned business prior to the IPO launch (*former family firm*).

The survival variables measuring the durations of the non-family businesses are reduced to two: ST1 measures the ST until crucial change occurs and ST2 measures the ST until observation ends. Due to the high occurrence of MorA as the main form of crucial change among the non-family businesses, no other survival variables would have made sense due to the small set of applicable cases.

Table 3.5 Variables describing the Sample of Non-Family Enterprises

Variable	Description
Descriptive categorical variables	
Year of IPO	Categorized by decade (1950´s, 1960´s, 1970´s, 1980´s)
Turnover at IPO	Categorized by size of turnover (<50mio DM, 50-99mio DM, 100-499mio DM, 500-999mio DM, >1bn DM)
Industry	Categorized by *Klassifikation der Wirtschaftszweige des Statistischen Bundesamts* (2008)
Descriptive numercial variables	
Age at IPO	Indicator for the age of the firm at IPO
Descriptive binary variables	
Former family firm	Indicator whether the firm was once a founding-family-owned enterprise before the IPO launch
Crucial Changes/Final States:	
No significant change	All firms that haven´t experienced any significant sharehgolder changes

(continued)

Table 3.5 (continued)

Variable	Description
MorA	All firms experienceing merger or acquisition as form of crucial change (failure)
Merger	Share of MorA-firms experiencing megrer as form of crucial change (failure)
Acquisition	Share of MorA-firms experiencing acquisition as form of crucial change (failure)
MorA by foreign firm	Share of MorA-firms experiencing merger or acquisition by a foreign firm as form of crucial change (failure)
MorA by family firm	Share of MorA-firms experiencing merger or acquisition by another family firm as form of crucial change (failure)
De-listing	All firms experiencing de-listing as form of crucial change (failure)
Bankruptcy	All firms experiencing bankruptcy as form of crucial change (failure)
Break-up	All firms experiencing corporate break-up as form of crucial change (failure)
Survival variables	
ST1	Survival time until crucial change occured (all failures)
ST2	Survival time until observation end (all survivors)

3.4.3.3 Introduction into the Categorical Variables

Categorical variables are usually defined by qualitative characteristics. As the term implies, the characteristics are assigned to categories which contain either verbal or alphabetical values. But not only verbal or alphabetical measures can be assigned to these kinds of variables. Categorical values can also contain a range of numerical values that are combined into a defined category. In these cases, the numerical value does not offer an individual, precise value unique to the corresponding subject, but rather more generalized information on the values which are assigned to the overall category. Hence, the variable gives the researcher a gross understanding of which range the corresponding value is situated, but not the detailed value. This applies to the descriptive categorical variables describing the year of IPO and turnover at IPO for both sample groups, as well as to the categorical variable describing the family shareholding quota at IPO.

The categorical variable describing the industry of economic activity, on the other hand, represents a verbal characteristic. This variable is common among both sample groups. In contrast to the categorical variables containing numerical values, these categories are not ordered, but rather of nominal nature.

The categorization complies with the *Klassifikation der Wirtschaftszweige*, the most recent edition published by the German *Statistisches Bundesamt* in 2008. This classification work is an official listing and classification of all relevant industries in Germany (Statistisches Bundesamt, 2008a). It has been developed in order to capture the full range of industries for the purpose of statistical analyses (Statistisches Bundesamt, 2008b, p. 3). The original language of the publication is German, although an English version is available and has been used for orientation in the translation of the industries (Statistisches Bundesamt, 2008c).

When comparing Tables 3.6 and 3.7, the categories coincide to a certain degree. Nevertheless, there are differences in the number of represented industries between the sample groups. Table 3.6 lists the categories of industries, represented by the sample of family enterprises. The total of 77 family businesses within the sample are active in seven different industries.

Table 3.6 Categories by Industry—Family Enterprises

Category by Industry	**Industry Description**
Cat. C	Manufacturing
Cat. F	Construction
Cat. G	Wholesale & Retail Trade
Cat. H	Transportation & Storage
Cat. J	Information & Communication
Cat. K	Financial & Insurance Activities
Cat. L	Real Estate Activities

Source: based on Statistisches Bundesamt (2008c, 2008d)

Table 3.7 shows the categories of industries for the comparison sample group of the non-family enterprises. Here, the field of economic activity ranges more widely compared to the family enterprise sample. A total of nine economic fields are represented. *Cat. D* and *Cat. Q* are unique to the comparison sample group of the current study.

Table 3.7 Categories by Industry—Non-Family Enterprises

Category by Industry	Industry Description
Cat. C	Manufacturing
Cat. D	Electricity, Gas, Steam & Air Conditioning Supply
Cat. F	Construction
Cat. G	Wholesale & Retail Trade
Cat. H	Transportation & Storage
Cat. J	Information & Communication
Cat. K	Financial & Insurance Activities
Cat. L	Real Estate Activities
Cat. Q	Human Health & Social Work Activities

Source: based on Statistisches Bundesamt (2008c, 2008d)

3.5 Methods of Data Analysis

3.5.1 Approaching the Research Questions

The methods of data analysis have been chosen in order to ensure the most appropriate examination of the research questions. Mixed methods of data analysis are applied for a holistic illumination of the samples. Firstly, the survival analysis has been conducted by means of Cox PH Models and Kaplan-Meier Survival Estimates. Subsequently, a qualitative approach has been applied in order to identify clusters and patterns. Given the lack of prior research in this specific field, the inductive approach allows for an in-depth screening of the data, and possibly opens up new frontiers for future research on stock-listed family business longevity.

Bringing the research questions back to mind:

How did German stock-listed family firms develop after IPO, with a main focus on longevity and family involvement?—Development of a model based on the long-term analysis of historical data ranging from 1950-2018

- *How long do families of publicly traded family firms maintain their influence through shares after IPO?*
- *How does family influence (shareholding quota) develop after IPO?*
- *In cases of dissolution or dilution, what were the reasons (sale/family exit, delisting, bankruptcy, etc.)?*

- *Are there beneficial factors/success factors for family firm survival (industry, number of families involved, age of firm, etc.)?*

The research focuses on longevity of post-IPO family enterprises, a purely quantitative approach. Softer questions, however, are also of interest, and these questions call for a more qualitative approach. Hence the data analysis is divided into two parts—the quantitative and the qualitative approach.

3.5.2 The Quantitative Approach—Survival Analysis

The quantitative approach commits itself to the actual question of how long the family IPO firms survive after stock market flotation in their original state. A survival analysis was conducted by applying Cox proportional hazards models in order to identify independent variables with significant effects on the defined survival times (dependent variables). For comparison reasons, the tests were applied to both samples equally and in the same way.

Initially, the independent variables were tested for correlation, in order to identify and exclude variables with high correlation. In further course, log-rank tests were conducted. This was necessary due to the large number of independent variables, especially for the sample of family businesses. Conducting these tests allowed a first identification of possible significant effects of the independent variables. Based on the initial selection by the log-rank tests, the actual survival analysis was conducted by applying Cox PH models. The analysis was applicable to only three of the seven defined dependent variables, due to too few observations. Based on the findings of the Cox PH tests, Kaplan-Meier survival graphs were established for the independent variables that were identified with significant effects on the corresponding survival times. These graphs allow for a more visual observation and understanding of the effects on the corresponding survival time.

In conclusion, tests of significance were conducted in order to identify other possible significant relations between the independent variables and the dependent variables, that weren't calculable by the Cox PH tests.

3.5.3 The Narrative Approach—Clusters, Patterns and Success Factors

The softer research questions concerning the development of family influence, possible reasons, or clusters, patterns, and success factors have been approached in a narrative manner. The goal was to combine the findings of the quantitative survival analysis with the observations from the narrative depiction of the samples, if possible.

The researcher approached the data in a more intuitive and *playful* way. By juggling and cross-referencing the data, clusters and patterns were observed, which brought forth new observations and insights. If existent, interesting cases out of the samples are brought up and introduced to the reader. By doing so, the analysis is complemented with actual firm histories, making the observations more concrete and tangible for the reader.

The observations from the narrative depiction are described as soft features, since there is no empirical evidence to support them. Yet in combination with the corresponding results from the empirical survival analysis, the soft observations support the findings.

References

Andres, C. (2008). Large shareholders and firm performance—An empirical examination of founding-family ownership. *Journal of Corporate Finance*, 14, 431–445.

Bremer, H. (1969). Grundzüge des deutschen und ausländischen Börsenrechts. In W. Kunkel, P. Lerche, W. Mieth & W. Vogt (Eds.), *Enzyklopädie der Rechts- und Staatswissenschaften*, pp. 1–205. Heidelberg: Springer.

Brown, J.M. (1970). Post-Offering Experience of Companies Going Public. *Journal of Business*, 3, 10–18.

Bundesgesetzblatt (1955). *Gesetz zur Bereinigung der auf Reichsmark lautenden Wertpapiere der Knversionskasse für deutsche Auslandsschulden (nr. 7)*. Bonn.

Carpentier, C. & Suret, J.-M. (2011). The survival and success of Canadian penny stock IPOs. *Small Business Economics*, 36, 101–121.

Churchill, G.A. & Brown, T.J. (2007). *Basic Marketing Research (6. Ed.)*. Mason, USA: South-Western College.

Commerzbank (1954–2000). *Wer gehört zu wem—Mutter- und Tochtergesellschaften von A-Z (1.-20. ed.)*. Commerzbank Berlin. Hamburg: Hanseatische Druckanstalt.

Deutsche Börse AG (2010). *1585–2010, Die Deutsche Börse feiert Jubiläum—eine Chronologie effizienter Märkte*. Düsseldorf: corps. Corporate Publishing Services GmbH. Retrieved from https://www.deutsche-boerse.com/resource/blob/321538/5d0c10548c7fe945fcff2a3d338d2856/data/jubilaeum425-1585_de.pdf

Fredebeul-Krein, T. (2012). *Koordinierter Einsatz von Direktmarketing und Verkaufsaussensdienst im B2B-Kontext—Grundlagen der explorativen Untersuchung*, pp. 65–92. Wiesbaden: Springer/Gabler.

Gambatese, J.A. & Hallowell, M. (2011). Enabling and measuring innovation in the construction industry. *Construction Management and Economics*, 29, 553–567.

Glaser, B.G. & Strauss, A.L. (2010). *Grounded Theory—Strategien qualitativer Forschung (3. ed)*. Bern: Huber.

Hair Jr., J.F., Celsi, M., Money, A., Samouel, P. & Page, M. (2016). *Essentials of Business Research Methods (3. Ed.)*. New York: Routledge.

Jain, B.A. & Kini, O. (2000). Does the Presence of Venture Capitalists Improve the Survival Profile of IPO Firms? *Journal of Business Finance & Accounting*, 27(9), 1139–1176.

Jain, B.A. & Kini, O. (2008). The Impact of Strategic Investment Choices on Post-Issue Operating Performance and Survival of US IPO Firms. *Journal of Business Finance & Accounting*, 35(3), 459–490.

Khurshed, A. (2000). *Discussion of* Does the Presence of Venture Capitalists Improve the Survival Profile of IPO Firms? *Journal of Business Finance & Accounting*, 27(9), 1177–1183.

Kiefer, N. M. (1988). Economic Duration Data and Hazard Functions. *Journal of Economic Literature*, 16, 646–679.

Klasa, S. (2007). Why Do Controlling Families of Public Firms Sell Their Remaining Ownership Stake? *Journal of Financial and Quantitative Analysis*, 42(2), 339–368.

Klein, S.B. (2000). Family Businesses in Germany: Significance and Structure. *Family Business Review*, 13(3), 157–182.

Koch, W. & Wegmann, J. (2000). *Praktiker-Handbuch Börseneinführung—Ablauf des Börsengangs mittelständischer Unternehmen—mit Erfahrungsberichten vom Neuen Markt (3. ed)*. Stuttgart: Schäffer-Poeschel.

Le Breton-Miller, I. & Miller, D. (2006). Why do some family businesses out-compete? Governance, long-term orientation, and sustainable capability. *Entrepreneurship Theory and Practice*, 30(6), 731–746.

Lumpkin, G.T., Brigham, K.H. & Moss, T.W. (2010). Long-term orientation: implications for the entrepreneurial orientation and performance of family businesses. *Entrepreneurship & Regional Development*, 22(3–4), 241–264.

Oakes, D. (2000). Survival Analysis. *Journal of the American Statistical Association*, 95(449), 282–285.

Presse- und Informationsamt der Bundesregierung (2015). *Deutsche Einheit—Regierungsdokumente und Erklärungen aus den Jahren 1989–1991*. Retrieved from https://archiv.bundesregierung.de/resource/blob/975236/237440/63b9cde71a07804a8ee297d1561cd1ed/2009-11-16-regierungsdokumente-20-jahre-dt-einheit-data.pdf?download=1.

Rau, S. B. (2013). Emotions Preventing Survival of Family Firms: Comments on Exploring the Emotional Nexus in Cogent Family Business Archetypes: Towards a Predominant Business Model Inclusive of the Emotional Dimension. In *Special Issue—A New Business Model: The Emotional Dimension of* Organizations, 3(3), De Gruyter, 425–432.

Rost, J. (2003). Zeitgeist und Moden empirischer Analysemethoden. In *Von Generation zu Generation*, pp. 21–31. Retrieved from https://www.ssoar.info/ssoar/bitstream/handle/document/50712/ssoar-2002-rost-Zeitgeist_und_Moden_empirischer_Analysemethoden.pdf?sequence=1&isAllowed=y&lnkname=ssoar-2002-rost-Zeitgeist_und_Moden_empirischer_Analysemethoden.pdf

Rudolph, B. (1992). Die Entwicklung der Börse von 1945 bis in die heutige Zeit. *Börse als Informationsdrehscheibe und Handelsplatz.* 15. Symposium zur Bankengeschichte am 5. Juni 1992 in der Frankfurter Wertpapierbörse-IHK, Frankfurt.

Schürmann, W. & Körfgen, Dr. K. (1987). *Familienunternehmen auf dem Weg zur Börse—Ein Leitfaden für potentielle Börsenkandidaten (2. ed).* Munich: C.H. Beck.

Schürmann, W. (1980). *Familienunternehmen und Börse—Emittieren, warum und wie?* Wiesbaden: Gabler.

Seibold, L.K.C. (2019). *Family Businesses´ Growth—Unpacking the Black Box.* Wiesbaden: Springer-Gabler Verlag.

Stafford, K., Bhargava, V., Danes, S.H., Haynes, G. & Brewton, K.E. (2010). Factors Associated with Long-Term Survival of Family Businesses: Duration Analysis. *Journal of Family and Economic Issues*, Vol. 31, 442–457.

Statistisches Bundesamt (2008a). *Klassifikation der Wirtschaftszweige—Gleiderung mit Erläuterung, Ausgabe 2008 (WZ 2008).* Wiesbaden, Germany. Retrieved from https://www.klassifikationsserver.de/klassService/jsp/common/url.jsf?variant=wz2008.

Statistisches Bundesamt (2008b). *Klassifikation der Wirtschaftszweige—mit Erläuterungen, Ausgabe 2008 (WZ 2008).* Wiesbaden, Germany. Retrieved from https://www.klassifikationsserver.de/klassService/jsp/common/url.jsf?variava=wz2008.

Statistisches Bundesamt (2008c). *German Classification of Economic Activities, Edition 2008 (WZ 2008).* Wiesbaden, Germany. Retrieved from https://www.destatis.de/DE/Methoden/Klassifikationen/Gueter-Wirtschaftsklassifikationen/Downloads/klassifikation-wz-2008-englisch.html.

Statistisches Bundesamt (2008d). *Kurzanleitung Wirtschaftszweigklassifikation.* Wiesbaden, Germany. Retrieved from https://www.bafa.de/SharedDocs/Downloads/DE/Wirtschafts_Mittelstandsfoerderung/unb_kurzanleitung_wirtschaftszweigklassifikation.html.

Sreejesh, S., Mohapatra, S. & Anusree, M.R. (2014). *Business Research Methods—An Applied Orientation.* Switzerland: Springer International.

Wilbon, A.D. (2002). Predicting survival of high-technology initial public offering firms. *Journal of High Technology Management Research*, 13, 127–141.

Part I
The Quantitative Analysis

Presenting the Results of the Quantitative Data Analysis

4

This chapter is committed to the presentation and interpretation of the results of the quantitative data analyses.[1] A detailed introduction to the applied methods of analysys is offered in Section 3.5, "Methods of Data Analysis". The chapter guides the reader through the statistical analysis, to present the comprehensive raw output given by the analyses in a first step and subsequently refining the findings to the significant observations and offering potential interpretation of and meaning to the findings. First the results for the non-family enterprises, the classic IPO firms, are presented. Then follows a discussion of the results for the family enterprises which are the heart of the study.

4.1 Chapter Overview

First, basic statistical measures were calculated for both samples, to develop a sensitivity and a feeling for the firms within the samples. Descriptive statistics such as the total number of observations per variable, the mean, the minimum

[1] For statistical analyses the researcher used the Stata 17.0 software. The researcher attended the VHB ProDok seminar on "Applied Regression Analysis," which offers in-depth knowledge and active experience in *Economic Duration Analysis* and *Hazard Functions* conducted with the Stata software. For further assistance, the researcher used literature by Kohler & Kreuter (2016) and Cleves et al. (2016).

Supplementary Information The online version contains supplementary material available at https://doi.org/10.1007/978-3-658-44303-0_4.

K. Stotmeister, *Publicly Traded Family Businesses*, Familienunternehmen und KMU, https://doi.org/10.1007/978-3-658-44303-0_4

and maximum values within the sample, and the corresponding standard deviations (SD) are presented in detail. Furthermore, the chapter gives insight into the distribution of IPOs over the decades, the firms´ turnover at the time of stock market flotation, the family shareholding structure for the focus sample, and the firms´ industries.

With a basic understanding of the firm characteristics per sample given by the descriptive measures, further necessary tests were conducted in preparation for the actual survival analysis. One core element of the research question is the examination of duration of *survival* of the firms in their original state as they entered the public market, and it comprises two parts: the *Cox Regression Analysis*[2] and the *Kaplan-Meier-Estimators.*

The Cox regression, or Cox proportional hazards model (PH), was conducted as the actual test for firms´ survival. These tests were applied to both samples. Then the previously defined significant variables by the Cox PH models were put into visible plots by means of KM-curves, to allow for closer examination of the effects of these independent variables. Finally, tests of significance were applied to examine the effects on the survival times that were not calculable by means of Cox PH models.

After presenting the results for both sample groups separately, the chapter brings together the significant findings, with the goal of comparing the insights. Finally, the focus lies solely on the significant findings identified by the previously explained tests, offering a summary of these as well as potential meaning and interpretation of the results.

4.2 Overview of the Combined Samples

The combined data set comprises a total of 116 businesses, divided into the sample group of stock-listed family businesses and the control sample group of stock-listed non-family businesses. According to the selection criteria for the samples, which are explained in detail in Section 3.3.3. "Derivation of Final Sample Groups," the samples represent the majority of economically relevant stock-listed firms in Germany, which launched an IPO within the designated timeline.[3]

[2] Cox regression is a partial likelihood approach as proposed by Cox (1972,1975), and is also known as Cox proportional hazards model.

[3] See Section 3.3.1. "Defining the Time Frame".

The sample group of the family controlled and owned businesses[4] is composed of a total of 77 businesses (66.4%) and the control sample of 39 businesses (33.6%). All firms either are currently or were at one point publicly traded at the German stock exchange *Deutsche Börse*. The analysis covers the time frame from 1950 until 2018, integrating firms into the data set that launched their Initial Public Offering within the period between 1950 and 1988.[5] This allows for a developmental phase of at least 30 years after IPO, offering a reasonable amount of time to evolve under the circumstances as a publicly traded firm.

4.3 The Sample of Non-Family Enterprises

4.3.1 Descriptive Statistics

The sample of non-family enterprises comprises 39 businesses which meet the IPO requirements equal to the sample of family businesses. The sample includes all firms that have not been defined as a family-owned or family-controlled firm at the time of the IPO launch. Hence, former family enterprises with a family shareholder block of <25% have also been assigned to this sample.

4.3.1.1 Categorical Variables

Equivalent to the introduction into the descriptive characteristics of the sample group of family enterprises, tables 4.1 through 4.3 represent the descriptive statistics of the non- family enterprises regarding the categorical variables.

As table 4.1 shows, nearly 75% of all firms allocated to this sample group launched their IPO in the 1980's (in absolute numbers: 29 firms). Four firms became stock listed in the 1970's and six in the 1960's.

Table 4.1 Year of IPO—Non-Family Enterprises

Year of IPO	N	%
1950´s	0	0
1960´s	6	15.4
1970´s	4	10.3
1980´s	29	74.4

4 For further information on the difference between family control and family ownership, see Section 2.5.1. "The Dilution Process".

5 For further information on sample criteria, see Section 3.3, "Data Collection Process".

Most non-family firms, namely ten firms in absolute numbers or roughly 29% of the entire sample, recorded a turnover at the time of IPO launch in the middle range. These are followed by eight and seven firms, resulting in 23% and 20% of the entire sample recording turnovers in the highest range of >1bn DM and the high range, respectively. Only ten out of the 39 non-family businesses were in the two lowest ranges of turnover at the time the firms experienced stock market flotation (see table 4.2).

Table 4.2 Turnover at IPO—Non-Family Enterprises

Turnover at IPO (in DM)	N	%
≥ 1 bn	8	22.9
500–999 mio	7	20.0
100–499 mio	10	28.6
50–99 mio	5	14.3
<50 mio	5	14.3

Table 4.3 shows the distribution of non-family businesses among the industries. Three industries have been identified as the main fields of economic activity among this sample. The manufacturing industry, with approximately 44%, represents the largest part of non-family businesses, followed by commerce and energy supply.

Table 4.3 Industry—Non-Family Enterprises

Industry	N	%
Manufacturing Industry	17	43.6
Energy Supply	6	15.4
Construction Industry	1	2.6
Commerce	7	18.0
Transportation & Storage	1	2.6
Information & Communication	2	5.1
Finance & Insurance	2	5.1
Real Estate	2	5.1
Health & Insurance Services	1	2.6

4.3.1.2 Metrical and Binary Variables

The comparison sample of non-family enterprises not only differentiates itself from the focus sample through its sample size, but also through the number of independent variables that are to be tested for significant effect on the dependent survival variables. The number of independent variables is far smaller than for the family businesses. Merely two independent variables concerning firms' specific characteristics have been identified. Hence, table 4.4 represents the firms' specific characteristics as well as the crucial changes/final states the firms experienced.

Table 4.4 Firm Specific Characteristics and Final States—Non-Family Enterprises

Independent Variable	N	M	SD	Min	Max
Age at IPO	39	57.05	39.32	0.00	166.00
Former family firm	39	0.46	0.51	0.00	1.00
No change	39	0.05	0.22	0.00	1.00
Merger	39	0.21	0.41	0.00	1.00
Acquisition	39	0.72	0.46	0.00	1.00
MorA by foreign firm	39	0.10	0.31	0.00	1.00
MorA by other family firm	39	0.08	0.27	0.00	1.00
De-listing	39	0.00	0.00	0.00	0.00
Bankruptcy	39	0.00	0.00	0.00	0.00
Break-up	39	0.03	0.16	0.00	1.00

The firm's specific characteristics comprise the age of the firm at the IPO launch and whether the firm was a former pre-IPO family business. On average, the non-family businesses were 57 years old at the time of their stock market flotation. The oldest firm counted 166 years at the time of IPO, while the youngest experienced flotation directly upon or after establishment. Of all non-family businesses, 46% were former family-owned businesses, hence nearly half of the comparison sample.

Only 5% of the sample remained in their original state until the end. Acquisition, as a form of crucial change, comprises 72% of all non-family businesses, 28 firms in total. Eight firms, equaling 21% of the total sample, became subject to merger. In total, 36 non-family firms experienced either acquisition or merger ending the survival period. Of these firms, 10% were merged or acquired by a foreign firm and 8% by a family firm, hence four and three firms in total numbers, respectively.

Of all non-family businesses, only one firm experienced a breakup as the final blow.

4.3.1.3 Survival Variables

The focus sample of family businesses examined seven survival variables. Many of these were connected to changes in shareholder structure regarding family ownership. These aspects are irrelevant for the comparison sample group, and so the number of dependent survival variables are fewer in comparison. The survival variables mainly analyze the survival times regarding the crucial changes that ended the lives of the non-family firms in their original states (see table 4.5).

Table 4.5 Survival Times and Frequencies—Non-Family Enterprises

Variable	M	Min	Max
ST until crucial change	12.14	1.00	46.00
Crucial change	0.95	0.00	1.00
ST until observation end	46.50	41.00	52.00
Survival with no change	0.05	0.00	1.00

The sample divides into two groups: firms that experienced a crucial change during the timeline of observation and firms that remained in their original state until the observation period ended, i.e. the survivors. In total, 37 firms—95% of the entire sample—experienced some sort of crucial change. The average survival time constitutes approximately twelve years, with a minimum ST of one year and a maximum ST of 46 years.

The group of survivors is far smaller, with merely two firms maintaining their original status. The mean ST is 46.5 years. The shortest ST until observation end is 41 years, hence stock market flotation was in the year 1977 for this particular firm. The firm with the longest ST of 52 years experienced IPO launch in 1966. Due to right-censoring, the actual ST is not definable.

4.3.2 Survival Analysis

4.3.2.1 Testing for Correlation between Independent Variables

Equivalent to the analysis approach for the sample group of family businesses, a correlation matrix has been established in order to check for correlation between the independent variables prior to conducting the Cox PH models. The relation between merger and acquisition has been identified with a high value for correlation of 0.81 (see table 4.6). Consequently, the variable *Merger* has been eliminated for further survival analyses.

Table 4.6 Correlation Matrix—Non-Family Enterprises

Variable	(1)	(2)	(3)	(4)	(5)	(6)	(7)	(8)	(9)
CatYofIPO (1)	1								
CatTOatIPO (2)	0.42	1							
AgeatIPO (3)	0.28	−0.04	1						
Merger (4)	−0.23	−0.24	0.13	1					
Acqu (5)	0.34	0.32	0.02	**−0.81**	1				
MorAforeign (6)	0.19	−0.01	0.13	−0.17	0.21	1			
MorAFF (7)	−0.1	−0.02	0.03	−0.15	0.18	−0.1	1		
Breakup (8)	0.09	0.16	−0.18	−0.08	−0.26	−0.05	−0.05	1	
FormerFF (9)	0.3	0.09	0.49	−0.22	0.35	0.03	0.12	−0.15	1

4.3.2.2 Log-Rank Tests

Log-rank tests have been conducted for all independent variables in connection with every dependent survival variable. The p-values of the tests are on display in table 4.7. Values below 0.05 indicate a significant relation between the two variables. The tests have identified several p-values below the critical threshold for ST1 (ST until crucial change), but no p-values have been pinpointed to indicate any significance for ST2 (ST until observation end). Therefore, a Cox PH model has only been calculated for ST1.

Table 4.7 Log-Rank Tests—Non-Family Enterprises

Variable	**ST1**	**ST2**
Year of IPO	**0.002**	0.368
Turnover at IPO	**0.002**	1.000
Age at IPO	0.064	1.000
Former family firm	**<0.001**	1.000
Acquisition	**0.005**	0.480
M or A foreign	0.110	1.000
M or A by family firm	0.848	0.480
Break-up	**0.004**	1.000
Industry	**0.006**	0.981

4.3.2.3 Cox Proportional Hazards Model

The Cox PH model (Cox 1972) is a partial likelihood approach which recognizes and deals with censoring. This is an important feature for model specification. The sample contains firms that have survived beyond the observation period. Hence, these firms have been identified with right-censored survival spells, meaning their survival duration has not ended within the observation period. Still, the duration must be integrated into the calculation. Because this method follows a multivariate approach, the independent variable can be checked for influence of several independent variables. In Cox regression, the hazard rates are conditional probabilities, since they involve certain events that have not yet occurred. This means that the coefficients of this model reflect the risk of the subject falling out within the observation period (Harhoff & Wagner, 2009; Ziegler et al, 2004). Hence, the hazard ratios (HR) indicate whether the independent variable has a risk-increasing or risk-minimizing effect on the ST. An HR>1 indicates that the corresponding independent variable has a risk-increasing effect on the dependent variable. This means the independent variable minimizes or reduces the total ST. An HR<1 consequently has the opposite effect, namely an increasing effect on the total ST of the firm. The values for Pseudo R^2 measure the goodness-of-fit. In general, they can take on a value between 0 and 1. The higher the value, the better the goodness-of-fit of the model. The p-values offer information on the level of significance of the HR-values.

Resulting from the outcomes of the log-rank tests, a Cox PH model has been conducted for the dependent variable ST1 (ST until crucial change) in connection with the identified independent variables. The hazard ratios are presented in table 4.8.

ST1: The Cox PH model has identified two independent variables with a p-value below the critical threshold, indicating the variable has a significant effect on the ST until the crucial change occurs. The turnover category of 50-99mio DM has been identified with an HR of 7.44, indicating that firms among this category of turnover at the time of the IPO launch have a significantly higher risk, or in this case a shorter ST, until the crucial change sets in. These results are in comparison to the reference category of >1bn DM. Hence, survival times until crucial changes tend to be shorter for smaller non-family firms with lower turnover.

The independent variable regarding whether a non-family firm was once a family-owned business prior to stock market flotation has been identified with an HR of 7.59. Accordingly, firms that have family firm roots are at higher risk, or more specifically have shorter survival times until a crucial change occurs after IPO launch.

Table 4.8 Cox Regression Analysis—Non-Family Enterprises

Variable	ST1
Year of IPO—1970´s	0.507 (−0.54)
Year of IPO—1980´s	6.183 (1.48)
Turnover 500–999 Mio DM	0.395 (−1.19)
Turnover 100–499 Mio DM	1.570 (0.70)
Turnover 50–99 Mio DM	7.44** (2.07)
Turnover <50 Mio DM	1.746 (0.46)
Age at IPO	1.006 (1.02)
Acquisition	1.640 (0.48)
Break-up	10.909 (1.32)
Former family firm	7.59* (1.67)
Energy Supply	7.334 (1.35)
Construction Industry	12.907 (1.49)
Commerce	4.850 (1.27)
Transportation & Storage	. (.)
Information & Communication	2.604 (0.70)
Finance & Insurance	0.720 (−0.17)
Real Estate	0.870 (−0.09)
Pseudo R2	0.257
N	35

*p<0.1, **p<0.05. ***p<0.01

4.3.2.4 Kaplan-Meier Estimation

KM plots have been generated for more detailed visual analysis. According to the procedure for the family firm analyses, the independent variables that have been identified with a significant effect for the non-family firms are on display in figures 4.1 and 4.2.

The survival lines until crucial change (ST1) of the firms categorized by turnover at the time of IPO launch are presented in the graph (see figure 4.1). It is apparent that the larger the firm regarding turnover is, the longer the survival times are. The firms within the category of 50-99mio DM, which has been identified as significant, have by far the shortest survival times. All firms within this category experienced a crucial change within the first ten years after IPO, followed by the category of the lowest turnover of <50mio DM. From there, the survival times get longer, the larger the turnover category. The only survivors beyond the observation end (right-censored spells) among the sample group of non-family enterprises were in the category of the largest turnover of >1bn DM at IPO launch.

Figure 4.2 plots the survival lines of the non-family businesses until crucial change (ST1), divided into whether the firm was a former family firm or not. The line representing the former family firms follows a constant decline. Within the

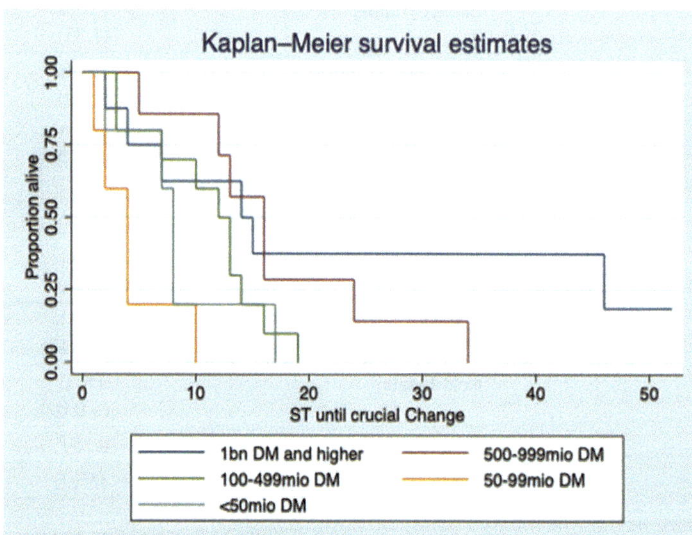

Figure 4.1 ST1—Category Turnover

first 16 years, approximately, all former family firms were subjected to a crucial change. The line representing the opposing group, i.e. the firms with no family background prior to IPO, shows the most intense decline takes place between roughly seven years and twenty years. After this threshold the survival times get longer with fewer cases. The survivors were all among this group.

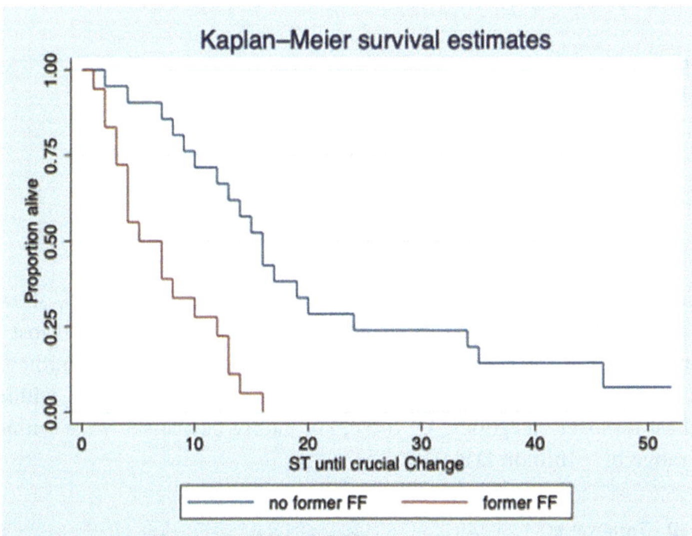

Figure 4.2 ST1—Former Family Firms

4.4 The Sample of Family Enterprises

4.4.1 Descriptive Statistics

A total of 77 businesses were assigned to this sample. All businesses were either in founding family control, meaning a company stake larger than 50% in family ownership, or in founding family ownership, meaning company stake between 25% and 50% in family ownership[6] at the time the business launched the IPO.

[6] See Section 2.5.1. "The Dilution Process" for an explanation of the difference between family control and family ownership.

4.4.1.1 Categorical Variables

Introducing the sample of family businesses, tables 4.9 through 4.12 display the absolute numbers (N) and the percentages of the given frequency distribution of the categorical variables *Year of IPO*, *Turnover at IPO*, *Shareholder Structure at IPO*, and *Industry*. According to table 4.9, the majority of IPOs were launched in the 1980´s. A total number of 62 stock market flotations took place in this decade, whereas merely one flotation from the 1950´s made it into the sample.[7]

Table 4.9 Year of IPO—Family Enterprises

Year of IPO	N	%
1950´s	1	1.3
1960´s	7	9.1
1970´s	7	9.1
1980´s	62	80.5

The distribution of turnover at the time of stock market flotation, shown in table 4.10, displays the highest frequency in middle-sized turnover. Most family businesses (N = 29) recorded a turnover between 100 and 500 million DM in the year of their individual IPO. Only 13 family businesses were within the two highest turnover categories. Of these, six family businesses were within the highest range of ≥ 1billion DM.

Table 4.10 Turnover at IPO—Family Enterprises

Turnover at IPO (in DM)	N	%
≥ 1 bn	6	8.3
500–999 mio	7	9.7
100–499 mio	29	40.3
50–99 mio	16	22.2
<50 mio	14	19.4

Table 4.11 displays the shareholder structure with respect to family ownership at the time of the IPO launch. A total number of 67 family businesses within the sample were family-controlled at the time. The vast majority of 56% noted a family share of even ≥ 75%. Only ten family businesses were merely family owned, with 25–50% of shares in family hands.

[7] In the 1980´s a trend towards going public had set in due to German banks promoting the development.

Table 4.11 Shareholder Structure at IPO—Family Enterprises

Family Shares at IPO	N	%
75–100%	43	55.8
51–74%	24	31.2
25–50%	10	13.0

The distribution of the family businesses among the industries is given in table 4.12. Apparent at first sight is the high frequency of economic activity in the manufacturing industry. Nearly 70% of all family firms are in a manufacturing business, followed by the Information & Communication industry.

Table 4.12 Industry—Family Enterprises

Industry	N	%
Manufacturing Industry	53	68.8
Construction Industry	3	3.9
Commerce	7	9.1
Transportation & Storage	2	2.6
Information & Communication	9	11.7
Finance & Insurance	2	2.6
Real Estate	1	1.3

4.4.1.2 Metrical and Binary Variables

Apart from the descriptive statistics of the categorical variables, characteristics for all metrical and binary variables have been calculated as well. These have been divided into three parts: firstly, firm specific characteristics, given in table 4.13; secondly, family involvement described in table 4.14; and thirdly, the final states at the time the firm either falls out of observation due to failure/crucial change or the observation period coming to an end, given in table 4.15.

Table 4.13 Firm specific Characteristics—Family Enterprises

Independent Variable	N	M	SD	Min	Max
Age at IPO	77	61.44	69.63	0.00	544.00
Reductions Total	77	1.23	0.99	0.00	4.00
Time Frame of Reductions	58	6.67	9.01	1.00	39.00

Looking at the firm specific characteristics, table 4.13 shows the total number (N), the mean (M), the standard deviation (SD), and the minimum (Min) and maximum value (Max) of the sample.

The mean age at IPO launch was 61 years. The variable shows a high value for standard deviation. This is due to the outliers of very old and very young family businesses. Some businesses basically entered the stock market with establishment, others after many years as a privately held firm. The oldest firm in the sample counted 544 years before stock market flotation, roughly 18 family generations after establishment.

The table displays a mean of 1.23 for the total number of reductions in shares held by the owning families. The calculations show a range between 0 and 4 reductions in shares. Hence, there are families that have never sold shares within the observation period. This explains the different number of observations for the variable regarding the time frame of reductions. This variable counts only 58 observations. Hence, since not all firms experienced reductions in family held shares, a total of 19 family businesses maintained their original shareholding quota.

Table 4.14 Family Involvement—Family Enterprises

Independent Variable	N	M	SD	Min	Max
Families Invested	77	1.21	0.68	1.00	5.00
Fam. Memb. Exec. Board at IPO	77	0.48	0.50	0.00	1.00
Fam. Memb. Sup. Board at IPO	77	0.18	0.39	0.00	1.00
Fam. Memb. both Boards at IPO	77	0.18	0.39	0.00	1.00
Fam. Memb. Exec. Board at Crucial Change	77	0.30	0.46	0.00	1.00
Fam. Memb. Sup. Board at Crucial Change	77	0.29	0.45	0.00	1.00
Fam. Memb. both Boards at Crucial Change	77	0.10	0.31	0.00	1.00

On average, 1.21 families were invested in the family business at the IPO launch, although up to five families have been accounted for in at least one case. The last six variables displayed in table 4.14 are binary variables. These explain whether a family member was operating on the board of managing directors or was part of the supervisory board, or whether family members were present in both committees at the time of IPO and at the time of crucial change, if given, otherwise at the time the observation ended (AO measures). In 48% of all family businesses, a family member was operating on the board of managing directors at the time of IPO. Furthermore, in 18% of all cases a family member was present on the supervisory board and in equally 18% of all cases on both boards.

No matter whether the firm experienced a crucial change or survived throughout the observation period, the table shows that for the last three the variables' relation does change in the end. The ratio between family members on the board of managing directors and the supervisory board are nearly identical (approximately 30%). In only 10% of all cases are family members present in both committees by the time the firm falls out of observation.

Resuming the calculated AO measures into the defined AO degrees,[8] 14% of all family businesses experienced no AO measures by family members and 16% experienced AO measures at the time of the IPO launch. A remarkable 70% of all family businesses experienced the highest level of AO—continuous AO measures throughout the observation timeline.

Table 4.15 Final States—Family Enterprises

Independent Variable	N	M	SD	Min	Max
Survival as family-controlled	77	0.19	0.40	0.00	1.00
Survival as family-owned	77	0.05	0.22	0.00	1.00
Merger or acquisition (MorA)	77	0.58	0.50	0.00	1.00
Merger	77	0.01	0.11	0.00	1.00
Acquisition	77	0.57	0.50	0.00	1.00
MorA by foreign firm	77	0.26	0.44	0.00	1.00
MorA by other family firm	77	0.08	0.27	0.00	1.00
Delisting	77	0.03	0.16	0.00	1.00
Bankruptcy	77	0.13	0.34	0.00	1.00
Dissolution	77	0.01	0.11	0.00	1.00

Regarding the descriptive characteristics of the independent variables describing the final states/crucial changes, 24% of all family businesses maintained their family firm status throughout the observation period. Hence, table 4.15 shows that 19% have even remained in family control (N = 15), whereas 5% remained family owned with a blocking minority (N = 4).

The remaining variables stand for the crucial changes the family businesses encountered. The vast majority of 45 firms, which makes 58% of the entire sample, were subjected to either merger or acquisition. Of these 45 firms, only one was merged with another firm, while the rest were all acquisitions. Furthermore, 26% of all firms within the sample were acquired by foreign firms and 8% by

[8] For further information, see Section 2.5.3. "The Concept of Active Ownership".

other family businesses. In absolute numbers, 20 of the 44 acquisitions were executed by foreign firms, which comprises nearly half of the cases. Acquisitions executed by other family businesses account for six cases.

Besides merger or acquisition, de-listings, bankruptcies, and dissolutions were among the spectrum of crucial changes, although merely two cases were de-listed during the observation period and only one firm experienced a dissolution. Bankruptcies account for ten failures among the sample.

4.4.1.3 Survival Variables

The survival analysis for the sample of family enterprises examines seven dependent variables. These are displayed in table 4.16 as the ST-variables, where ST stands for survival time.[9] The variables below the ST-variables are the corresponding event indicators. These are variables, as the name suggests, that indicate whether the event applies to the observation or not. They are necessary for the Cox regression model to recognize censored data.

Table 4.16 Survival Times and Frequencies

Variable	M	Min	Max
ST until 1. Reduction	8.21	1.00	34.00
Reductions YES	0.74	0.00	1.00
ST until Crucial Change	11.40	1.00	40.00
Crucial Change YES	0.75	0.00	1.00
ST until Observation End	32.11	30.00	39.00
Survival as FF YES	0.26	0.00	1.00
ST until Death as Listed Firm	14.07	1.00	33.00
Death as Listed Firm YES	0.17	0.00	1.00
ST until Death as Firm	12.36	1.00	25.00
Death as Firm YES	0.14	0.00	1.00
ST until Death as Family Firm	10.62	1.00	40.00
Death as FF YES	0.58	0.00	1.00
ST after 1. Reduction until MorA	4.47	1.00	39.00
MorA YES	0.58	0.00	1.00

Taking a look at the first two variables, the table shows that 57 firms within this sample have experienced at least one reduction in the family/-ies´ block

[9] An overview and explanation of the variables is given in Section 3.4. “Data and Variables”.

of shares. These account for 74% of the entire sample. On average these firms survived about 8 years until the first reduction of shares took place.

The mean ST until a firm experienced crucial change is 11.4 years and caused 75% of the sample to fail (N = 58). Furthermore, the average ST for family businesses that survived until the observation period ended is roughly 32 years. This is the case for 26% of all family enterprises, hence for the 19 family firm survivors. The shortest ST is identified with 30 years, the longest with 39 years. In conclusion, the firm with the longest ST launched its IPO in the year 1979. All family firm IPO launches prior to 1979 failed within the observation period.

The next two survival times measure the duration until the firm fails as a publicly listed firm and as a firm in itself. Failure as a *listed* firm integrates all firms that experienced de-listing, bankruptcy, or firm dissolution. Failure as a firm includes bankruptcies and firm dissolutions. For these dependent variables the mean ST is 14 and 12 years, respectively.

The last dependent variable measures the ST for all family businesses that have experienced a reduction in family-held shares until either a merger or acquisition took place.[10] This dependent variable measures the actual ST until a family firm loses its family firm status due to excessive dilution of family influence. Merger or acquisition were reasons for failure for 58% of the entire sample (N = 45). On average, once the reduction process was initiated, the firms only survived in family ownership for 4.5 years until final takeover.

4.4.2 Survival Analysis

4.4.2.1 Testing for Correlation between Independent Variables

Prior to conducting the extensive survival analysis, the independent variables used for the duration regression were tested for correlation.[11] The independent variables used in a Cox PH model should preferably show low correlation between one another. Table 4.17 displays the correlation matrix for the independent variables used in the model. Mostly there are no high correlations to be found, except for one. The variables *Acquisition* and *Merger or Acquisition* are highly correlated with a value of 0.97. Hence, the variable *MorA* has been eliminated for further analyses.

[10] Mergers and acquisitions are treated equally in this work.

[11] Compare to Hair et al. (2018), Hair et al. (2016) & Schlittgen (2012).

Table 4.17 *Correlation Matrix—Family Enterprises*[12]

Variable	(1)	(2)	(3)	(4)	(5)	(6)	(7)	(8)	(9)
(1) CatYofIPO	1								
(2) CatTOatIPO	−0.19	1							
(3) CatSharehatIPO	0.05	−0.14	1						
(4) FamInv	0.14	−0.07	−0.03	1					
(5) AgeatIPO	−0.29	0.07	−0.05	−0.15	1				
(6) RedTot	−0.16	0.11	−0.14	−0.17	0.17	1			
(7) TFofRed	−0.1	0.11	−0.28	0.07	−0.03	0.59	1		
(8) FMEBatIPO	−0.06	0.18	−0.15	−0.07	0.05	0.04	−0.03	1	
(9) FMSBatIPO	0.07	−0.21	0.28	−0.1	−0.11	−0.22	−0.26	−0.45	1
(10) FMbothBatIPO	0.16	0.03	−0.19	0.05	0.07	0.16	0.11	−0.45	−0.22
(11) FMEBatCrChangeobsend	−0.03	0.18	−0.05	−0.12	0.17	0.11	−0.08	0.39	−0.31
(12) FMSBatCrChangeobsend	0.04	−0.13	0.14	0.06	−0.06	0.05	−0.13	−0.15	0.45
(13) FMbothBatCrChangeobsend	0.15	−0.11	−0.03	0.02	−0.02	−0.26	−0.01	0.01	−0.16
(14) noAO	−0.19	0	0.14	0.15	−0.05	−0.02	0.13	−0.4	−0.2
(15) AOatIPO	0.04	0.08	−0.2	−0.08	−0.1	0.01	0.1	0.08	0.17
(16) ContAO	0.11	−0.07	0.05	−0.05	0.12	0	−0.18	0.24	0.02
(17) SurvFamOwned	0.11	0.09	−0.11	0.19	−0.12	0.24	0.39	0.13	−0.11
(18) Survival	0.22	−0.12	−0.16	0.05	−0.09	−0.23	0.38	0.23	−0.04

(continued)

[12] Table 4.17 displays an excerpt of the correlation matrix. For entire matrix, see Appendix III in the Electronic Supplementary Material.

Table 4.17 (continued)

Variable	(1)	(2)	(3)	(4)	(5)	(6)	(7)	(8)	(9)
(19) MorA	−0.19	0.08	0.08	−0.21	0.2	0.47	−0.46	−0.03	−0.01
(20) Merger	−0.11	0.07	−0.09	−0.04	−0.02	0.09	0.2	0.12	−0.05
(21) Acqu	−0.16	0.07	0.11	−0.2	0.2	0.45	−0.51	−0.06	0
(22) MorAforeign	−0.03	0.22	−0.18	−0.18	0.03	0.22	−0.14	0.02	0.03
(23) MorAFF	−0.08	0	0.04	0.05	0.05	0.18	0.16	0.01	−0.01
(24) Delist	−0.04	0.07	0.1	−0.05	−0.05	−0.21	.	0.01	−0.08
(25) Bnkrpcy	0.12	−0.06	0.07	0.28	−0.17	−0.25	0.22	−0.29	0.12
(26) Diss	−0.28	0.17	−0.09	−0.04	0.02	−0.14	.	0.12	−0.05

Variable	(10)	(11)	(12)	(13)	(14)	(15)	(16)	(17)	(18)	(19)
(1) CatYofIPO										
(2) CatTOatIPO										
(3) CatSharehatIPO										
(4) FamInv										
(5) AgeatIPO										
(6) RedTot										
(7) TFofRed										
(8) FMEBatIPO										
(9) FMSBatIPO										
(10) FMbothBatIPO	1									
(11) FMEBatCrChangeobsend	0.06	1								

(continued)

Table 4.17 (continued)

Variable	(10)	(11)	(12)	(13)	(14)	(15)	(16)	(17)	(18)	(19)
(12) FMSBatCrChangeobsend	0	−0.41	1							
(13) FMbothBatCrChangeobsend	0.28	−0.22	−0.22	1						
(14) noAO	−0.2	−0.27	−0.26	−0.14	1					
(15) AOatIPO	−0.11	−0.29	−0.28	−0.15	−0.18	1				
(16) ContAO	0.24	0.43	0.42	0.23	−0.62	−0.66	1			
(17) SurvFamOwned	0.04	−0.15	0.11	−0.08	−0.1	0.22	−0.1	1		
(18) Survival	−0.11	0.02	0.04	0.2	−0.23	−0.07	0.23	0.41	1	
(19) MorA	0.06	0.15	0.01	−0.23	0.04	−0.01	−0.02	−0.28	−0.68	1
(20) Merger	−0.05	0.18	−0.07	−0.04	−0.05	−0.05	0.08	−0.03	−0.07	0.1
(21) Acqu	0.07	0.11	0.02	−0.22	0.05	0	−0.04	−0.27	−0.66	**0.97**
(22) MorAforeign	−0.05	−0.06	−0.05	−0.01	0.01	0.15	−0.13	−0.14	−0.34	0.5
(23) MorAFF	−0.01	0.13	0.03	−0.1	0.02	−0.13	0.09	−0.07	−0.17	0.25
(24) Delist	−0.08	−0.11	0.08	−0.06	0.17	−0.07	−0.07	−0.04	−0.09	−0.19
(25) Bnkrpcy	0.12	−0.25	−0.07	0.12	0.17	0.15	−0.25	−0.09	−0.22	−0.46
(26) Diss	−0.05	0.18	−0.07	−0.04	−0.05	−0.05	0.08	−0.03	−0.07	−0.14

4.4.2.2 Log-Rank Tests

The list of independent variables is quite extensive. There is therefore a given risk of overfitting the regression model. Overfitting the model may lead to misleading output, for example throgh regression coefficients or p-values. But in order to take all the variables into account, without neglecting variables with possible significant effects on the dependent variables, log-rank tests were run before conducting the Cox PH models.

The survival analysis examines seven dependent variables. Hence, for every independent variable, a log-rank test has been run against every dependent variable. Table 4.18 displays the p-values given by the log-rank tests for all independent variables and the seven dependent variables. Taking the p-values of these tests under consideration, the independent variables that have been found to have a probable significant effect on the dependent variable (ST), have been used for further examination.

By applying a median split, the metrically scaled independent variables were divided into two categories. Otherwise, the log-rank test is not applicable to metrical variables.

Table 4.18 Log-Rank Tests—Family Enterprises

Variable	ST1	ST2	ST3	ST4	ST5	ST6	ST7
Year of IPO	0.775	0.946	**0.033**	0.966	0.980	0.834	0.591
Turnover at IPO	0.234	0.102	0.833	0.626	0.463	0.050	0.558
Shareholder Str. at IPO	0.461	0.188	0.949	0.148	**0.046**	0.188	**0.049**
Families Involved	0.295	0.991	0.693	0.155	0.076	0.418	0.931
Age at IPO	0.514	0.694	0.255	0.343	0.322	0.936	0.748
Reductions Total	**<0.001**	0.293	0.549	0.057	0.088	**0.026**	**<0.001**
Time Frame of Reductions	**0.004**	0.104	0.812	0.161	0.161	**0.041**	**<0.001**
FMEB at IPO	0.555	0.135	0.112	**0.035**	**0.020**	0.600	0.651
FMSB at IPO	0.428	0.409	0.968	0.471	0.272	0.595	**0.005**
FM both Boards at IPO	0.076	0.478	0.533	0.551	0.387	0.635	0.354
FMEB at Crucial Change	0.447	0.632	0.927	0.131	0.186	0.173	0.470

(continued)

Table 4.18 (continued)

Variable	ST1	ST2	ST3	ST4	ST5	ST6	ST7
FMSB at Crucial Change	0.839	0.830	0.596	0.545	0.410	0.924	0.901
FM both Boards at Cr. Change	0.162	0.232	0.109	0.745	0.557	0.123	0.849
no AO	0.951	0.305	0.064	**0.043**	0.123	0.947	0.821
AO at IPO	0.502	0.857	0.202	0.485	0.400	0.862	0.394
continuous AO	0.621	0.364	0.454	**0.040**	0.071	0.926	0.370
Survival	**<0.001**	**<0.001**	**0.007**	**<0.001**	**0.001**	**<0.001**	**0.002**
Survival Fam.-Control	**<0.002**	**<0.002**	0.247	**0.002**	**0.009**	**<0.002**	.
Survival Fam.-Owned	0.888	**0.017**	**0.044**	0.248	0.272	**0.039**	**0.002**
Merger	**0.003**	0.951	1.000	0.664	0.690	0.774	0.478
Acquisition	**<0.001**	**<0.001**	**0.023**	**0.006**	**0.007**	**<0.001**	**<0.001**
M or A foreign	**<0.001**	**0.004**	**0.044**	0.095	0.116	**<0.001**	0.113
M or A by Family Firm	**<0.001**	0.221	0.060	0.387	0.453	0.061	0.625
De-listing	0.089	0.895	0.201	**0.047**	0.523	0.184	.
Bankruptcy	0.212	0.095	1.000	**<0.001**	**<0.001**	**0.017**	0.013
Dissolution	0.380	0.485	1.000	**0.004**	**0.004**	0.505	.
Industry	0.678	**0.026**	0.154	**<0.001**	**<0.001**	0.614	0.826

4.4.2.3 Cox Proportional Hazards Model

Initially, histograms were analyzed in order to check for distribution among the independent variables. The metrical variables *Age at IPO* and *Time Frame of Reductions* have been identified with a considerable "right-skewness."[13] This unequal distribution is due to single extreme values. In order to reduce the effect of the outliers, a log-transformation of the variables was performed.

The Cox regressions were successful for three of the seven defined dependent variables. An overview of these is given in table 4.19. Due to small sample sizes and partially very few events in connection with the survival variables, convergence problems led to a lack of results for the dependent variables ST3, ST4, ST5, and ST7.

[13] See Appendix V in the Electronic Supplementary Material.

Table 4.19 Survival Variables—Family Enterprises

ST	Definition
ST1	Survival time until 1. reduction in family held shares
ST2	Survival time until crucial change (MorA, bankruptcy, de-listing, dissolution)
ST3	Survival time until observation end as family firm (right-censored; survival as family firm)
ST4	Survival time until death as listed firm (de-listings, bankruptcies, dissolutions)
ST5	Survival time until death as firm (bankruptcies, dissolutions)
ST6	Survival time until death as family firm (MorA)
ST7	Survival time after 1. reduction until MorA

The values in table 4.20 represent the hazard ratios. These figures indicate which effect the independent variable has on the dependent variables.

ST1: Three significant effects have been identified for ST1. The HR>1 for the independent variable *Reductions Total* indicates that the variable has a risk-increasing effect on the dependent variables. Hence, the more reduction steps of the family block of shares took place, the shorter the survival time. With HR<1, the family businesses that remained in family control (family shareholding quota >75%) throughout the observation period show longer survival times. The final identified significant effect with a p-value <0.05 and an HR of 3.361 given for ST1 is the effect that merger or acquisition by another family business reduces the survival time by more than threefold.

ST2: There is only one independent variable that has a significant effect on the ST until crucial change occurs (ST2), yet this effect is highly significant with a p-value below 0.01. The longer the time frame (TF) over which reductions took place, the longer the survival times of the firms. With an HR of 0.522, a longer time frame of reductions doubles the survival time.

ST6: Three variables have been identified with significant effects on the survival time until death as a family firm (ST6), hence until merger or acquisition occurred (dilution). The variable *Reductions Total* has an HR of 2.378, indicating a risk-increasing effect on the ST until the family business got merged or acquired. A high number of reductions in family shares reduces firm ST in family ownership by more than a double. On the other hand, the variable *Time Frame of Reductions* has been found to have a risk-decreasing effect with an HR of 0.291, and with a p-value below 0.01. This effect is highly significant. A large time frame of reductions in family shares increases the survival time for family firms that have been merged or acquired in the end *by more than half.* Finally, the variable *Acquisition* has been identified with a significant effect with p<0.05 and an HR of 10.79, implying that family businesses being subject to acquisitions show far shorter survival times.

The number of observations for these three Cox regressions is 58, instead of the total of 77 within the sample of family enterprises. This is due to the fact that not all family businesses experienced reductions. For these three dependent variables though, reductions-related independent variables have been identified with significant effects. Hence the number of valid observations is limited to the firms that in fact had experienced reductions in shares.

Table 4.20 Cox Regression Analysis—Family Enterprises

Variable	ST1	ST2	ST6
Reductions total	1.874* (1.96)		2.378* (1.90)
Time frame of reductions	1.047 (0.19)	0.522*** (−2.97)	0.291*** (−2.77)
Survival fam.-control	0.296* (−1.85)	. (.)	. (.)
Merger	3.082 (0.92)		
Acquisition	1.169 (0.3)	0.793 (−0.33)	10.79** (2.23)
M or A foreign	1.232 (0.65)	0.930 (−0.19)	1.004 (0.01)
M or A by family firm	3.361** (2.35)		
Turnover 500–999 Mio DM		0.776 (−0.33)	0.895 (−0.16)
Turnover 100–499 Mio DM		0.855 (−0.23)	1.023 (0.03)
Turnover 50–99 Mio DM		0.439 (−1.08)	0.638 (−0.63)

(continued)

4.4.2.4 Kaplan-Meier Survival Estimation

The Kaplan-Meier survival curves were plotted for the independent variables that were identified with significant effects on the dependent variables by the Cox

Table 4.20 (continued)

Variable	ST1	ST2	ST6
Turnover <50 Mio DM		0.415 (−1.13	0.499 (−0.97)
Survival fam.-owned		. (.)	
Construction Industry		1.536 (0.62)	
Commerce		1.357 (0.50)	
Transportation & Storage		2.110 (.)	
Information & Communication		1.869 (1.11)	
Finance & Insurance		0.707 (−0.31)	
Pseudo R2	0.081	0.183	0.189
N	58	58	58

*p<0.1, **p<0.05. ***p<0.01

PH models. They measure and visualize the time until failure occurs in reference to the independent variable. For the following KM estimates, the samples were divided into two groups by median split, in order to generate comparability.

4.4.2.4.1 Survival Time until first Reduction (ST1)

The graph in figure 4.3 plots the survival lines of the family enterprises regarding the number of total reductions of family-owned shares during the observation period with respect to the *ST until 1. reduction.* Family businesses that experienced many reductions clearly have a far shorter survival span until the first reduction than family firms that experienced fewer reductions. The line reflecting the family firms with a higher number of reductions drops drastically within the first few years, indicating that several families sold a certain number of shares within the first couple of years after IPO. Within this group, the maximum ST until the first reduction is around 13 years. The line reflecting the survival line of the firms that experienced fewer reductions of shares, on the other hand, displays a regularly declining line until around 13 years, indicating that also for this group several families sold shares within the first couple of years after IPO. The thirteen years also mark about the same time the group with the higher number of total reductions experienced their maximum ST until first reduction. After this 13-year cut, the survival times until the family/-ies sold their first stake got longer. A certain proportion survived beyond the observation period without experiencing any reductions, with a conditional maximum survival time of 40 years.

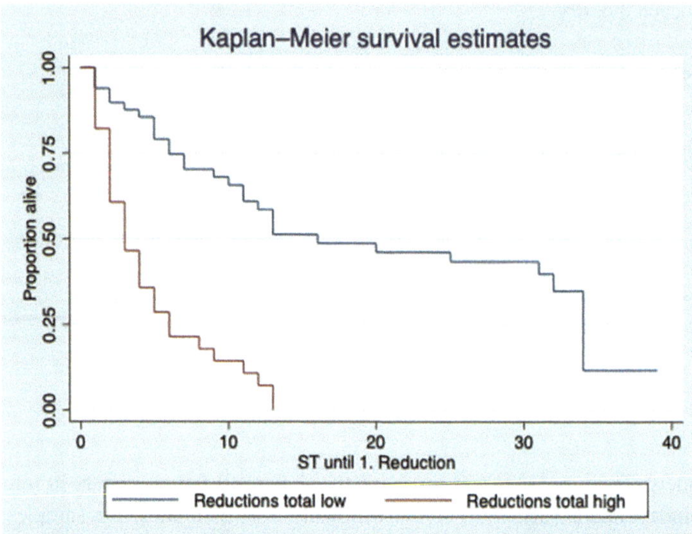

Figure 4.3 ST1—Reductions Total

Whether a family firm survived in family control beyond the observation cut-off is shown in figure 4.4. The line representing all firms that did not survive as family-controlled, i.e. all firms with family stake between 25–50%, shows a breaking point at around 13 years, similar to the graph in figure 4.3. Many family businesses in the group represented by this line experienced the first reduction in family-owned shares within the first couple of years after IPO. After around 13 years, survival times got longer until the first shares were sold. A small proportion survived beyond observation with a conditional maximum ST of approximately 33 years. The other line reflects the survival times until the first reductions in family-owned shares for the survivors in family control. Here again the thirteen-year mark catches the eye. Among the survivors the first reductions took place after roughly 13 years. After this drop there was a long period of stability. The largest proportion of about 50% of the family-controlled survivors remained in their original shareholding state for at least thirty years without any reductions. Nearly 25% of all family-controlled survivors did not experience any reductions, with a conditional ST of roughly 40 years.

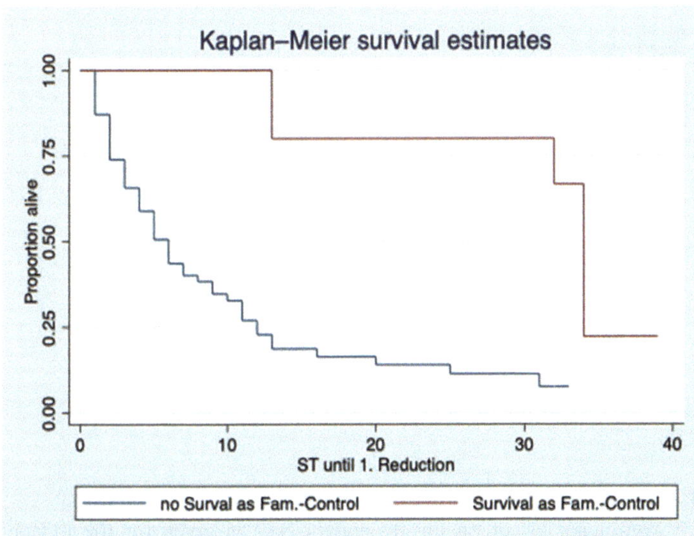

Figure 4.4 ST1—Survival as Family-Controlled

Figure 4.5 plots the survival lines for the dependent variable *ST until first reduction* in connection with the third independent variable with a significant effect (hence whether a merger or acquisition by another family firm took place). 50% of the family businesses that experienced merger or acquisition by another family firm are identified with a very short ST until first reduction in family-owned shares. For this group, the graph displays a maximum survival time of approximately four years until the family/-ies sold off stock. Among the group of firms that were not subjected to merger or acquisition by another family firm, the 13-year threshold appears once again. Most firms in this group have short survival times up until the threshold, whereafter the survival times get longer with another drop at approximately 34 years of *ST until first reduction.*

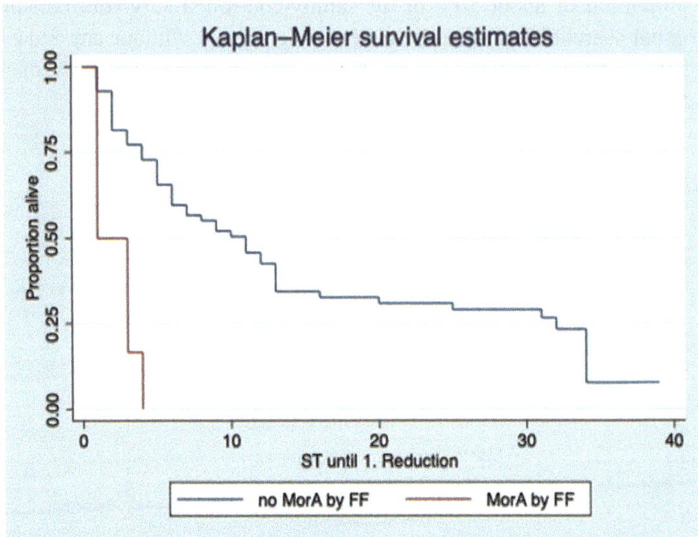

Figure 4.5 ST1—Merger or Acquisition by other Family Firm

4.4.2.4.2 Survival Time until Crucial Change (ST2)

The only significant effect on the dependent ST2 is given for the independent variable *time frame of reductions*. The graph in figure 4.6 displays the effects that a short TF of reductions has on the ST until crucial change leads to failure, as well as the effect given by a long TF of reductions. Both lines show a similar course. Once again, the most failures occur within roughly the first 13 years, rather short survival times until crucial change. Yet the line reflecting long TF of reductions indicates that the firms initially survived a couple years longer than the firms with a shorter TF of reductions. Still, in the end, all firms identified with a long TF of reductions, did experience a crucial change, i.e. they failed. The family businesses with a shorter TF of reductions experienced most crucial changes in the first 13 years, but after this threshold the survival times get longer, with a small proportion of survivors with a conditional ST of approximately 34 years. This finding implies that the surviving family businesses survived longer before selling off first stock, hence only shortly before the observation ended in 2018 did the surviving firms reduce shares. This in turn explains the short TF of reductions.

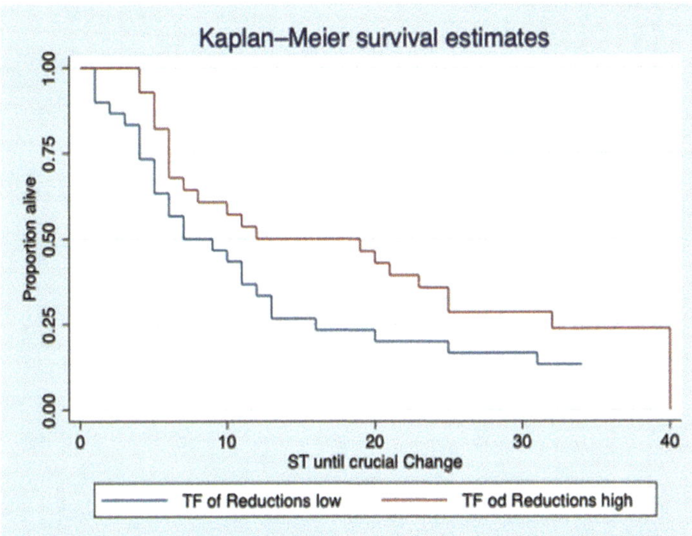

Figure 4.6 ST2—Time Frame of Reductions

4.4.2.4.3 Survival Time until Death as Family Firm (ST6)

Three independent variables have been identified with significant effects on the *ST until death as a family firm.* The graph featured in figure 4.7 plots the effects of the total number of reductions on the ST until death as a family firm (dilution through MorA). The sample was divided into low and high numbers of total reductions. At first sight, the firms with a higher number of reductions have shorter survival times until death as a family firm, although they survive longer in the beginning. Of this group, all firms fail as a family firm in the end, with the longest survival time being 40 years. There are some cases of family businesses with fewer reductions in family-owned shares that experienced death shortly after IPO. In fact, there is a constant decline among the proportion alive in the first thirteen years. Roughly 40% experienced merger or acquisition within these years. After this threshold the survival times get longer—nearly 50% of the group of family firms with few reductions in total experience a conditional ST of roughly 40 years.

Furthermore, the variable regarding the time frame of reductions has been identified as highly significant for effect on the ST until death as a family firm. Figure 4.8 displays the graph for these effects. The firms with a short time frame

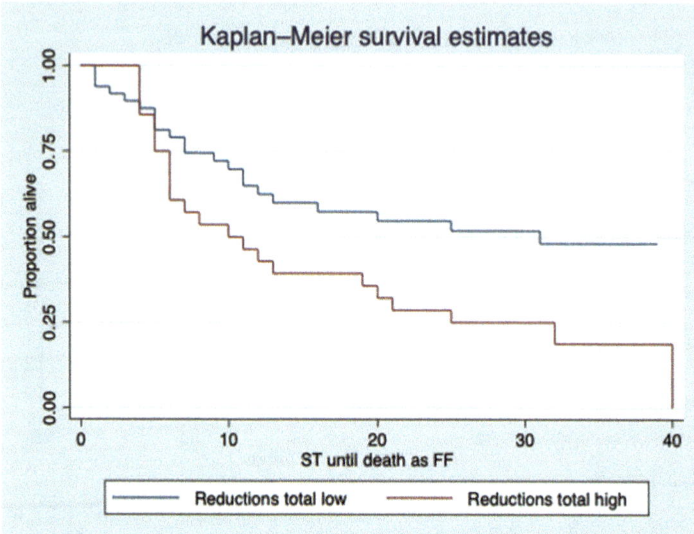

Figure 4.7 ST6—Reductions Total

of reductions experience death as a family firm mostly within the first 13 years. For the years after this mark, the survival times get longer, with a conditional maximum ST of approximately 34 years for firms that have not experienced death as a family firm. The firms with a longer TF of reductions have survived initially for a couple of years longer, but then a rapid decline is visible in the graph until roughly the 13-year threshold. Afterwards these periods get longer, with the final proportion experiencing death after a ST of 40 years.

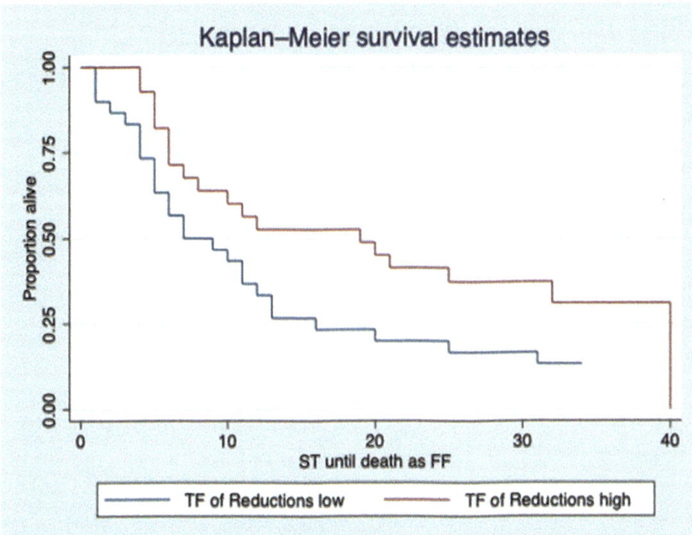

Figure 4.8 ST6—Time Frame of Reductions

Figure 4.9 plots the effect that acquisition as a form of crucial change has on the ST until death as a family firm. What emerges most clearly is the wide gap between the groups of family businesses that were acquired during observation and the family businesses that did not experience acquisition. Most family businesses experienced acquisition as the form of crucial change. The strongest decline is visible within the first 13 years or so. More than 75% of the firms in this group experienced acquisition within this time. Subsequently, the survival times get longer, with a maximum ST of forty years. The group of firms that have not been identified with acquisition as the form of crucial change are very few and have far longer survival times, with nearly the entirety surviving beyond observation with a conditional ST of nearly 40 years.

In conclusion, when observing the KM plots, one finds one commonality in all the graphs: the 13-year threshold. It appears that the first 13 years after IPO launch bear a higher risk of family businesses facing failure. Once the firms survive beyond this theoretical threshold, the risk of failure appears to decrease, and survival chances appear to increase.

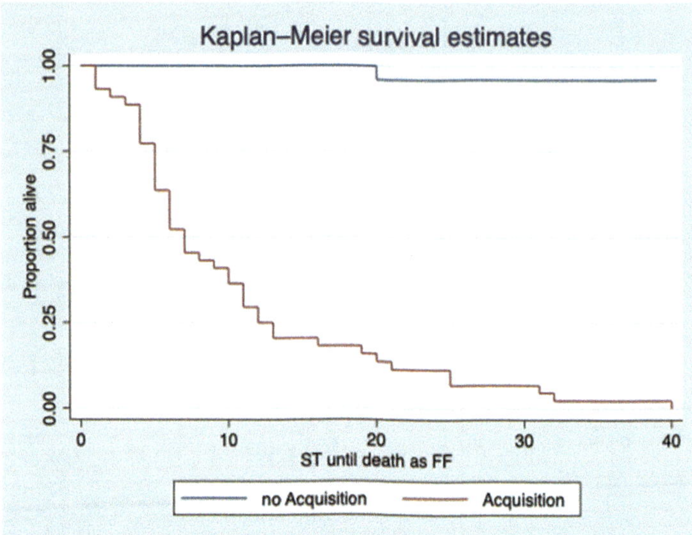

Figure 4.9 ST6—Acquisition

4.4.3 Tests of Significance

Due to convergence problems, Cox PH models were not calculable for four of the seven pre-defined survival variables. In order to check for possible significant relations between the independent variables and these specific survival variables, tests of significance were conducted.

The survival variables under examination regard *survival as family firm*, *death as a listed firm*, *death as a firm* and *death as a family firm (MorA)*.[14]

4.4.3.1 Chi^2 Tests of Independence

The chi^2 tests of independence have been applied to measuring the relations between the categorical variables and the survival variables. The results are presented in table 4.21. The table displays the p-values given by the tests. A significant relation is proposed by a p-value <0.05. Furthermore, the percentage of firms to which the categorical variable applies is on display, as well as the absolute number of observations.

---

[14] See table 4.19.

Table 4.21 *Chi^2 Tests of Independence—Family Enterprises*

		ST3 Survival as family firm			**ST 4 Death as listed firm**		
Variable	Characteristics	%	N	p	%	N	p
Year of IPO	1950´s	0.00	0	0.301	0.00	0	0.815
	1960‘s	0.00	0		14.29	1	
	1970‘s	14.30	1		28.57	2	
	1980‘s	29.00	18		16.13	10	
Turnover at IPO	>1 bn	50.00	3	0.218	0.00	0	0.406
	500–999 m	0.00	0		0.00	0	
	100–499 m	31.03	9		20.69	6	
	50–99 m	25.00	4		12.50	2	
	<50 m	14.29	2		7.14	1	
Shareholder str. at IPO	75–100%	30.23	13	0.356	11.63	5	0.152
	51–74%	20.83	5		29.17	7	
	25–50%	10.00	1		10.00	1	
Fam. mem. on exec. Board at IPO	No	15.00	6	**0.041**	25.00	10	**0.048**
	Yes	35.14	13		8.11	3	
Fam. mem. on sup. Board at IPO	No	25.40	16	0.755	15.87	10	0.616
	Yes	21.43	3		21.43	3	

(continued)

Table 4.21 (continued)

		ST3 Survival as family firm			**ST 4 Death as listed firm**		
Fam. mem. on both boards at IPO	No	26.98	17	0.319	15.87	10	0.616
	Yes	14.29	2		21.43	3	
Fam. mem. on exec. Board at cr. ch./obs. end	No	24.07	13	0.851	22.22	12	0.055
	Yes	26.09	6		4.35	1	
Fam. mem. on sup. Board at cr. ch./obs. end	No	23.64	13	0.738	18.18	10	0.631
	Yes	27.27	6		13.64	3	
Fam. mem. on both boards at cr. ch./obs. end	No	21.74	15	0.079	15.94	11	0.517
	Yes	50.00	4		25.00	2	
no AO	No	27.69	18	**0.046**	13.85	9	0.067
	Yes	0.00	0		36.36	4	
AO at IPO	No	25.00	16	0.533	15.62	10	0.429
	Yes	16.67	2		25.00	3	
continuous AO	No	8.70	2	**0.043**	30.43	7	**0.042**
	Yes	30.19	16		11.32	6	

(continued)

Table 4.21 (continued)

		ST3 Survival as family firm			ST 4 Death as listed firm		
Industry	Manufacturing	22.64	12	0.216	16.98	9	0.363
	Construction	0.00	0		0.00	0	
	Commerce	28.57	2		14.29	1	
	Transportation & Storage	100.00	2		0.00	0	
	Information & Communication	22.22	2		22.22	2	
	Finance & Insurance	50.00	1		0.00	0	
	Real Estate	0.00	0		100.00	1	

		ST5 Death as firm			ST7 Merger or acquistion		
Variable	Characteristics	%	N	p	%	N	p
Year of IPO	1950´s	0.00	0	0.982	100.00	1	0.363
	1960‘s	14.29	1		85.71	6	
	1970‘s	14.29	1		57.14	4	
	1980‘s	14.52	9		54.84	34	
Turnover at IPO	>1 bn	0.00	0	0.295	50.00	3	0.071
	500–999 m	0.00	0		100.00	7	
	100–499 m	20.69	6		48.28	14	
	50–99 m	6.25	1		62.50	10	
	<50 m	7.14	1		78.57	11	
Shareholder str. at IPO	75–100%	9.30	4	**0.032**	58.14	25	0.270

(continued)

Table 4.21 (continued)

		ST3 Survival as family firm			ST 4 Death as listed firm		
	51–74%	29.17	7		50.00	12	
	25–50%	0.00	0		80.00	8	
Fam. mem. on exec. Board at IPO	No	22.50	9	**0.032**	60.00	24	0.773
	Yes	5.41	2		56.76	21	
Fam. mem. on sup. Board at IPO	No	12.70	8	0.398	58.73	37	0.913
	Yes	21.43	3		57.14	8	
Fam. mem. on both boards at IPO	No	12.70	8	0.398	57.14	36	0.624
	Yes	21.43	3		64.29	9	
Fam. mem. on exec. Board at cr. ch./obs. end	No	18.52	10	0.104	53.70	29	0.196
	Yes	4.35	1		69.57	16	
Fam. mem. on sup. Board at cr. ch./obs. end	No	16.36	9	0.410	58.18	32	0.942
	Yes	9.09	2		59.09	13	
Fam. mem. on both boards at cr. ch./obs. end	No	13.04	9	0.360	62.32	43	**0.043**

(continued)

Table 4.21 (continued)

		ST3 Survival as family firm			ST 4 Death as listed firm		
	Yes	25.00	2		25.00	2	
no AO	No	12.31	8	0.192	58.46	38	0.747
	Yes	27.27	3		63.64	7	
Ao at IPO	No	12.50	8	0.259	59.38	38	0.946
	Yes	25.00	3		58.33	7	
continuous AO	No	26.09	6	0.058	60.87	14	0.846
	Yes	9.43	5		58.49	31	
Industry	Manufacturing	13.21	7	0.263	60.38	32	0.367
	Construction	0.00	0		100.00	3	
	Commerce	14.29	1		57.14	4	
	Transportation & Storage	0.00	0		0.00	0	
	Information & Communication	22.22	2		55.56	5	
	Finance & Insurance	0.00	0		50.00	1	
	Real Estate	100.00	1		0.00	0	

ST3 Survival as family firm: The chi^2 tests of independence revealed significant associations between the variables *FM on Executive Board at IPO, no AO* and *continuous AO* and the survival as a family firm. A higher degree of family involvement has therefore been found to be beneficial for survival as a family firm.

ST4 Death as listed firm: A significant association has also been identified between the degree of family involvement and the occurrence of death as a listed firm. Family businesses that experienced death as a listed firm (de-listing, bankruptcy, and dissolution) rarely have family members on the Executive Board at the time of the IPO launch, and rarely have continuous AO measures exerted by the family.

ST5 Death as firm: Furthermore, a significant association has been found between the shareholder structure at the time of the IPO launch and FM on the Executive Board at IPO and the occurrence of death as a firm itself (bankruptcy and dissolution). Most firms that experienced bankruptcy or dissolution were owned by a family shareholding quota between 51–74%. None of these firms were owned by a quota of 25–50%. Here also, the lack of family involvement supports the occurrence of death as a firm.

ST7 after 1. Red. until merger or acquisition: Finally, a significant association between the occurrence of MorA and lack of FM on both Boards at crucial change/observation end has also been identified. 62% of all family businesses that experienced MorA didn´t have family members on both Boards at the time that the firm was acquired.

4.4.3.2 T-Tests

For further analysis of the survival variables, t-tests have been calculated in order to identify possible significant effects of the metrical variables. The test offers information as to whether the metrical variable differs and to what extent, depending on whether or not the incident occurred. Table 4.22 displays the mean values of the corresponding independent variable, dividing into occurrence and nonoccurrence (Yes/No) of the survival variable. Furthermore, a p-value below 0.05 indicates whether the difference between occurrence and nonoccurrence is significant.

Table 4.22 T-Tests—Family Enterprises

		ST3 Surv. as fam. firm		**ST4 Death as listed firm**	
Variable	Characteristics	M	p	M	p
Families involved	No	1.19	0.683	1.14	0.052
	Yes	1.26		1.54	
Age at IPO	No	3.62	1.000	3.76	**0.024**
	Yes	3.62		2.94	
Reductions total	No	1.36	**0.045**	1.39	**0.002**
	Yes	0.84		0.46	
Time frame of reduction	No	1.37	**0.016**	1.45	**0.050**
	Yes	2.17		2.57	
		ST5 Death as firm		**ST7 Merger or acqu.**	
Variable	Characteristics	M	p	M	p
Families involved	No	1.14	**0.022**	1.38	0.067
	Yes	1.64		1.09	
Age at IPO	No	3.72	0.103	3.35	0.088
	Yes	3.09		3.82	
Reductions total	No	1.35	**0.011**	0.69	**0.000**
	Yes	0.55		1.62	
Time frame of reduction	No	1.45	**0.050**	2.27	**0.001**
	Yes	2.57		1.29	

ST3 Survival as family firm: The family businesses that survived beyond the observation period (right-censored spells) had 0.84 reduction steps of family-owned shares on average, contrary to family firms that did not survive, with an average of 1.36 reduction steps. This difference is significant with a p-value of 0.045. The time frame of reduction has been identified with a significant effect, indicating far shorter periods of share reductions for the firms that did not survive, compared with an average reduction TF of 2.17 for the survivors with a p-value of 0.016.

ST4 Death as listed firm: The t-tests have identified three independent variables with significant effects for the family businesses that experienced death as a listed firm. Firstly, the variable explaining age at IPO shows a p-value of 0.024

with a mean value of 3.76 for the firms that did not experience death as a listed firm and 2.94 for firms that did. Hence, the age of the firm at the time of IPO was significantly higher for the firms that did not experience this form of death. Secondly, the number of total share reductions as well as the TF of reductions had p-values <0.05. These values indicate that the reduction steps in total are significantly higher for the firms that did not experience death as a listed firm. The TF of reductions, on the other hand, are significantly shorter, hence the firms that experienced death as a listed firm had less reductions in total and longer time frames of reductions.

ST5 Death as firm: The family businesses that experienced death as a firm had significantly more families involved, with a p-value of 0.022. For these cases, two independent variables (reductions total and TF of reductions) have also been identified with significant effects. Consequently, the effects are similar to the previous survival variables. Family businesses experiencing death as a firm as a crucial change during the observation period had significantly fewer reduction steps of family held shares in total, and significantly longer time frames between share reductions than family businesses that haven't experienced this form of crucial change.

ST7 after 1. Red. until merger or acquisition: Mergers or acquisitions have been defined as the official death as a family firm, due to loss of family influence through the dilution process.[15] For this survival variable, table 4.13 displays two variables with p-values below the crucial threshold of 0.001. The difference in the number of total reductions in shares is highly significant, hence the firms that experienced MorA during the observation period had more reduction steps than the opposing firms. Furthermore, contrary to the findings for the previously discussed survival variables, these cases have been found to have had shorter time frames of share reductions.

In conclusion, the independent variables regarding reductions in shares and TF of reduction have been identified with significant effects for all four survival variables. Nevertheless, the most outstanding variable is that the family businesses that experienced MorA as a crucial change, therefore losing their status as a family firm due to dilution of family influence, have reversed signs in comparison to the other cases. These have been found to have a higher number in total reduction steps and a shorter TF of share reductions.

---

[15] For further information, see Section 2.5.1. "The Dilution Process".

4.5 Comparing Results of both Samples

This subchapter commits itself to setting the findings of both samples by the previously discussed analyses into comparison, as far as comparable results are available and allow for conclusive evaluation.

Initially, the descriptive statistics of both samples are contrasted, offering a direct comparison of the sample characteristics. The significant findings resulting from the survival analysis are then brought into direct relation, as far as the data and the results allow.

4.5.1 Comparing the Descriptive Statistics

The IPO distribution by decade is similar for both samples. The largest proportion of stock market flotations, namely more than 70%, were registered in the 1980´s. There is merely a slight difference given regarding the 1960's—the non-family businesses registered their IPO with a moderately larger proportion in this decade, compared to the family businesses (Tabel 4.23).

Table 4.23 Year of IPO—Family vs. Non-Family Enterprises

	Family Firms		Non-Family Firms	
Year of IPO	N	%	N	%
1950´s	1	1.3	0	0
1960´s	7	9.1	6	15.4
1970´s	7	9.1	4	10.3
1980´s	62	80.5.2	29	74.4

When comparing the distribution of the firms by level of turnover at the time of IPO (see table 4.24), the majority of family businesses with more than 80% were small- to mid-sized firms. On the other hand, the majority of the non-family enterprises were in the middle to large range of turnover. What both sample groups have in common, however, is that the largest proportion of each group has been assigned to the middle-size category of 100-499mio DM.

Table 4.24 Turnover at IPO—Family vs. Non-Family Enterprises

	Family Firms		**Non-Family Firms**	
Turnover at IPO (in DM)	N	%	N	%
≥ 1 bn	6	8.3	8	**22.9**
500–999 mio	7	9.7	7	**20.0**
100–499 mio	29	**40.3**	10	**28.6**
50–99 mio	16	**22.2**	5	14.3
<50 mio	14	**19.4**	5	14.3

In the case of family businesses, Manufacturing is the main field of economic activity (nearly 70% of all firms). This is by far the largest cluster, distantly followed by the Information & Communication industry with 12%. The non-family businesses show a more balanced distribution. Even here, though, Manufacturing dominates at 44%, followed by Commerce and Energy Supply. Furthermore, the group of non-family businesses has been active in a wider range of industries—the categories of Energy Supply and Health & Insurance Services only apply to this group (see table 4.25).

Table 4.25 Industry—Family vs. Non-Family Enterprises

	Family Firms		**Non-Family Firms**	
Industry	N	%	N	%
Manufacturing Industry	53	**68.8**	17	**43.6**
Energy Supply	0	0.0	6	**15.4**
Construction Industry	3	3.9	1	2.6
Commerce	7	9.1	7	**18.0**
Transportation & Storage	2	2.6	1	2.6
Information & Communication	9	**11.7**	2	5.1
Finance & Insurance	2	2.6	2	5.1
Real Estate	1	1.3	2	5.1
Health & Insurance Services	0	0.0	1	2.6

Observing the differences in crucial changes given in table 4.26, the sample group of family businesses shows a higher rate of survival with 24%. Among the non-family businesses, merely 5% remained in their original state until the observation period came to an end. Furthermore, 72% of non-family businesses experienced an acquisition as the form of crucial change, whereas this form of crucial change accounts for a smaller proportion of 57% for the family businesses. On the other hand, a larger proportion of the family firms that experienced merger or acquisition were in fact merged or acquired by a foreign firm, with 26% accounting for the family businesses compared to 10% for the comparison group.

Table 4.26 Crucial Changes—Family vs. Non-Family Enterprises

	Family Firms		**Non-Family Firms**	
Crucial Changes	**N**	**M**	**N**	**M**
Survival / no change	77	**0.24**	39	0.05
Merger	77	0.01	39	0.21
Acquisition	77	0.57	39	**0.72**
MorA by foreign firm	77	**0.26**	39	0.10
MorA by other family firm	77	0.08	39	0.08
De-listing	77	0.03	39	0.00
Bankruptcy	77	0.13	39	0.00

When considering the firm-specific characteristics, merely one mentionable difference meets the eye—the focus group of family businesses has a maximum age of 544 years at the time of stock market flotation, which surpasses the maximum age of the non-family businesses by far (see table 4.27). Although in the end, the average age at IPO does not vary considerably.

Table 4.27 Firm Characteristics—Family vs. Non-Family Enterprises

	Family Firms			**Non-Family Firms**		
Firm-Specific Characteristics	**N**	**M**	**Max**	**N**	**M**	**Max**
Age at IPO	77	61.44	**544.00**	39	57.05	166.00

Both sample groups have two survival variables in common. These are the most important survival variables with respect to the research question—*how long do the firms survive in their original state after stock market flotation and how long have they survived so far?* The descriptive statistics are displayed in table 4.28, whereas the results of the survival analysis will be set into comparison in table 4.29 (Section 4.5.2.1.).

The average survival times until crucial change are similar for both groups, although the event indicator shows that in the end, 95% of all non-family businesses were subjected to a form of crucial change, whereas a crucial change occurred in only 75% of the family businesses. The non-family businesses have been identified with an average survival time until observation ended of nearly 47 years and a maximum ST of 52 years. This indicates that even though the sample group of non-family businesses has a smaller survivor rate (5%), the surviving firms registered their IPO´s earlier than the family businesses, going back to 1966. Therefore, the non-family businesses have longer survival times until observation end. The family businesses show shorter survival times until the observation ends, but they have a higher survival rate of 25%.

Table 4.28 Survival Times and Frequencies—Family vs. Non-Family Enterprises

	Family Firms			**Non-Family Firms**		
Survival Variables	**M**	**Min**	**Max**	**M**	**Min**	**Max**
ST until crucial change	11.40	1.00	40.00	12.14	1.00	46.00
Crucial change	0.75	.	.	**0.95**	.	.
ST until observation end	32.11	30.00	39.00	**46.50**	41.00	52.00
Survival with no change	**0.25**	.	.	0.05	.	.

4.5.2 Comparing the Results of the Survival Analysis

The survival analyses for the sample groups differ in scale, due to the research question and the exploratory background of the study and therefore, the more elaborate range of variables given for the main sample group of family businesses.

4.5.2.1 Comparing the Results of the Cox PH Models

The number of dependent survival variables differs between the sample groups. As displayed in table 4.28, the most important survival variables with respect to the research question are equal for both samples. Due to convergence problems, however, the survival variable measuring the ST until observation end was not calculable for the sample of family firms. Additionally, the log-rank tests did not identify any independent variables with a possible significant effect on the survival variable ST until observation end for the non-family businesses, so no Cox PH model was calculated. Hence, the most relevant survival variable offering grounds for comparison is the survival time until crucial change.

The independent variable of the time frame of reductions of family-owned shares has been identified as the only independent variable with a high significance for the ST of family businesses until crucial change occurs with an HR of 0.522. Hence, this variable has a risk-reducing effect. A longer TF of reductions doubles the ST before crucial change occurs.

The Cox PH model identified the independent variables regarding turnover of 50-99mio DM at IPO and whether a non-family firm was a former family-owned business with significant effects on the ST until crucial change for the comparison group. With a HR of 7.44, the turnover category of 50-99mio DM has a risk-increasing effect, reducing the ST until crucial change of non-family businesses. Additionally, non-family firms with a family background have been identified with a very similar effect.

In conclusion, the Cox PH models did not identify any independent variables with a significant effect on the ST until crucial change that is applicable to both sample groups. The only independent variable with a significant effect, which both sample groups have in common, is the variable regarding turnover at IPO. Yet it only shows significance with respect to the ST until crucial change for the non-family businesses.

Table 4.29 Cox Regression Analysis—Family vs. Non-Family Enterprises

	Family Firms	Non-Family Firms
Variable	**ST until crucial change**	**ST until crucial change**
Time Frame of Reductions	0.522***	.
	(−2.97)	.
Turnover 50–99 Mio DM	0.439	7.44**
	(−1.08)	(2.07)
Former family firm	.	7.59*
	.	(1.67)
N	58	35
*p<0.1, **p<0.05. ***p<0.01		

4.5.2.2 Kaplan-Meier Estimation

The Kaplan-Meier plots take up the independent variables that have been identified as having a significant effect on the corresponding ST, hence comparison between the samples is difficult.

Taking table 4.28 into consideration, one independent variable applies to both samples, but has been identified with a significant effect on the ST until crucial change only for the non-family businesses. This variable concerns the category of turnover at IPO between 50-99mio DM. This being the only common denominator, KM plots showing the survival lines of both sample groups divided into the categories of turnover at IPO are contrasted in figure 4.10.

The graph shows that the family businesses assigned to the category of turnover at IPO between 500-999mio DM have all failed within approximately the first 13 years. Furthermore, all family businesses of the very small turnover size of <50mio DM failed in the end, although the survival times did last longer—up to 40 years. Family firm survivors are present within the remaining categories, although the category with the largest turnover at IPO of >1bn DM ultimately has the largest proportion of survivors.

The KM plot displaying the survival lines of the non-family businesses paints a somewhat different picture. Survival times in general are shorter—small- to middle-sized firms all fail within twenty years. As the size of the firm at IPO grows, the survival times get longer. In the end, the only survivors among the non-family businesses were all very large firms to begin with, with a turnover at the time of stock market flotation of >1bn DM.

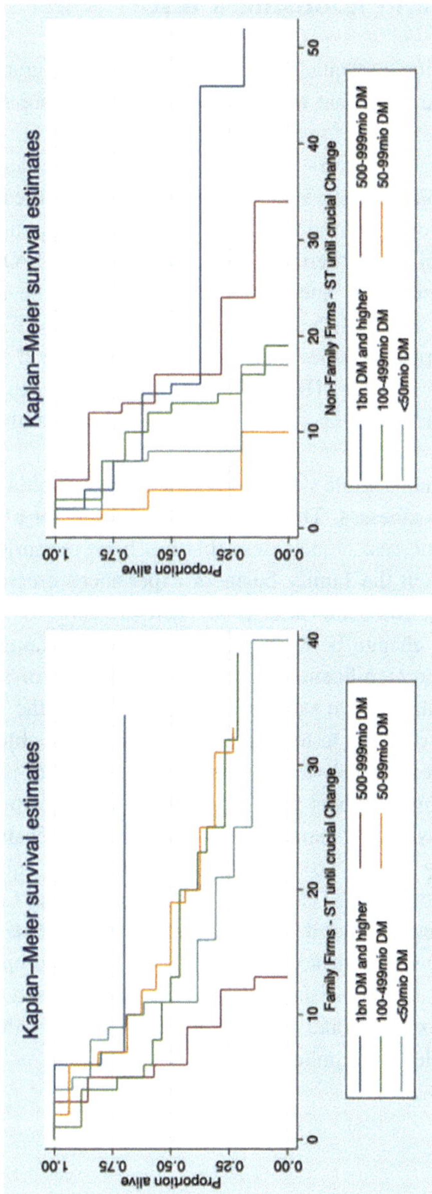

Figure 4.10 ST until Crucial Change—Family vs. Non-Family Enterprises

4.6 Sensitivity and Robustness Test

So far, the aim underlying the quantitative analysis was integrating the width of variables given by the data, due to the explorative background of the study. Especially regarding the sample of family enterprises, the spectrum of variables is substantial. Although Log Rank tests have been conducted, in order to reduce the overall number of variables to the variables with possible significant effects, the Cox PH analysis is yet confronted with a large number of independent variables. This bears the risk of bias. Furthermore, the distribution of IPO´s among the family enterprises is considerably uneven. Merely one IPO has been registered in the 1950´s, followed by seven in the 1960´s and seven in the 1970´s. A strong increase in IPO´s took place in the 1980´s, comprising more than 80% of all family firm IPO´s of the sample. Hence, further tests have been conducted in order to verify the findings of the initial survival analysis of the family firm sample.

Initially, due to the small sample sizes, it was considered combining the data of family and non-family businesses. This would have allowed for a slightly larger sample size of 116 businesses. Nonetheless this has been discarded. The target variable is the point, when the family business experiences crucial change and therefore loses the family firm status after IPO. There are certain overlaps regarding the forms of crucial change between the family and non-family businesses. Nevertheless, there is one significant difference—the dilution of shares—which is only relevant for the family firm sample. Hence, combining the samples poses difficulties because they can´t be tested for the same target variable.

Hence, the spectrum of control variables has been reduced to relevant exogenous variables. The target variables have been reduced to the most crucial for the sample of family businesses, namely to ST until crucial change (ST2) and ST until death as family firm (ST6). The initial procedure is equivalent to the procedure followed in the extended Cox analyses. By conducting Log Rank tests, the spectrum of variables is filtered for possible relevance. Based on the outcome, Cox PH models were run, tested for goodness of fit by comparison of AIC and BIC, and Cox-Snell residuals, the models were adjusted and the procedure repeated. In case the Cox PH model was not an appropriate fit, the Accelerated Failure Time (AFT) model was applied.

Table 4.30 Log-Rank Tests

Variable	ST2	ST6
Year of IPO	0.946	0.834
Turnover at IPO	0.102	0.050
Shareholder Str. at IPO	0.188	0.188
Cat. AO	0.991	0.780
Age at IPO	0.694	0.936
Reductions Total	0.293	**0.026**
Time Frame of Reductions	0.104	**0.041**

The results of the Log Rank tests show that only the variables regarding reductions have been identified with a possible effect on ST6. The variable regarding the turnover at IPO is marginal with a p-value of 0.050 for ST 6. Hence, Cox PH models have been conducted for both target variables. Furthermore, the Log Rank tests have revealed high probability values for the year of IPO. These values indicate that the decade of IPO doesn´t have an influence on the survival times. Hence, there is a very small risk of bias due to the uneven distribution of data according to decade.

4.6.1 Survival Time until Crucial Change

Initially, the variables Year of IPO, Reductions Total and Time Frame of Reductions have been integrated into the Cox PH model for ST2. As expected, the confidence interval is large for the variable regarding the year of IPO. Furthermore, AIC and BIC have a value >300.00 for this model. Hence, in a second run the model excluded the variable Year of IPO (Table 4.31).

Table 4.31 Results Cox PH Models—ST2

	1. Run	2. Run
Variable	**ST until crucial change**	**ST until crucial change**
Year of IPO—Cat. 2	0.626	.
Year of IPO—Cat. 3	1.301	.
Year of IPO—Cat. 4	0.853	.
Reductions Total	**2.384*****	**2.206*****
Time Frame of Reductions	**0.860*****	**0.868*****
N	58	58

*p<0.1, **p<0.05. ***p<0.01

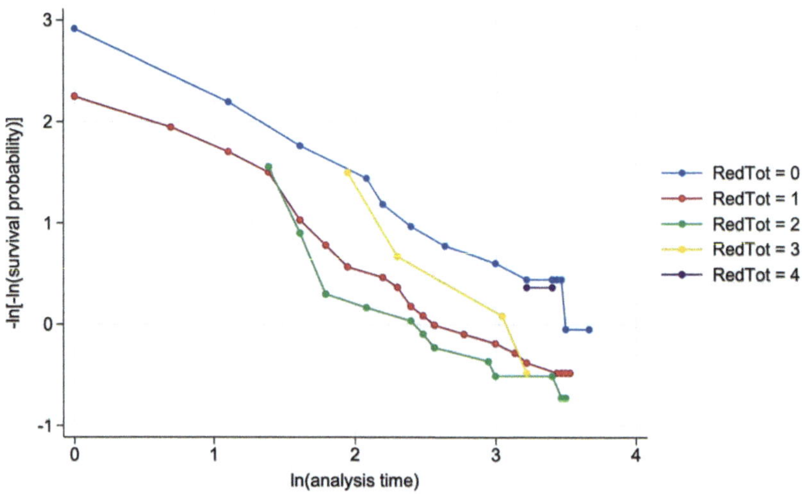

Figure 4.11 Proportional Hazards ST2

The lines are parallel when the proportional hazards are verified. The plot in figure 4.11 supports this. In a further step, the goodness of fit was tested by means of Cox-Snell residuals. An appropriate goodness of fit of the model is indicated when the dynamic line remains on the angle bisector. The plot in figure 4.12 indicates an inappropriate fit of the model, due to the deviating line. Furthermore, the AIC and BIC values are lower than in the first run, but still beyond the value of 300.0.

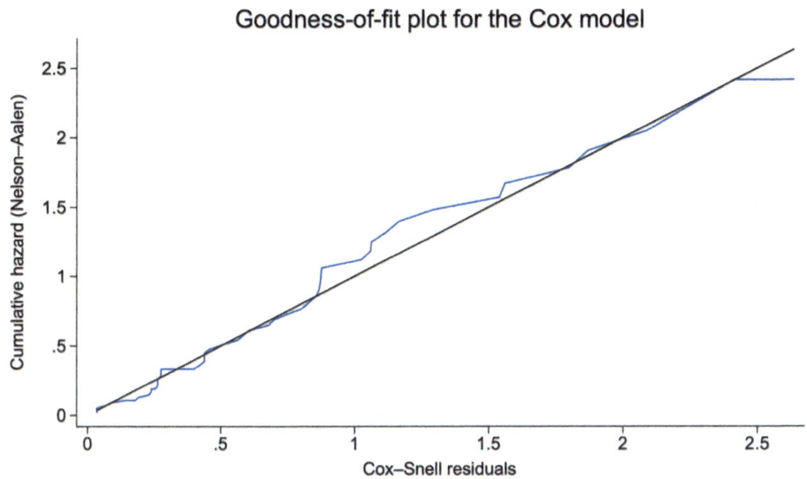

Figure 4.12 Goodness of Fit—Cox PH Model ST2

Due to the inappropriate fit of the Cox model, an Accelerated Failure Time (AFT) Model has been conducted, integrating the variables Reductions Total and Time Frame of Reductions into the model. Given the coefficients for the variable Time Frame of Reductions, the value for interpretation of these is 1.1170318. This value indicates that if the time frame increases by one unit, the expected survival time rises by 11.7%. The goodness of fit by means of Cox-Snell residuals indicates a systemic error, as visualized by the deviation from the angle bisector. Nevertheless, the values for AIC (155.8) and BIC (162.0) for this model are lower in comparison to the values given for the Cox PH models. Hence, the AFT model has a better fit (Table 4.32) (Figure 4.13).

Table 4.32 Results AFT Model—ST2

Variable	coefficent	p-value	95% conf. interval	
Reductions Total	−.6555	0.006	−1.126	−.185
Time Frame of Reductions	.1107	0.000	.0563	.1651

The survival function (see figure 4.14), evaluated at overall means of covariates, and the histogram (see figure 4.15) show a severe drop in the first approximate 13 years after IPO. After this threshold survival times get longer

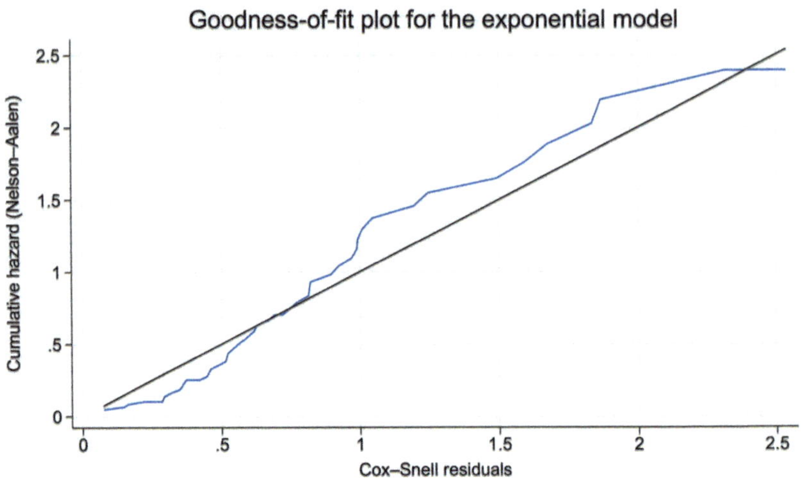

Figure 4.13 Goodness of Fit—AFT Model ST2

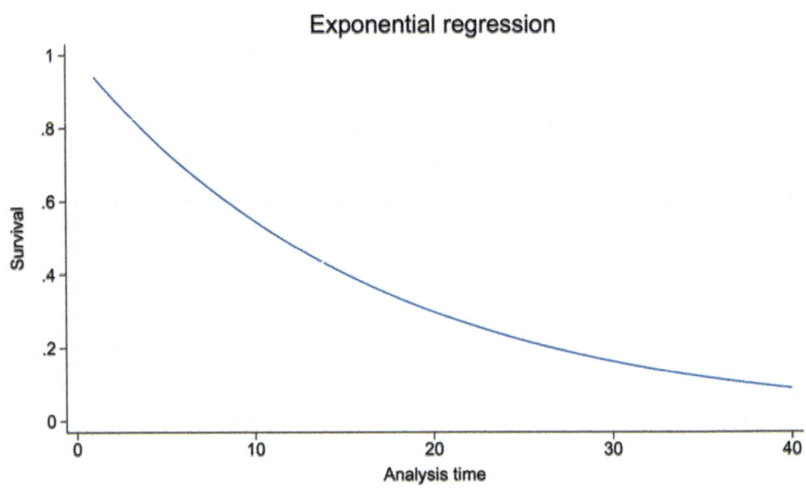

Figure 4.14 Survival Function—ST2

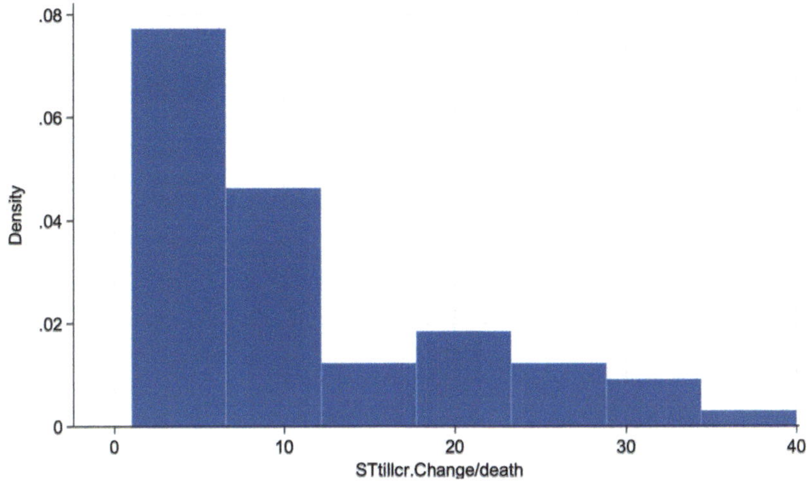

Figure 4.15 Failures ST2

and incidents farther apart. This finding supports the observations derived from the Kaplan-Meyer estimators.

4.6.2 Survival Time until Death as Family Firm

The same procedure has been applied for the survival time until death as family firm, which equals dilution of family shares below the critical point of 25%. These comprise all acquisitions. The Log-Rank results indicate a marginal probability value for the turnover at the time of IPO. Hence, next to the variables Reductions Total, Time Frame of Reductions and Year of IPO, the categorical variable Turnover at IPO has been integrated into the Cox PH model. Comparable to the first run of the model for ST2, the confidence intervals for Year of IPO and Turnover at IPO are quite large, signaling that the coefficient estimates have a high insecurity. The values for AIC and BIC lay at 285.4 for AIC and 303.9 for BIC. In the second run the model excluded the variable Year of IPO. The AIC (282.6) and BIC (294.9) values are slightly lower in this run, meaning this model has a slightly better fit. In a third run, the variable Turnover at IPO was excluded from the model, revealing once again a slightly better fit with AIC (278.2) and BIC (282.3) (Table 4.33).

Table 4.33 Results Cox PH Models—ST6

	1. Run	2. Run	3. Run
Variable	**ST until death as FF**	**ST until death as FF**	**ST until death as FF**
Year of IPO—Cat. 2	0.282	.	.
Year of IPO—Cat. 3	0.976	.	.
Year of IPO—Cat. 4	0.612	.	.
TO at IPO—Cat 3	2.254	1.966	.
TO at IPO—Cat. 4	2.808	2.311	.
TO at IPO—Cat. 5	1.179	1.351	.
TO at IPO—Cat. 6	1.189	1.237	.
Reductions Total	**3.263*****	**2.603*****	**2.518*****
Time Frame of Reductions	**0.815*****	**0.832*****	**0.838*****
N	58	58	58
*p<0.1, **p<0.05. ***p<0.01			

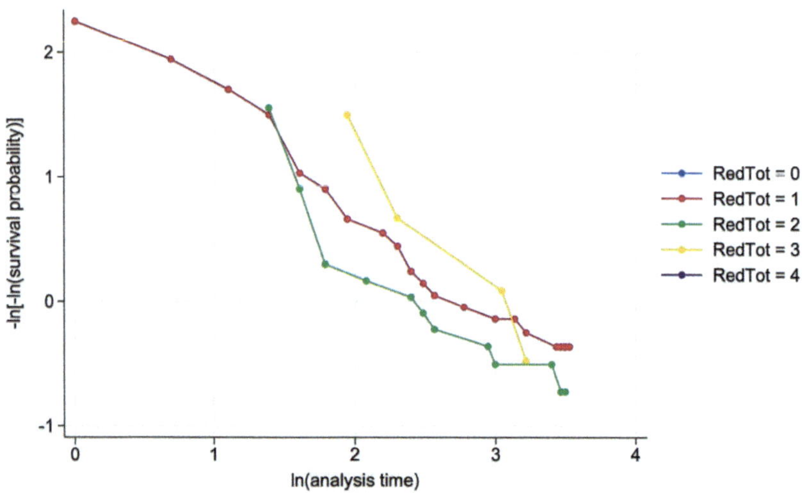

Figure 4.16 Proportional Hazards ST6

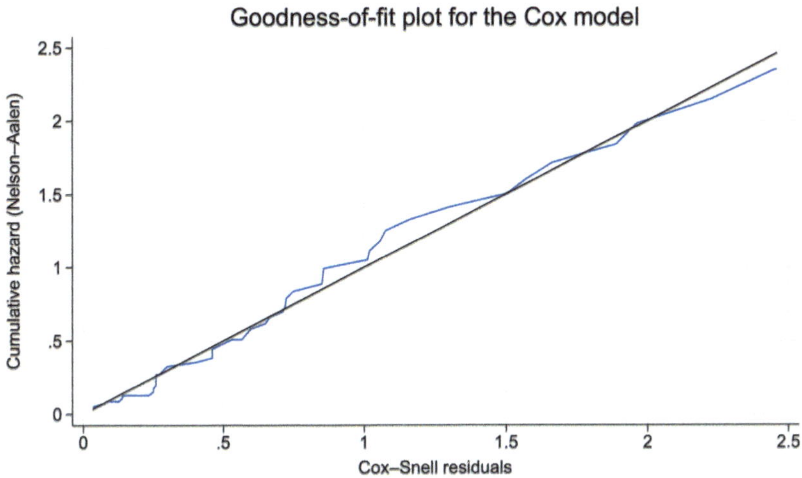

Figure 4.17 Goodness of Fit—Cox PH Model ST6

The plot in figure 4.16 shows mostly parallel lines with few crossovers at the edges, which indicates that the assumptions of the hazard ratios are confirmed. The goodness of fit plot by means of Cox-Snell residuals in figure 4.17 shows slight deviations from the angle bisector.

Nonetheless, an AFT model integrating the variables Reductions Total and Time Frame of Reduction was run for comparison. An interpretation of the coefficient value for the variable Reductions Total can be derived from the value 0.47486634. This indicates that if the value of Reductions Total increases by one unit, the expected survival time decreases by 53%. The values for AIC (150.4) and BIC (156.6) are considerably lower than the values given for the Cox models. Hence, in this case too the AFT model is the more appropriate model, even though the goodness of fit plot reveals deviations from the bisector (see figure 4.18) (Table 3.34).

Table 4.34 Results AFT Model—ST6

Variable	coefficent	p-value	95% conf. interval	
Reductions Total	−.7447	0.004	−1.2468	−.2427
Time Frame of Reductions	.1324	0.000	.0692	.1955

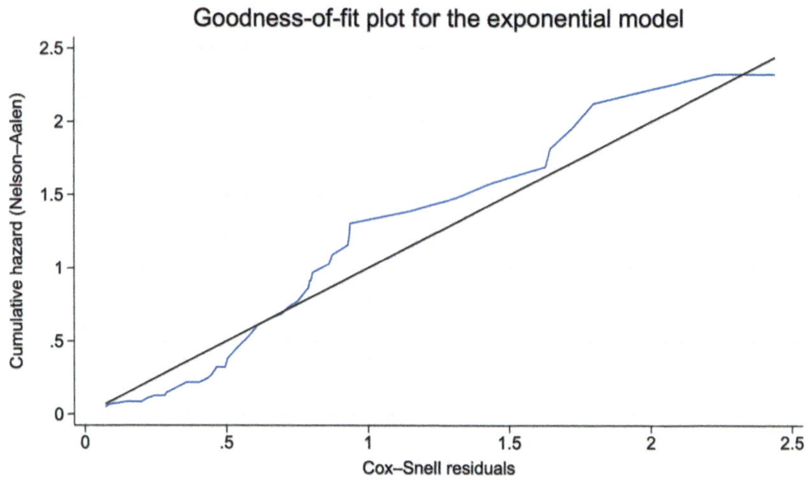

Figure 4.18 Goodness of Fit—AFT Model ST6

The survival function featured in figure 4.19 and the histogram visualizing the distribution of failures according to survival times (see figure 4.20) show a similar development to the cases underlying crucial change. The 13-year threshold catches the eye, which indicates most failures occur with the first 13 years after IPO.

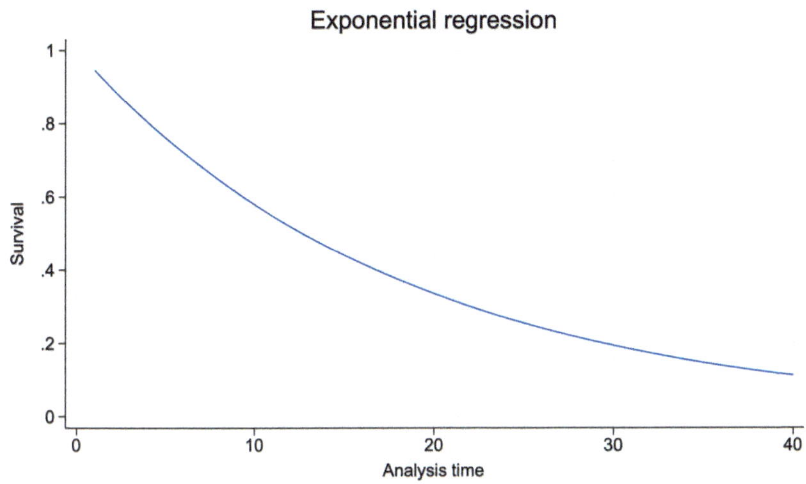

Figure 4.19 Survival Function—ST6

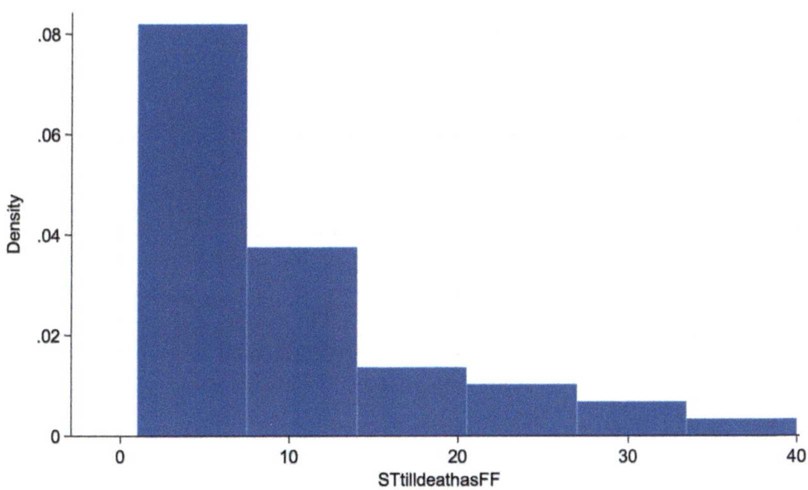

Figure 4.20 Failures ST6

4.6.3 Drawing Conclusions from the Sensitivity and Robustness Check

Starting with the width of data on stock-listed family businesses flowing into the extended survival analysis in Section 4.4.2., which comprised log rank tests, Cox PH analyses and Kaplan-Meyer estimates, this chapter reduced the data to few core variables. In order to check for robustness of the previous results, further Cox models were run in smaller format. The results support the findings in Section 4.4.2. Nevertheless, the tests for goodness of fit revealed that the models were not the appropriate choice for the given data. Hence, AFT models were conducted which were identified with a better fit. The AFT models equally support the findings from the previous analyses. A low number of total reductions and a long time frame of reductions have been found to be highly significant in increasing the chance of stock-listed family firm survival. Furthermore, with a probability value of slightly > 0.1, the category of turnover between 100–499 mio is marginally outside of the significant probability range. This attribute has been identified as a soft success factor in Section 5.3.2.2. As stated in Section 6.2., one major limitation of this study is the small sample size. For future research, an expansion of the sample would be advisable in order to receive more accurate results. Nevertheless, the analyses offer a valuable glimpse of direction.

4.7 Summary of Significant Findings

The significant findings for this chapter are presented in a compacted overview for the sample of the family-owned businesses (see table 4.30). Only the most significant results are displayed in the table in connection with the corresponding dependent and independent variables. The table is divided by method of analysis. Hence, the hazard ratios are given for the Cox PH models and the p-values for the chi^2 tests of independence and t-tests. Due to the smaller scope of analysis for the sample group of the non-family businesses, a compacted overview is offered in table 4.8.

The quantitative analyses have revealed a number of interesting findings. Among the sample of non-family enterprises, a total of 95% of all IPO firms experienced crucial change within the observation period. Merely 5% survived unaffected by public life. Most prominent for the sample of non-family enterprises, though, is the influence the *former* family connection has on the IPO

Table 4.35 Summary of Significant Findings—Family Enterprises

	ST1	ST2	ST3	ST4	ST5	ST6	ST7
	until 1. reduction	**until crucial change**	**until observation end**	**until death as listed firm**	**until death as firm**	**until death as FF**	**after 1. red. Until MorA**
Cox PH Model (HR)							
Reductions total	1.874*	.	.	.	.	2.378*	.
Time frame of reductions	.	0.522***	.	.	.	0.291***	.
Survival as fam.-controlled	0.296*	.	.	.	.	.	.
Acquisition	.	.	.	.	.	10.79**	.
MorA by family firm	3.361**	.	.	.	.	.	.
Chi Tests of Independence (p-values)							
Shareholder str. at IPO 75–100%	.	.	.	.	0.032	.	.
Fam. mem. on exec. board at IPO	.	.	0.041	0.048	0.032	.	.
Fam. mem. on both boards at cr. ch./obs. end	.	.	.	.	.	.	0.043
T-Tests (p-values)							
Families involved	.	.	.	.	0.022	.	.
Log age at IPO	.	.	.	0.024	.	.	.
Reductions total	.	.	.	0.002	0.011	0.045	0.001
Log time frame of reductions	.	.	.	0.05	0.05	0.016	0.001

firm. Nearly half of all non-family firms were categorized as former family businesses pre-IPO. All of these firms experienced crucial change within the first sixteen years following stock market flotation.

The analyses examining the sample of family businesses have revealed a higher survival rate among the sample of family businesses (24%), compared with their non-family counterparts. The Cox PH analysis identified two main influencing factors for increasing the chance of family firm survival: a low number of total reductions, and a long time frame of reductions. Furthermore, the Kaplan-Meier Estimates illustrate a 13-year high-risk phase after IPO, in which the occurrence of failure/death is more frequent. The tests of significance reveal a pattern of influencing factors, in which a high shareholding quota at IPO, the application of AO measures, and the age at IPO all have a positive effect on the chance of family firm survival (Table 4.35).

References

Cleves, M., Gould, W.W. & Marchenko, Y.V. (2016). *An Introduction to Survival Analysis Using Stata (3. ed).* Texas: Stata Press.

Cox, D.R. (1972). Regression Models and Life-Tables. Read before the *Royal Statistical Society*, London, 187–202.

Cox, D.R. (1975). Partial Likelihood. *Biometrika,* 62 (2), 269–276.

Hair Jr., J.F., Black, W.C., Babin, B.J. & Anderson, R.E. (2018). *Multivariate Data Analysis (8. ed).* Andover, UK: Cengage.

Hair Jr., J.F., Celsi, M., Money, A., Samouel, P. & Page, M. (2016). *Essentials of Business Research Methods (3. ed).* New York: Routledge.

Harhoff, D. & Wagner, S. (2009). The Duration of Patent Examination at the European Patent Office. *Management Science*, 55 (12), 1969–1984.

Kohler, U. & Kreuter, F. (2016). *Datenanalyse mit Stata—Allgemeine Konzepte der Datenanalyse und ihre praktische Anwendung.* Berlin: De Gruyter.

Schlittgen, R. (2012). *Angewandte Zeitreihenanalyse mit R (2. ed).* München: Oldenbourg.

Ziegler, A., Lange, S. & Bender, R. (2004). Überlebenszeitanalyse: Die Cox-Regression. *Deutsche Medizinische Wochenschrift,* 129, T1–T3.

Part II

The Narrative Analysis

The Narrative Depiction of the Samples

5

Chapter 4 commits itself purely to presenting the results of the quantitative analysis conducted for this study and summarizing the significant findings in connection to the research questions. This chapter, however, follows a more intuitive, narrative approach. The data is juggled and screened from different angles, which allows for putting different aspects and findings into relation with each other. Furthermore, the researcher dives into the special cases and introduces the firms and their extraordinary developments or features. For instance, the surviving family businesses and their characteristics are taken into account and introduced in detail.

In conclusion, the goal is to bring the significant findings of quantitative nature of Chapter 4 into connection with the firms, their backgrounds, and the findings of this chapter. By doing so, the researcher aims at adding a sense of life and dynamism to the mathematical side of the study, and therefore bring the results of both perspectives into a holistic analysis of the research questions.

5.1 Chapter Overview

First, the classic publicly traded companies (the non-family businesses) are examined. The analysis cross-references the extracted variables related to size, age, and so on, in order to discover conspicuous relations, clusters, or patterns pertaining to the longevity of publicly traded non-family enterprises. Second, the analysis approaches the actual IPO firm of interest, i.e. the family enterprise with all its diverse features. The researcher provides an overview of the sample of family enterprises. This overview is divided into the specifics of IPO distribution within

K. Stotmeister, *Publicly Traded Family Businesses*, Familienunternehmen und KMU, https://doi.org/10.1007/978-3-658-44303-0_5

the sample, and the interplay between IPO distribution and longevity. Both are set into relation with economic milestones throughout German history along the timeline. The descriptive characteristics are then categorized by the individual firm specifics, such as age at IPO or size of firm at the time of stock market flotation. The next large topic comprises family involvement, leaving space for analysis of the effects of the number of families invested in the firm, of the shareholder structure at IPO, and the question of whether one or more family members were active as officer/s or director/s at the time of IPO, as well as at the time of crucial change/observation end (active ownership). After a discussion of family involvement, comes attention to the dilution process of family influence, with an analysis of possible effects of the total number of share reductions during the observation period and the time frame of these reductions. Then the crucial changes that occur will be introduced. Finally, the family firm survivors will be examined in order to determine common success factors.

If the analysis allows, a summary of the identified clusters, patterns and success factors will complete the qualitative analysis.

5.2 Introducing the Non-Family Enterprises

The typical publicly traded firm is a non-family-owned business. Regarding the historic development of stock market flotations, many were state-owned at the time or also formerly, pre-IPO family owned. They all differ from family enterprises in the sense that they lack one crucial feature: family influence. This feature may be of advantage or disadvantage.

5.2.1 Overview of the Sample

5.2.1.1 Interplay between IPO Distribution and Economic Milestones

The sample representing non-family businesses is smaller than the one for family businesses. While the family firm sample comprises 77 firms, the comparison sample comprises 39 firms. Nevertheless, the IPO distribution shows conclusive similarities to the IPO distribution of the family businesses (see Figure 5.4). The first firm of this sample to launch an IPO was *Volkswagen AG* shortly after the regeneration phase following WWII: the *Wirtschaftswunder*—in 1961. The years following WWII were hopeful and optimistic. Still, the repercussions of the war still had a severe impact on the monetary capacity as well as the mental

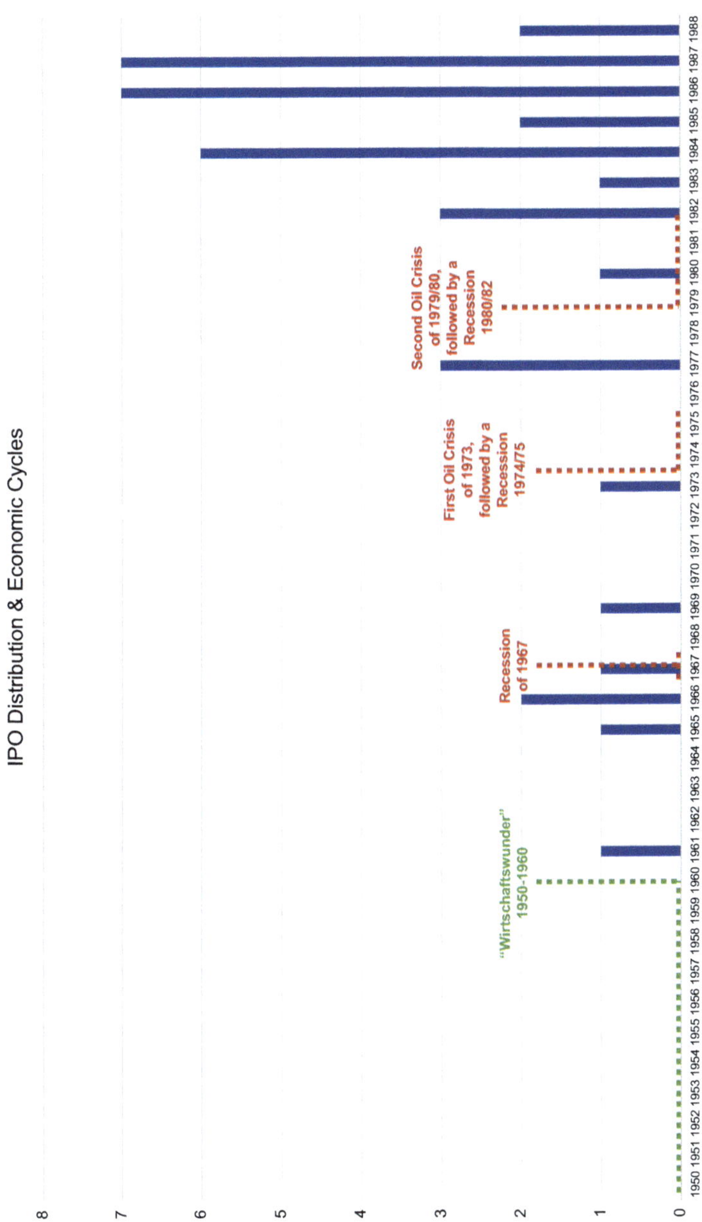

Figure 5.1 IPO Distribution & Economic Cycles—Non-Family Enterprises. (Source: Author´s own figure, partially appended by Frankfurter Allgemeine Zeitung (2010), Bundeszentrale für politische Bildung (2016) and Heilemann (2019)).

and physical capacities of the German people.[1] The German people were still cautious in pursuing new business ventures, even though they were hungry to thrive. It wasn't until the 1960s that normality finally set in.

Comparable to the IPO distribution among the family businesses, there is a detectable pattern with respect to the large crises and resulting recessions (see Figure 5.1). Only a few stock market flotations were launched between 1950 and the early 1980s. Next to *Volkswagen AG* (1961), the firms *Vereinigte Elektrizitäts- und Bergwerks AG* (1965), *Lufthansa AG* (1966), *Vereinigte Elektrizitätswerke Westfalen AG* (1966), *Deutsche Klinik für Diagnostik AG* (1967) and *Horten AG* (1969) entered the public market in the 1960s.

Only four firms in the sample became stock-listed in the 1970´s, which were *Badenwerk AG* (1973), *Joh. Friedrich Behrens AG* (1977), *BayWa AG* (1977) and *ASKO Deutsche Kaufhaus AG* (1977).

The real IPO boom ignited in the 1980s, after the recession from the Second Oil Crisis in 1979–80. Equally for both samples, the first year with a greater number of IPO launches was 1984, followed by 1986 as the year with the most IPO´s recorded for both samples.

5.2.1.2 Interplay between IPO Distribution and Longevity

The variables describing the sample of the non-family firms differ from those describing the family firm sample. Yet for both, longevity is the focus.

After Germany regained economic stability, a wave of privatization began.[2] Many state-owned firms became stock-listed after the *Wiederaufbau.* Figure 5.2a/b shows that the first IPO firms, especially in the 1960´s, have very long survival times. *Volkswagen AG, Vereinigte Elektrizitäts- und Bergwerke AG, Lufthansa AG* and *Vereinigte Elektrizitätswerke Westfalen AG* were the first businesses within the sample to experience stock-market flotation. These firms were all state-owned at the time of IPO. The state then took the opportunity to reduce ownership gradually, and therefore the survival times of these firms are exceptionally long. As long as the state was involved, crucial changes such as bankruptcies did not occur. The firms either ended in merger or acquisition or remained in free float after a full exit by the state.

One crucial variable refers to whether the stock-listed firm was a family firm prior to IPO. In the 1960´s and 1970´s only two firms were identified as former family firms. These were *Horten AG* (1969) and *Joh. Friedrich Behrens AG*

---

[1] Also see Bundeszentrale für politische Bildung (2002) and Bundeszentrale für politische Bildung (2016).

[2] Also see Peter (2009).

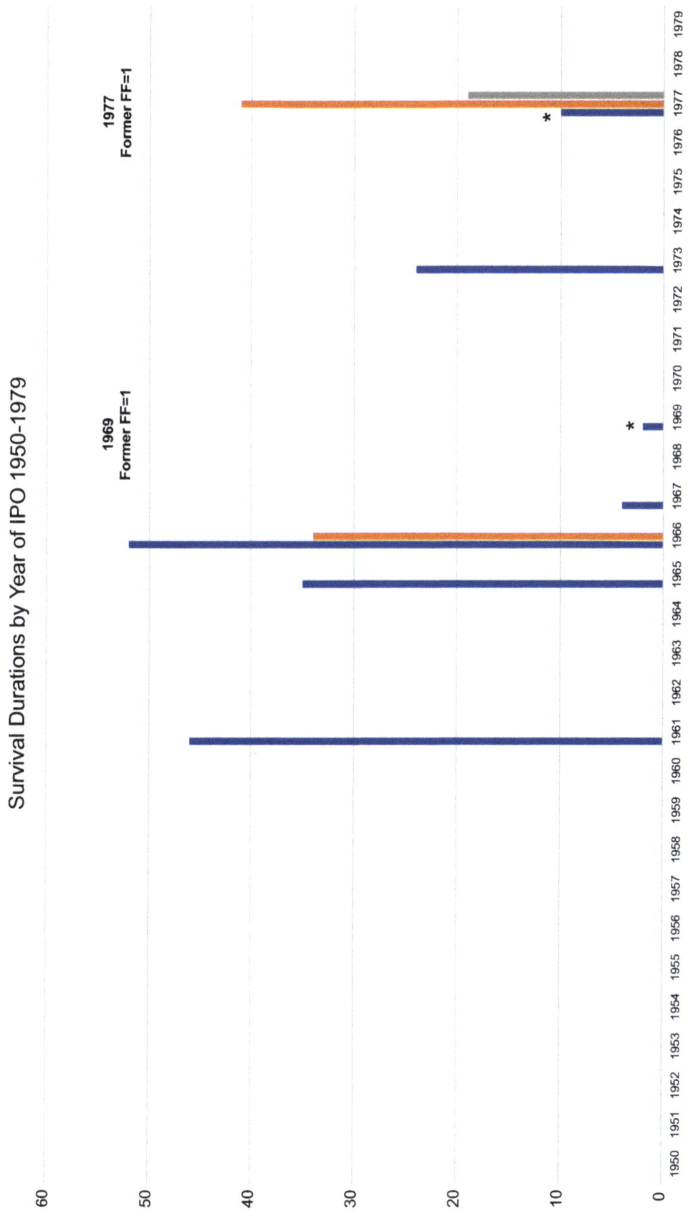

Figure 5.2a Survival Durations by Year of IPO—1950–1979. (Source: Author´s own figure)

(1977). The survival times until crucial change occurred were remarkably short in comparison to the other IPO firms of this time (see Figure 5.2a). Moving along the timeline to the 1980´s, 16 more IPO firms have been identified as former family businesses (see Figure 5.2b). Here again, the survival times are rather short in comparison to the firms without family background. This finding has been identified as significant by the Cox PH model.[3] From this finding, one may conclude that former family businesses achieve a certain degree of attractiveness for acquiring firms, since all of these pre-IPO family businesses became subject to MorA.

A remarkable cluster finds itself in the IPO firms of the year 1984. All IPO firms of this IPO-heavy year have been categorized as former family firms. Furthermore, among the non-family firms as well, 1984 and 1986 have been identified as the IPO-heaviest years.

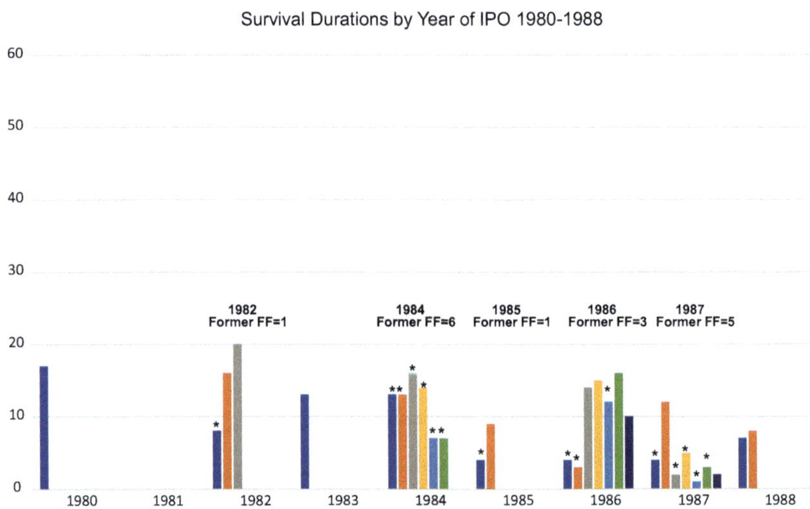

Figure 5.2b Survival Durations by Year of IPO—1980–1988. (Source: Author´s own figure)

[3] For further information, see Section 4.4.4. "Cox Proportional Hazards Model".

5.2.2 Possible Influence Factors

5.2.2.1 Does the Age at IPO influence Longevity?

The average age at IPO launch has been defined as 57 years for the non-family businesses, a slightly lower value compared with the average age of 61 years for the sample of family businesses. When examining the very old firms, the average survival time until crucial change is also slightly lower, with eight years for the non-family businesses and nearly 11 years for the very old family businesses. Overall, there is only one interesting finding: Nearly all old non-family businesses which were established prior to the 20th century are former family businesses (see Table 5.1).[4]

Regarding the very young non-family businesses (younger than 10 years at the time of stock market flotation), there is nothing remarkable (see Table 5.2). When comparing with the sample of very young family businesses though, the share of very young non-family IPO-firms is considerably lower than among the family businesses. While nearly 16% of family businesses were below ten years of age

Table 5.1 The oldest Non-Family Enterprises

Year of IPO	Enterprise	Year of Establishment	Years of Survival at Stock Market	Former Family Firm	Final State
1977	ASKO Deutsche Kaufhaus AG	1880	19		MorA/A
1984	Carl Schenk AG	1881	16	✔	MorA/A
1984	Schmalbach-Lubeca AG	1898	7	✔	MorA/A
1985	Schumag AG	1830	4	✔	MorA/A
1986	Feldmühle Nobel AG	1885	4	✔	MorA/A
1986	Felten & Guilleaume AG	1820	12	✔	MorA/A
1987	Stixi AG	1886	1	✔	MorA/A
1987	Linotype AG	1887	3	✔	MorA/M

[4] The original shareholding structure of the *ASKO Deutsche Kaufhaus AG* could not be identified at the time of establishment, hence the missing value for the variable *Former Family Firm*.

at the time of the IPO launch, not even 8% of the non-family firms were young IPO-firms. Although, when considering the form of crucial change, the share is nearly identical for the acquisitions (MorA/A). As a result, the difference lies in the higher share of early post-IPO bankruptcies among the family businesses (see Section 5.3.2.1.).

Table 5.2 The youngest Non-Family Enterprises

Year of IPO	Enterprise	Year of Establishment	Years of Survival at Stock Market	Former Family Firm	Final State
1967	Deutsche Klinik für Diagnostik AG	1967	4		MorA/A
1982	Electronic 2000 Vertriebs-AG	1982	8	✔	MorA/A
1982	Monacchia Grundstücks-AG	1982	20		MorA/A

5.2.2.2 What about the Size at IPO?

The sample of non-family businesses contains proportionally many large IPO-firms. More than 20% of these IPO firms recorded a turnover >1bn DM at the time of stock market flotation. Among the sample of family-owned businesses, on the other hand, merely 8% had achieved such a size by the time of IPO. At this point, state ownership and the connected privatization wave comes into play again. Nearly all large IPO firms were state-owned at the time of IPO. The five firms with the longest survival times were all state-owned and were partially privatized over time (see Figure 5.3). These firms were *Deutsche Lufthansa AG*, *Volkswagen AG*, *Vereinigte Elektrizitäts- und Bergwerks AG*, *Vereinigte Elektrizitätswerke Westfalen AG* and *Badenwerk AG*. These outliers are all categorized as large to very large firms with TO above 500mio DM. Comparable to the distribution among the sample of family-owned businesses, most IPO firms recorded a TO in the mid-range between 100-499mio DM.

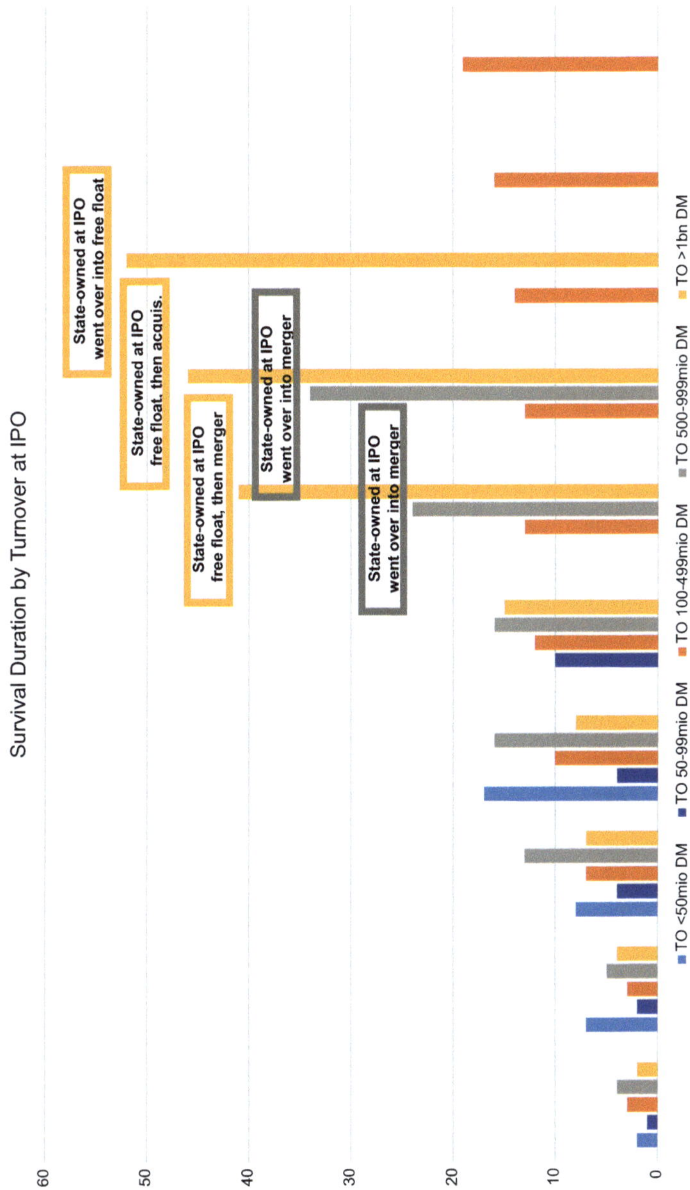

Figure 5.3 Survival Duration by TO at IPO—Non-Family Enterprises. (Source: Author´s own figure)

Table 5.3 Failures—Mergers or Acquisitions—Non-Family Enterprises

Year of IPO	Enterprise	Survival time until MorA	Megers	Acqu.	Former Family Firm
1961	Volkswagen AG	46		✔	
1965	Elektrizitäts- und Bergwerks AG	35	✔		
1966	Vereinigte Elektrizitätswerke Wetsfalen AG	34	✔		
1967	Deutsche Klinik für Diagnostik AG	4		✔	
1969	Horten AG	2		✔	✔
1973	Badenwerk AG	24	✔		
1977	Joh. Friedrich Behrens AG	10		✔	✔
1977	ASKO Deutsche Kaufhaus AG	19	✔		
1980	AGAB AG für Anlagen und Beteiligungen	17		✔	
1982	Electronic 2000 Vertriebs-AG	8		✔	✔
1982	Main-Gaswerke AG	16	✔		
1982	Monacchia Grundstücks-AG	20		✔	
1983	Etienne Aigner AG	13		✔	
1984	Konrad Hornschuch AG	13		✔	✔
1984	Kolbenschmidt AG	13	✔		✔
1984	Carl Schenck AG	16		✔	✔
1984	Leifheit AG	14		✔	✔
1984	Schmalbach-Lubeca AG	7		✔	✔
1984	MotoMeter AG	7		✔	✔
1985	Schumag AG	4		✔	✔
1985	Deutsche Beteiligungs AG	9		✔	
1986	Feldmühle Nobel AG	4		✔	✔
1986	Antriebstechnik G. Bauknecht AG	3		✔	✔
1986	VIAG AG	14	✔		
1986	AVA Allg. Handelsges. der Verbraucher AG	15		✔	

(continued)

Table 5.3 (continued)

Year of IPO	Enterprise	Survival time until MorA	Megers	Acqu.	Former Family Firm
1986	Felten & Guilleaume Energietechnik AG	12		✔	✔
1986	Industrieverwaltungsgesellschaft AG	16		✔	
1986	Mineralbrunnen Überkingen-Teinach AG	10		✔	
1987	SABO-Maschinenfabrik AG	4		✔	✔
1987	Schwabengarage AG	12		✔	
1987	Stelcon AG	2		✔	✔
1987	Boge AG	5		✔	✔
1987	Stixi AG	1		✔	✔
1987	Linotype AG	3	✔		✔
1988	Fernheizwerk Neukölln AG	7		✔	
1988	SPAR Handel-AG	8		✔	

5.2.3 Overview of the Crucial Changes

The most clearly dominant form of crucial change which occurred among the non-family businesses is MorA (see Table 5.3). Out of 39 firms within the sample, a total of 36 experienced merger or acquisition during the observation period. This equates to over 90% of all crucial changes. The dominance of MorA as the form of crucial change applies to both samples. Certain differences do lie in the strong occurrence among the non-family firms and the higher share of mergers compared to the family businesses. Approximately 22% of all cases of MorA were mergers. Among the family businesses, mergers comprised only 2%. A striking observation is that most mergers among the non-family businesses concerned firms from the energy supply industry. This may explain the differing dominance in comparison to the family businesses, of which not a single firm came from this industry.

All in all, only one other firm experienced another form of crucial change (see Table 5.4). The story evolving around the *Co op AG* was rather gripping—a story of embezzlement and betrayal which led to the company breakup in 1989.[5]

In comparison to the nineteen surviving family businesses, the sample of non-family businesses comprises only two firms that survived throughout the observation period without significant changes—the *Lufthansa AG* and *Baywa AG* (see Table 5.4). It must be clarified that the *Lufthansa AG* was under state ownership at the time of the IPO launch and became privatized during the observation period, ending in free float.[6]

Table 5.4 Failures—Break-up & no significant Changes—Non-Family Enterprises

Year of IPO	Enterprise	Survival times	Break-up	No change/ constant free float	Former Family Firm
1966	Lufthansa AG	52		✔	
1977	BayWa AG	41		✔	
1987	co op AG	2	✔		

5.2.4 The Influence of being a former Family Enterprise

Non-family businesses with pre-IPO family backgrounds have been found to have significantly lower survival times until crucial change occurred than IPO-firms without family backgrounds. Looking back on the analysis, the feature of a non-family IPO-firm being a former family firm has been clearly identified as significant. Not only are nearly half of all IPO firms of this sample ($N = 18$) former family-owned businesses, but they have also all experienced merger or acquisition within relatively few years of stock market flotation. The Cox analysis supports this finding.[7] One can only speculate on the reasons. As previously stated, former family businesses appear to be very attractive to potential acquirers. This also applies to the sample of family businesses. Since many of these former

[5] Also see Manager Magazin (2001), Fiedler (2016) and Capital (2019).

[6] Privatization hasn´t been defined as a form of crucial change, hence *Lufthansa AG* has been found to experience no significant change during the observation period. For further information, see Section 2.5.2. "The Concept of Crucial Change".

[7] For further information, see Section 4.4.4 "Cox Proportional Hazards Model" and "Kaplan-Meier Estimation".

family-owned businesses are very old, they have achieved a degree of maturity which may be beneficial. This may concern brand recognition through a prestigious and traditional trademark, product and/or service quality, firm reputation, and many more aspects.

5.2.5 Clusters, Patterns and Influence Factors

The sample of non-family businesses differs from the family firm sample in several ways. These differences are mainly due to the special features of family firms under closer examination with respect to the research questions and the focus on longevity of the publicly traded family-owned businesses. Hence, the dimension of variables, and therefore possible clusters, patterns, or influence factors are far smaller compared to the analysis of the family businesses. Table 5.5 summarizes the soft features resulting from the qualitative analysis of the non-family firms. Only firm-specific factors could be taken into account, since family involvement and the dilution process of family influence are not applicable.

Table 5.5 Summary of soft Features describing Firm Survival

Firm-specific influence factors
Nearly all very old IPO-firms have been identified as former family-owned businesses (except for one missing value).
Mature firms with a higher age at IPO appear to be desirable to acquiring firms. Nearly all old-aged firms once had a family background.
State-owned IPO-firms have been identified with the longest survival times, due to extended privatization phases into free float or until crucial change.

5.3 Introducing the Family Enterprises

Previously, family influence has been found to play a crucial role regarding post-IPO longevity of non-family firms. The Cox PH analysis has identified former family businesses to be at significantly higher risk of failure/death. This brings us to the main sample of interest—German stock-listed family businesses—in search of clusters and patterns that describe longevity as a publicly traded family-owned business.

5.3.1 Overview of the Sample

5.3.1.1 Interplay between IPO Distribution and Economic Milestones

Most family enterprises of our sample of 77 companies became stock listed in the 1980's. Hence, 62 registered their IPO between 1980 and 1988. Merely one family business within the sample was initially stock-listed in the 1950's. Shortly after the Official Market was opened at the German Stock Exchange in Frankfurt in 1949, the *Kienzle Uhrenfabrik AG* was the first of all family businesses of the sample to experience flotation in 1951.

In the following decade, seven further stock market flotations took place—*G.M Pfaff AG* (1960), *WOLKO Schuhfabrik AG* (1961), *Westag & Getalit AG* (1961), *Pschorrbräu AG* (1961), *Neckermann Versand KGaA* (1963), *Pegulan-Werke AG* (1964) and *Braun AG* (1964).

Another seven IPOs were launched in the 1970s for *Dyckerhoff & Widmann AG* (1972), *ALTANA Industrie-Aktien und Anlagen AG* (1977), *Herlitz AG* (1977), *Leffers AG* (1977), *Progress-Werk Oberkirch AG* (1978), *Drägerwerk AG* (1979) and *Mauser Waldeck AG* (1979).

When observing the IPO distribution by year, there is a pattern following the German economic cycles and connected milestones (see Figure 5.4). The German economy experienced a strong economic upswing in the 1950's—the *Wirtschaftswunder.* This post-war economic rehabilitation led to new wealth and optimism among the German people, also affecting the need and desire of company growth and expansion.[8] The *Kienzle Uhrenfabrik AG* is the only family enterprise within the sample that launched an IPO this early in the economic rehabilitation phase after WWII. In order for firms to launch a reasonable and successful IPO, the firms had to deliver a certain level and continuity of performance.[9] Especially with respect to performance continuity, the economic cycles play a crucial role. This effect is visible, as seen in Figure 5.4. Even among the early decades of the observation period with very few cases of IPO´s, the effects of the crises and following recessions are clearly displayed. The big boom of stock market flotations took place after the recession of 1980–82, and before the *German Wiedervereinigung* in 1989, which also marks the upper cutoff for stock market flotations for this study.[10]

---

[8] Compare with Hewel (1980), Frankfurter Allgemeine Zeitung (2010), Bundeszentrale für politische Bildung (2016) and Heilemann (2019).

[9] Also see Frankfurter Allgemeine Zeitung (2018).

[10] For further information, see Section 3.3.1. "Defining the Time Frame".

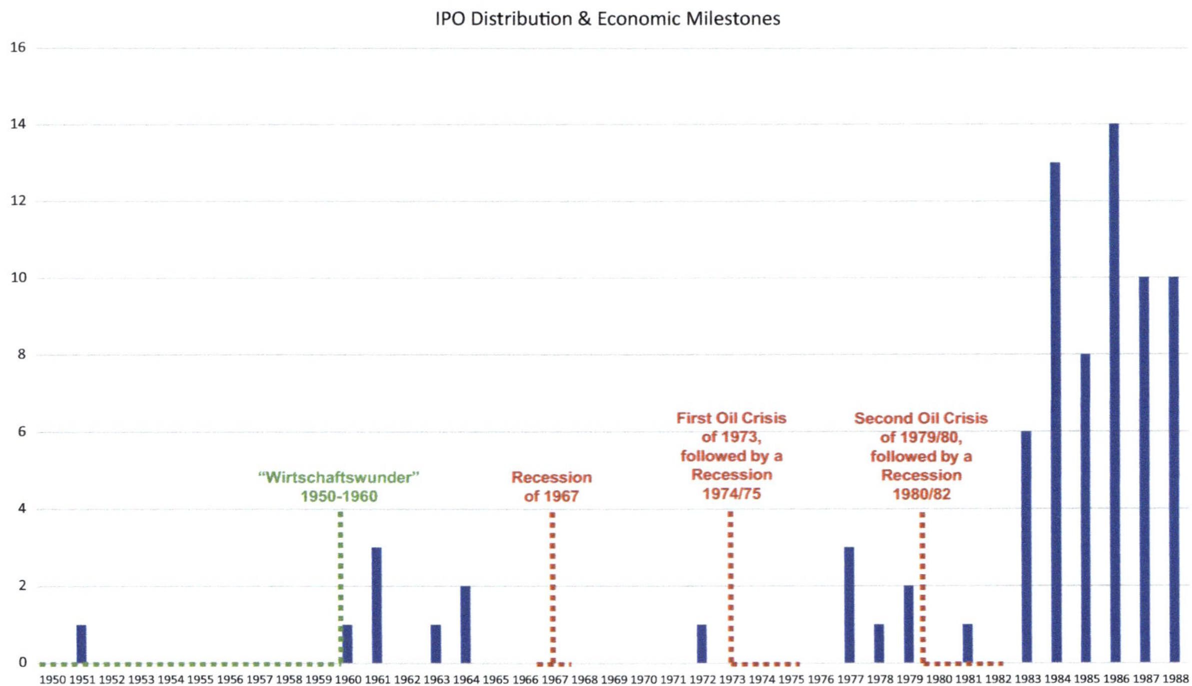

Figure 5.4 IPO Distribution & Economic Milestones—Family Enterprises. (Source: Author´s own figure, partially appended by Frankfurter Allgemeine Zeitung (2010), Bundeszentrale für politische Bildung (2016) and Heilemann (2019))

Economic crises and the accompanying recessions are periods that have been avoided in the past for IPO launches.

5.3.1.2 Interplay between IPO Distribution and Longevity

The longest surviving family business in family control[11] in the sample is *Drägerwerk AG*, with 39 years and ongoing. The company was founded in 1889 and experienced stock market flotation in 1979. Hence, there was a ninety-year maturation phase before the firm became a publicly listed family enterprise. This equates to approximately three to four generations of family ownership until the firm was successfully brought to the German Stock Exchange. By the time of the observation end in 2018, the family still held a major block of >70% ordinary shares, guaranteeing family influence through voting rights—the firm being nearly 130 years of age and the family in its fifth generation of ownership.

Figure 5.5a/b displays the survival times of all firms within the family enterprise sample, clustered by year of IPO launch and with reference to the economic crises and recession phases. The survival duration of *Drägerwerk AG* is given in Figure 5.5a, marked with $FC = 1$. This indicates that the firm ended the observation under family control (FC), which was the case for only one firm within this year. Furthermore, *Drägerwerk AG* was the only family firm to survive the heavy recession of the early 1980´s.

Westag & Getalit AG surpassed *Drägerwerk AG* by one year in survival duration, although this firm became subject to acquisition in 2001 and therefore failed to survive as a publicly listed family business. Referring to the development of the shareholder structure,[12] the family held a 100% stake at the time of IPO launch. In that process they reduced to >75%, and in further then in 1994 to >50%, until the majority of shares was acquired by a foreign firm in 2001. The reduction phase was quite extensive with 40 years—implying at least one change of generation. This leaves space for speculation. Possibly the family members reduced shares successively due to need of liquidity or the desire for a partial family exit, which both may have come with the generation change, such as inheritance tax payments or lack of interest in the firm. Nonetheless, *Westag & Getalit AG* survived at least three large recessions after entering the stock market.

---

[11] For further information, see Section 2.5.1. "The Dilution Process."

[12] The detailed shareholder quotas for the sample of family enterprises are summarized in Appendix I in the Electronic Supplementary Material.

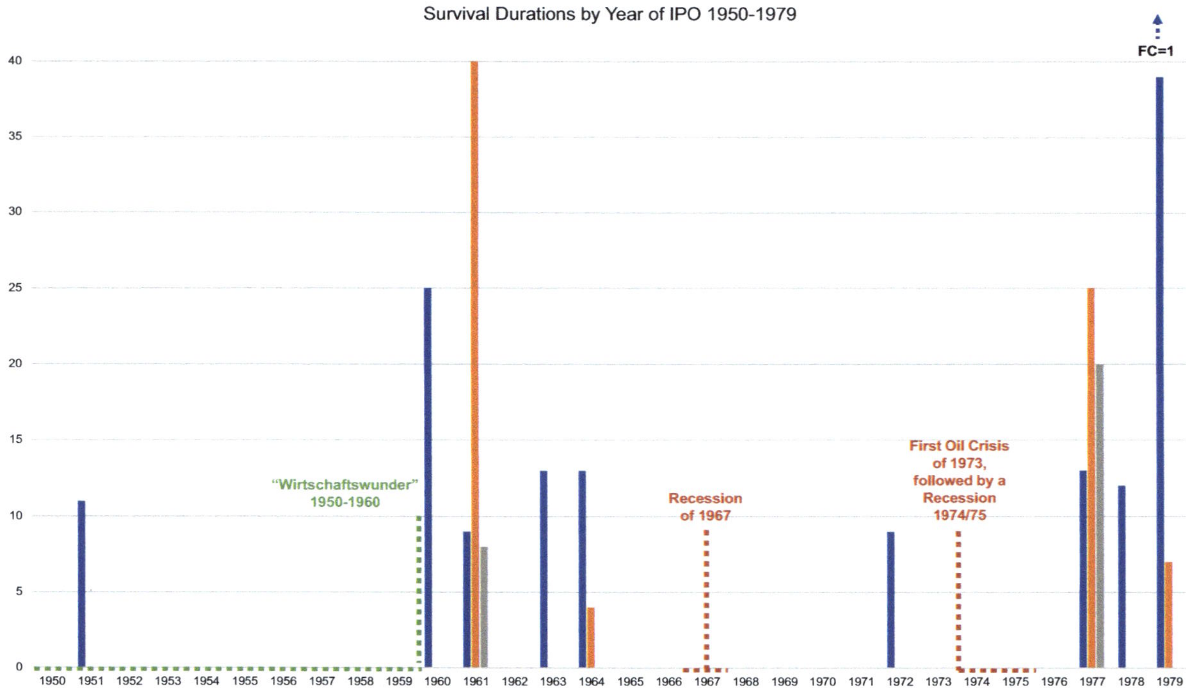

Figure 5.5a Survival Durations by Year of IPO 1950–1979—Family Enterprises. (Source: Author´s own figure, partially appended by Frankfurter Allgemeine Zeitung (2010), Bundeszentrale für politische Bildung (2016) and Heilemann (2019))

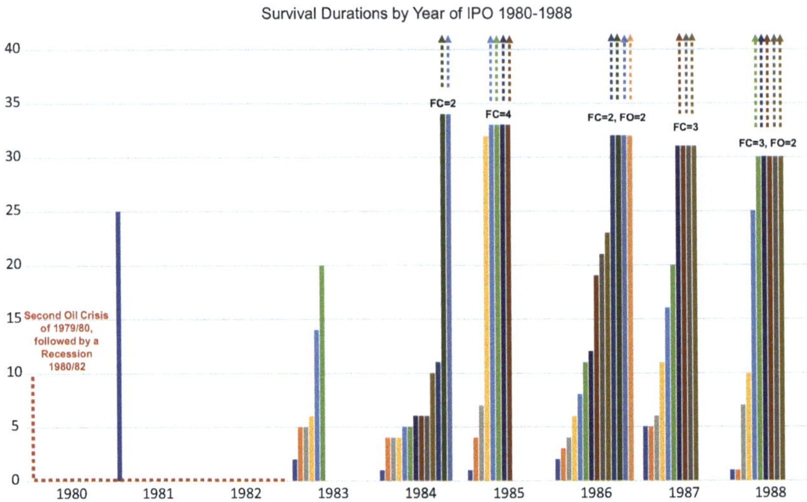

Figure 5.5b Survival Durations by Year of IPO 1980–1988—Family Enterprises. (Source: Author´s own figure, partially appended by Frankfurter Allgemeine Zeitung (2010), Bundeszentrale für politische Bildung (2016) and Heilemann (2019))

Continuing on the time axis, the big flood of IPOs was initiated shortly after the recession of 1980–82 (see Figure 5.5b). Most IPOs were launched in 1984 and 1986. Of all 19 surviving family businesses, 18 firms experienced IPO launch between 1984 and 1988. The years 1985 and 1988 have been identified as IPO years with a very strong survival rate. 50% of all firms with an IPO launch in 1985 survived throughout the observation period as family-controlled (FC = 4). Equally, 50% of all firms with flotation in 1988 survived beyond the upper cutoff, although three firms ended in family control and two firms ended in family ownership (FC = 3, FO = 2).

In conclusion, Figures 5.5a/b allow several observations at first glance. Firstly, recessions have a clear effect on IPO behavior. During and after recessions the IPO behavior slows down. This observation especially applies to the earlier decades. Secondly, only two IPO firms out of 15 of the early post-war decades (pre-1980´s) have been identified with long survival times, of which only one survived throughout the observation period. The majority of long-term survivors launched their IPOs in the 1980's. These firms have the potential to survive for many more years.[13]

[13] The further development of the surviving family businesses would be of great value for future follow-up research.

5.3.2 Possible Influence Factors

5.3.2.1 Does the Age at IPO influence Longevity?

The average age at IPO has been identified as 61 years with a high value for standard deviation (see Table 4.13, Chapter 4). This is due to the outliers of very old and very young family businesses, though especially with respect to the very old. The oldest family business in the sample, *Pschorrbräu AG,* goes back to 1417, and with 544 years had the highest age at the time of IPO. In total, 19 family enterprises were established before the twentieth century, although only *Pschorrbräu AG* was established earlier than the 19th century.

Table 5.6 offers an overview of the 19 oldest family enterprises of the sample, including year of IPO, year of establishment, number of years the firm survived as a publicly traded family business in its original state, and which final state the firm experienced by the end of the observation period.

As Table 5.6 gives insight into the old firms with establishment prior to the 20th century, Table 5.7 offers an overview of the family businesses that were very young at time of the IPO launch. Hence, family businesses that experienced stock market flotation within the first ten years after establishment have been assigned to this cluster.

When observing both Tables with a focus on the final states, the domination of bankruptcies among the very young family IPO-firms is striking.[14] This stands to reason when considering the advantage of maturity of the old firms that have already grown and survived for decades or even centuries—even surviving the drastic circumstances accompanying two world wars and severe recessions. Three of these very old family businesses—*Drägerwerk AG, Henkel KGaA* and *Hornbach AG*—survived throughout the observation period in family control, hence with a final family shareholder quota >50%.[15]

The main form of crucial change for this group of family businesses is acquisition (MorA/A). This indicates a certain attractiveness for acquiring firms, likely due to an established and healthy business structure, strong client base or popularity of a traditional, possibly prestigious family firm brand.[16] By further speculation, when a private firm becomes listed, the firm may gain more visibility with potential acquirers. Company valuation becomes easier due to legal

---

[14] Prior research has found that young and small firms tend to suffer from the liability of newness and smallness. See Freeman et al. (1983), Wiklund et al. (2013).

[15] For further information, see Section 2.5.1. "The Dilution Process".

[16] Also see Rauschendorfer et al. (2021), Beck et al. (2020), Beck & Prügl (2018), Lude & Prügl (2018), Zellweger et al. (2012) and Zellweger et al. (2010).

Table 5.6 The oldest Family Enterprises

Year of IPO	Family Enterprise	Year of Establishment	Years of Survival as private Ent.	Years of Survival at Stock Market	Final State
1951	Kienzle Uhrenfabrik AG	1822	129	11	MorA/A
1960	G.M. Pfaff AG	1862	98	28	MorA/A
1961	Pschorrbräu AG	1417	544	8	MorA/A
1961	WOLKO Schuhfabrik AG	1889	72	9	Diss
1972	Dyckerhoff & Widmann AG	1865	107	11	MorA/A
1979	Mauser Waldeck AG	1896	83	7	MorA/A
1979	Drägerwerk AG	1889	90	39 ongoing	Surv./FC
1983	Joseph Vögele AG	1836	147	6	MorA/A
1983	Wella AG	1880	103	20	MorA/A
1984	Zanders Feinpapiere AG	1829	155	5	MorA/A
1984	Garny AG	1813	171	5	MorA/A
1984	Nino AG	1897	87	5	MorA/A
1984	Sinn AG	1850	134	4	MorA/A
1985	FAG Kugelfischer Georg Schäfer KGaA	1896	89	7	MorA/A
1985	König & Bauer AG	1817	168	32	MorA/A
1985	Peter Temming AG	1895	90	1	Delist
1985	Henkel KGaA	1876	109	33 ongoing	Surv./FC
1986	Schneider Rundfunkwerke AG	1889	97	12	MorA/A
1987	Hornbach AG	1877	110	31 ongoing	Surv./FC

Table 5.7 The youngest Family Enterprises

Year of IPO	Family Enterprise	Year of Establishment	Years of Survival at Stock Market	Final State
1977	ALTANA Industrie-Aktien und Anlagen AG	1977	13	Delist.
1983	GfC AG für Computersysteme in der Medizin	1973	5	Bankr.
1983	Treuwo Verwaltungs-AG	1979	2	Bankr.
1984	MCS Modulare Comp. Und Software Syst. AG	1974	10	MorA/A
1984	BCT Computer AG	1976	1	Bankr.
1986	Irmen & Richter Textil AG	1986	2	MorA/A
1986	Greiffenberger AG	1986	32 ongoing	Surv./FO
1986	Escada AG	1978	23	Bankr.
1986	Technocell AG München	1983	8	Bankr.
1987	Pegasus Beteiligungen AG	1985	16	MorA/A
1988	Computer 2000 AG	1983	1	MorA/A
1988	Oppermann Versand AG	1980	1	MorA/A

requirements for firm transparency and publicity. Interested acquirers could initiate a gradual takeover by acquiring >30% and therefore securing a blocking influence. Another reason why an IPO may increase attention of potential acquirers is that they can follow the share price development and can thereby evaluate value fluctuations. This reasoning supports findings by Klasa (2007).[17]

A considerable number of these firms have been identified with survival durations of less than 10 years. This finding is worth being emphasized—many of these firms survived for more than hundred years as private enterprises and experienced family exit within a few years after IPO. This suggests a certain

[17] For further information, see Section 2.2.2. "Status Quo on Stock-Listed family Enterprise Longevity".

willingness of the family to sell their remaining stock in the company. Considering that the old firms were established in the 19th century, the owning family/-ies would at least be in the fourth to fifth generation. Interest in and commitment to the firm may have disintegrated over time due to the accompanying responsibilities and restrictions given by the strict rules and regulations as a publicly traded firm, leading to a lower emotional threshold towards an exit through sale. This, in combination with the higher pressure to sell by potential acquirers due to the attributes that come with suddenly being a publicly traded firm, may explain the short survival times after IPO for old and established family businesses.

In conclusion, old family IPO-businesses appear to be attractive to potential acquirers and appear to have a lower threshold towards family exit by means of sale, whereas very young family IPO firms appear more likely to suffer from bankruptcy.

5.3.2.2 What about the Size at IPO?

Due to restricted availability of data, the sole size indicator used for this study is the volume of turnover given at the time of the IPO launch. The data has been sorted into categories ranging from turnover below 50mio DM to more than 1bn DM.[18]

Figure 5.6 displays the survival times categorized by the turnover volume at the time of the IPO launch. The category with the largest survival rate is the one representing the largest firms with >1bn DM turnover in the year of the individual IPO. In total, six family businesses were assigned to this category. Three of these have survived in FC beyond the defined observation end in 2018.

The category of TO between 500-999mio DM comprises not a single case of family firm survival. Most family businesses have been assigned to the middle range category, representing firms with a TO at IPO launch between 100-499mio DM. In total, 29 family businesses recorded a TO within this range at the time of stock market flotation. Nine of these firms survived beyond the observation end, seven of which remained under family control and two in family ownership. This equals a survival rate of 31%.

Furthermore, sixteen family businesses registered a TO between 50-99mio DM. In comparison, these are quite small IPO firms. Yet, this TO category represents four survivors, hence a survival rate of 25%. A very interesting finding is given when observing the smallest category of turnover. Firstly, the firm with the longest survival time measured in this study was assigned to this category

[18] For further information, see Section 3.4.3.1. "Variables describing the Sample of Family Enterprises".

with a TO <50mio DM at IPO—*Westag & Getalit AG*—although the firm became subject to acquisition in 2001. Furthermore, two survivors were assigned to this group of small IPO-firms—*Greiffenberger AG* (FO) and *Bijou Brigitte modische Accessoires AG* (FC) remained in family ownership until the observation end.[19]

Although surviving family businesses have been identified in nearly all categories of turnover at IPO, a certain tendency is apparent. Maturity and stature of the firm appear to have a positive effect on longevity of publicly traded family enterprises.

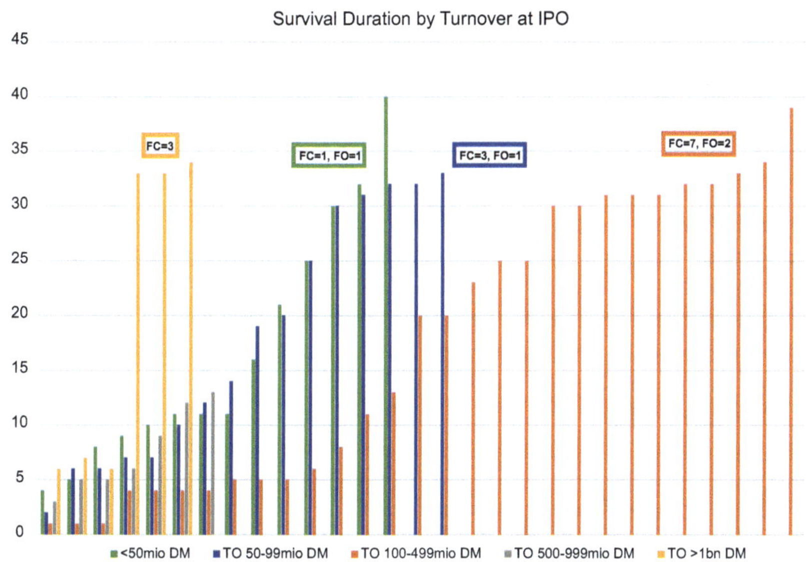

Figure 5.6 Survival Duration by TO at IPO. (Source: Author´s own figure)

[19] One family firm is exempt from display in Figure 5.6 due to lack of data on turnover at IPO.

5.3.3 The Depiction of Family Involvement—from the Beginning to the End

5.3.3.1 Number of Families Involved

So far, the focus has been on firm-specific factors. Now, the focus turns to the complementing other half of the family firm construct—the family. Does family involvement have an effect on firm longevity? Can the family overpower external influences and disruptive elements that may come with stock market flotation? Is there a recipe for a successful and long public corporate life in family hands?

Among other familial factors, the number of families invested in the firm at the time of IPO has been noted. The average number of families among the family businesses is 1.21, with a range between one and five families.[20] Hence, one or two families represent the average. Only very seldomly did the number exceed the average. *Treuwo Verwaltungs-AG* had the largest family involvement with five families invested in the firm. Yet they filed for bankruptcy only three years after stock market flotation. Four families were involved in the founding of *SAP AG.* Among the surviving family businesses, this is the only case exceeding the average. Over time, the number of invested families decreased. In the end, the firm counts as family-owned, including the family foundations.

To recapitulate, 15 of all surviving firms were owned by only one family. Two firms were owned by two families and just one firm by four families. Hence, the number of invested families doesn´t appear to have any noticeable effect, since the average for surviving as well as for failing family firms lies around 1.2 for both.

5.3.3.2 Shareholder Structure at IPO

The shareholder structure of the family businesses plays a key role in the analysis and therefore in answering the research questions. The initial shareholder quota by the invested family was defined at the time of the IPO launch. The quotas were analyzed in annual intervals along the designated timeline in order to define relevant changes within the shareholder structure and to define the duration of the family business remaining in family ownership.

When comparing the survivors and failures, the ratios concerning the shareholding quotas at the time of the IPO launch vary. A direct comparison is offered in Figure 5.7. In nearly 70% of the surviving family business cases, the family/-ies held >75% of shares in the company at the time of the IPO launch. In 26% the families held the majority of shares ranging between 50.1% and 75%, and

[20] For further information, see Section 4.4.1.2. "Metrical and Binary Variables," Table 4.14.

in just 5% of all surviving cases were the family's owners of 25–50% of shares with a blocking minority. Hence, 95% of all surviving family businesses were under family control to begin with. The distribution among the failing family businesses shows differences. Here, only approximately 50% of all firms were owned by families with a major block of >75% shares. In 33% of the cases the families held 50.1–75% of shares. The proportion of shareholding quotas between 25–50% lies here at 15%.

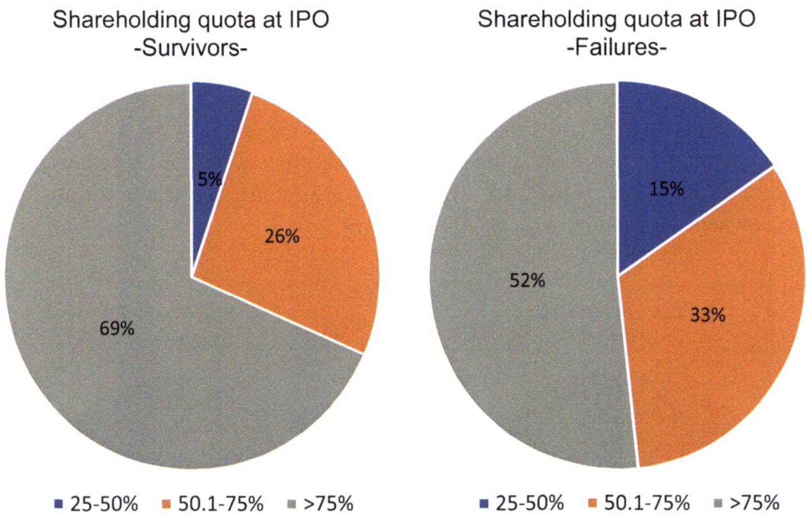

Figure 5.7 Shareholding quota at IPO—Survivors vs. Failures. (Source: Author´s own figure)

The differences in the distribution among the shareholding quotas between both groups leave room for interpretation. It appears that the surviving firms have stronger family involvement with respect to ownership from the beginning. The share of ownership quotas >75% is considerably higher compared to the failing family businesses. The share of minority ownership between 25–50% is considerably smaller compared to the failures. In these cases, the family/ies still own a significant share in the firm, yet they are no longer the sole decision-makers. They have the power to block decisions but lack the power of full influence. In the end, they can be a "poison pill" for acquisition efforts.

In conclusion, a higher degree of family ownership at the time of IPO launch appears to increase chances of survival.

5.3.3.3 Active Ownership

Another familial factor of family influence is active ownership (AO), i.e. shareholding family members taking active measures in order to control and influence the firm's development, such as being a member of the Executive or Supervisory Board.[21]

Figure 5.8 displays the distribution according to AO measures for the surviving family firms on the one side, as well as for the failing family firms on the other. The graphs show considerable differences between the degree of involvement and control through AO. Among the surviving family businesses 84% experienced continuous AO, from the beginning until the end. Hence, at least one family member was a member either of the executive or the supervisory board, or in several cases even of both boards, at the time of IPO and at the time of observation end. In 11% of cases the family members were active at the time of IPO, but at the end of the observation period, the family was no longer represented among either board. Merely 5% of all surviving family businesses maintained their ownership standing without AO measures.

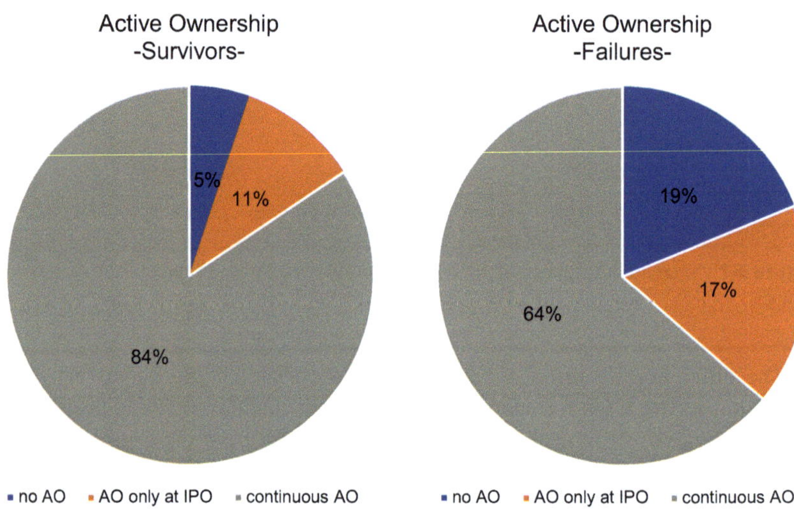

Figure 5.8 Active Ownership—Survivors vs. Failures. (Source: Author´s own figure)

[21] For further information, see Section 2.5.3. "The Concept of Active Ownership".

Among the failing family businesses, on the other hand, are far more cases of no AO (nearly 20%). Nevertheless, even among the failing family businesses there was a quota of 64% of continuous AO. In conclusion, even though family members were still active in either case, the family/ies decided to sell a major block of shares to outside acquirers, thereby diluting family influence into eventual non-existence. Possibly the families were seeking exits due to lack of a suitable successor,[22] lack of interest in the firm, or need for capital due to inheritance tax or other financial distress, among other reasons.[23]

When comparing the two largest categories of failure—MorA and bankruptcy—the family businesses underlying bankruptcy have the highest share of no AO measures (see Figure 5.9). In 30% of all bankruptcy cases, no family member took influence through membership on the Boards. Equally, for 30% of the firms AO was practiced at the time of IPO. Continuous AO measures were maintained for merely 40% of all bankruptcy firms. Among the MorA firms, nearly 70% experienced family involvement by continuous AO. This high level of AO among the mergers and acquisitions leaves further room for interpretation. Here again, several reasons may have led to the family's decision to sell the major block of shares. Nevertheless, it implies a certain willingness and openness towards an exit through sale.

In conclusion, a high degree of AO has been identified among all categories. A high degree of AO also appears to be necessary in the pursuit of family firm survival.

---

[22] Also see Parker (2016).

[23] For further information, see Section 1.3. "Family Enterprises Entering the Public Market—How Much Tension Can a Family Enterprise Take?".

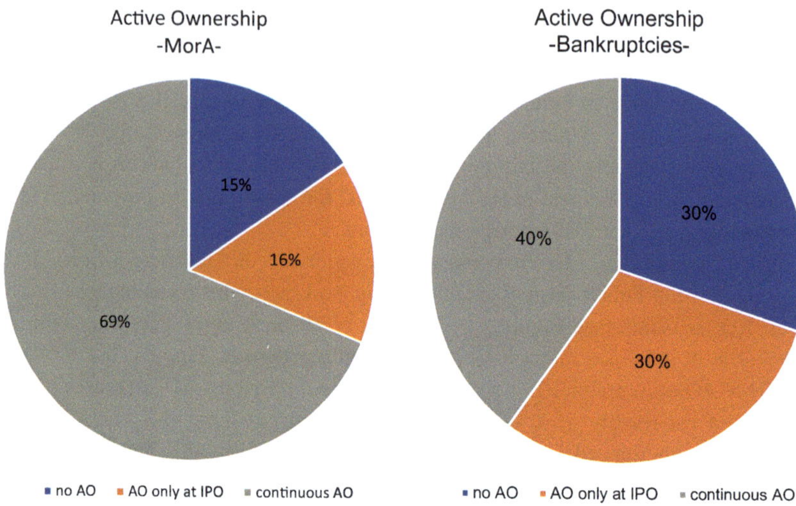

Figure 5.9 Active Ownership—MorA and Bankruptcies. (Source: Author´s own figure)

5.3.4 The Dilution Process of Family Influence

5.3.4.1 Total Number of Reductions

The firm-specific descriptive characteristics displayed in Table 4.13 of Chapter 4 include the number of reductions in family-held shares and the time frame from the initial reduction of stock until the crucial change or observation end sets in. These have been identified with significant effects on the survival times as family-owned firms after stock market flotation by the Cox PH models.[24] In general, in order for a family business to experience merger or acquisition (MorA), at least one reduction in family-owned shares must have taken place—leading to the exit sale of the family.

[24] For further information, see Section 4.4.2.3. "Cox Proportional Hazards Model" and 4.7. "Summary of Significant Findings".

The numbers of family-share reduction steps vary for the entire sample, from no reductions at all to 4 reductions.[25] Firstly, when observing the sales behavior of the surviving family businesses, nearly 50% have maintained their original shareholding quota (see Figure 5.10). For six firms, one sales step was recorded and for three of the surviving firms, two sales steps were recorded. In one case, however, a total of four share reductions were noted. This was *Marschollek, Lautenschläger und Partner AG*. They started off with a strong family ownership which was diluted over a long period of time of nearly 30 years, until in the end the family shareholding quota was between 25–50%.

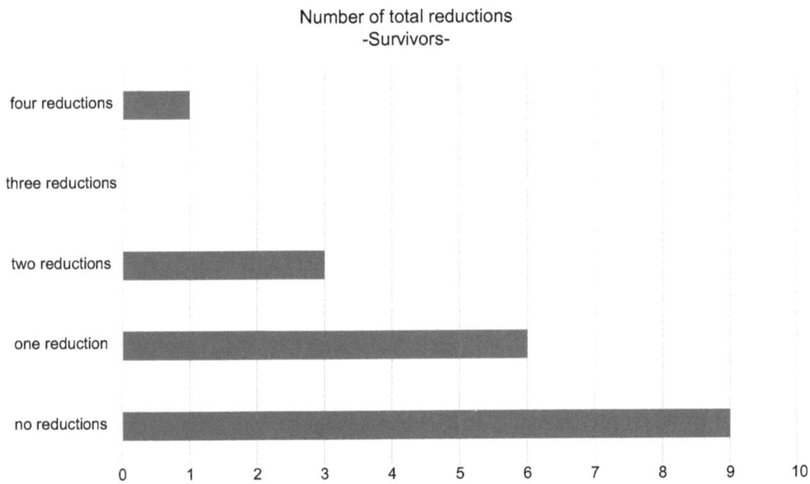

Figure 5.10 The Dilution Process of Family Influence—Survivors. (Source: Author´s own figure)

[25] Please note that the reduction steps have been derived from publications by Saling Aktienführer and Wer gehört zu wem?-Commerzbank. Only significant changes in the shareholding quotas have been acknowledged. The information provided by the publication sources shows a certain degree of variance, hence the researcher had to make a judgment call about whether the changes were of impact or not. As a result, the numbers of total reductions are approximate values.

All family businesses that experienced a steady shareholding quota held by the family without any mentionable reductions were all in family control to begin with. Hence, the initial shareholding quota at the time of IPO was >50% in all nine cases. Furthermore, by cross-checking with family involvement, these firms have all had a continuous AO. One can conclude that the family showed a high level of involvement from the beginning until the end. Table 5.8 offers an overview of these cases of high family involvement, which managed to avoid dilution of family influence.

Table 5.8 High Involvement Survivors

Year of IPO	Firm	Degree of AO
1979	Drägerwerk AG	continuous AO
1985	Axel Springer Verlag AG	continuous AO
1986	Edding AG	continuous AO
1987	Adolf Ahlers AG	continuous AO
1987	Hans Einhell AG	continuous AO
1987	Hornbach AG	continuous AO
1988	Bijou Brigitte modische Accessoires AG	continuous AO
1988	Schwälbchen Molkerei Jakob Berz AG	continuous AO
1988	Landshuter Kunstmühle AG	continuous AO

A total of 45 family businesses became subject to MorA as a form of crucial change. In nearly half of these cases the family/ies followed through with an ad hoc exit, which means the families sold a major block of shares at once, therefore diluting their influence to below 25% in one blow (see Figure 5.11). The one-step sale implies that the family/-ies approached the topic of sale with an intention to exit. Taking this observation one step further, one may conclude that the family/-ies may have decided to launch an IPO for exit reasons, leading to short survival times because a short-term sale was anticipated. But after cross-referencing with the survival times of these ad hoc sales firms, no conspicuous factors were detected. One may therefore conclude that the family/-ies were confronted with a very convincing purchasing price or were possibly in need of cash.[26]

[26] For further information, see Section 1.3. "Family Enterprises Entering the Public Market—How Much Tension Can a Family Enterprise Take?".

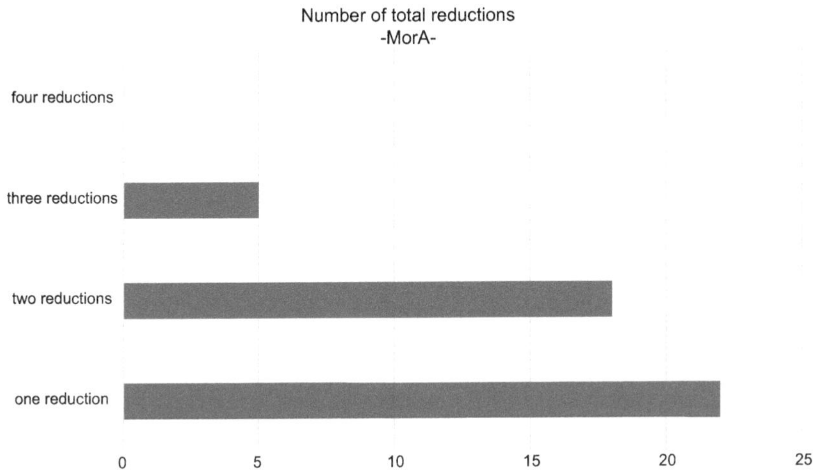

Figure 5.11 The Dilution Process of Family Influence—MorA. (Source: Author´s own figure)

The third block worth mentioning are bankruptcies. All in all, 10 firms entered bankruptcy during the observation period. A major block of these firms was not subjected to sales of family shares. This occurred for seven firms (see Figure 5.12). And yet, at one point the firms found themselves in financial distress. The degree of family influence varied. Only two firms experienced continuous AO. The remaining companies either had no family AO at all or only at the time of IPO (see Table 5.9). Hence, AO reasons don't appear to have an impact on the probability of bankruptcy for publicly traded family businesses.

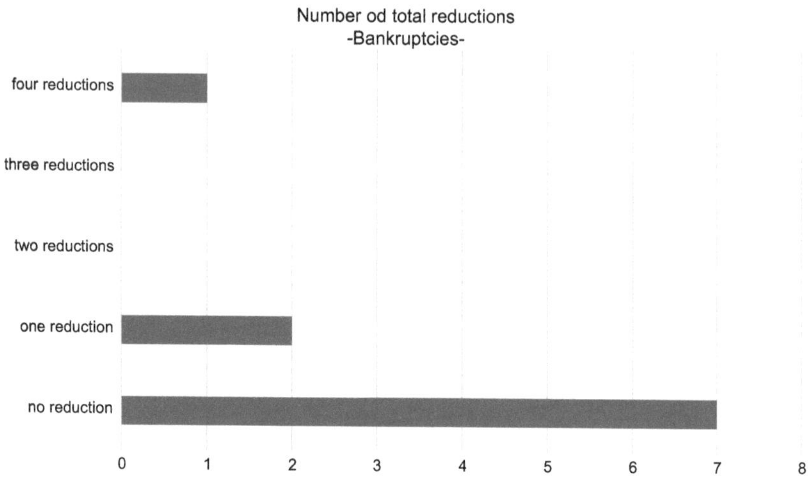

Figure 5.12 The Dilution Process of Family Influence—Bankruptcies. (Source: Author´s own figure)

Table 5.9 No Dilution among Bankruptcy Firms

Year of IPO	Firm	Degree of AO
1983	GfC AG für Computersysteme in der Medizin	no AO
1983	Treuwo Verwaltungs-AG	no AO
1984	BCT Computer AG	no AO
1986	Traub AG	continuous AO
1986	Technocell AG München	AO only at IPO
1987	BBS Kraftfahrzeugtechnik AG	continuous AO
1988	Kunert AG	AO only at IPO

5.3.4.2 Time Frame of Reductions

Coming from the total number of reductions of family-shares, this leads us directly to the associated topic of the time frames of reductions. Which firms exited the firm all at once? Over which timeline did the surviving family businesses reduce shares?

Many families reduced their block of shares in the firm over several years or even decades. All in all, these share reductions occurred in 58 cases. In some cases, the time frame of reduction was still ongoing, due to the elapsed observation period. The mean value determined by the calculation for the variable *Time Frame of Reduction* is nearly seven years. The average ST before the firm experienced any form of crucial change was 11 years.

Table 5.10 focuses on the family businesses that had the minimum time frame of share reductions, namely company sale all at once. The table shows the year of IPO, the firm, and the number of years the firm survived as an unchanged stock-listed company, until all family shares were sold down to a level <25%.

As previously stated in connection with the total number of reductions (see Subsection 5.3.4.1.), survival times vary widely. Hence, there appears to be no correlation between the phenomenon of the ad hoc company sale and the survival times. As a result, deriving a tendency regarding motives for these quick sales is impossible.

Table 5.10 Ad hoc Company Sales

Year of IPO	Family Enterprise	Survival time until MorA/A	Final State
1951	Kienzle Uhrenfabrik AG	11	MorA/A
1964	Pegulan-Werke AG	13	MorA/A
1972	Dyckerhoff & Widmann AG	9	MorA/A
1978	Progress-Werk Oberkirch AG	12	MorA/A
1979	Mauser & Waldeck AG	7	MorA/A
1981	Knürr AG Mechanik für die Elektronik	25	MorA/A
1983	Wella AG	20	MorA/A
1983	Hagen Batterie AG	5	MorA/A
1984	YMOS AG Industrieprodukte	5	MorA/A
1984	Hegener & Glaser AG	11	MorA/A
1984	Nino AG	5	MorA/A
1984	Sinn AG	4	MorA/A
1984	ADV/ORGA F.A Meyer AG	6	MorA/A
1985	FAG Kugelfischer Georg Schäfer KGaA	7	MorA/A

(continued)

Table 5.10 (continued)

Year of IPO	Family Enterprise	Survival time until MorA/A	Final State
1985	Peter Temming AG	1	MorA/A
1986	Irmen & Richter Textil AG	2	MorA/A
1987	Pegasus Beteiligungen AG	16	MorA/A
1987	Puma Rudolf Dassler Sport AG	3	MorA/A
1987	Biotest AG	31	MorA/A
1988	Computer 2000 AG	1	MorA/A
1988	Macrotron AG für Datenerfassungssysteme	10	MorA/A
1988	Oppermann Versand AG	1	MorA/A

The quantitative analysis reveals a highly significant relationship between the time frame of reductions and the survival time until crucial change sets in. Hence, a longer time frame of reductions can double survival time until crucial change occurs.[27]

Worth noting are the family businesses that started their public life as family-controlled firms (>50% family shares) but ended as family-owned firms (25–50% family-shares).[28] *Greiffenberger AG, Fresenius AG, SAP AG* and *Marschollek, Lautenschläger und Partner AG* experienced reductions in family-shares but did remain in family ownership through the end of the observation period. Except for *Greiffenberger AG*, the time frames of reduction stretched over a long period of time with up to four reduction steps, but with only small blocks of shares being sold at a time (see Table 5.11). These firms have been defined as weak survivors.

[27] See Section 4.4.2.3. "Cox Proportional Hazards Model".

[28] For further information, see Section 2.5.1. "The Dilution Process".

Table 5.11 Dilution from Family Control to Family Ownership—weak Survivors

Year of IPO	Firm	TF of Reductions (years)	Number of Red.	ST until 1. Red (years)
1986	Greiffenberger AG	1	1	32
1986	Fresenius AG	26	2	6
1984	Marschollek, Lautenschläger und Partner AG	29	4	1
1988	SAP AG	22	2	8

Finally, the rest of the sample that has not been identified with any reductions in family shares and therefore doesn't provide data on time frames of reduction is displayed in Table 5.12a/b. The firms' survival times and final states all vary. Naturally, family firms that have been subjected to merger or acquisition cannot be among this group. It is worth mentioning that of all ten cases of bankruptcies, seven did not reduce family shares. Furthermore, of all 15 cases of family firm survival in FC, nine did not reduce shares (also see Tables 5.8 and 5.9).

In conclusion, the time frame of share reductions plays a significant role for the survival time until crucial change and, therefore, until failure as a stock-listed family business. The longer the time frame of reductions, the higher the chance of survival.

Table 5.12a Family Enterprises without Reductions—Survivors

Year of IPO	Firm	Survival Time	Final State
1979	Drägerwerk AG	39 ongoing	FC
1985	Axel Springer Verlag AG	33 ongoing	FC
1986	Edding AG	32 ongoing	FC
1987	Adolf Ahlers AG	31 ongoing	FC
1987	Hans Einhell AG	31 ongoing	FC
1987	Hornbach AG	31 ongoing	FC
1988	Bijou Brigitte modische Accessoires AG	30 ongoing	FC
1988	Schwälbchen Molkerei Jakob Berz AG	30 ongoing	FC
1988	Landshuter Kunstmühle AG	30 ongoing	FC

Table 5.12b Family Enterprises without Reductions—Failures

Year of IPO	Firm	Survival Time	Final State
1961	WOLKO Schuhfabrik AG	9	Dissolution
1977	ALTANA Industrie-Aktien und Anlagen AG	33	De-Listing
1983	Gestra AG	14	De-Listing
1983	GfC AG für Computersysteme in der Medizin	5	Bankruptcy
1983	Treuwo Verwaltungs-AG	3	Bankruptcy
1984	BCT Computer AG	1	Bankruptcy
1986	Traub AG	11	Bankruptcy
1986	Technocell AG München	8	Bankruptcy
1987	BBS Kraftfahrzeugtechnik AG	20	Bankruptcy
1988	Kunert AG	25	Bankruptcy

5.3.5 Overview of Crucial Changes

The concept of crucial change was introduced in Section 2.5.2. Crucial change refers to a severe disruption a firm experiences that leads to new structural patterns in ownership, sturdy and healthy firm development, or legal status. The occurrence of crucial change leads to failure of the stock-listed family firm. A total of 58 family businesses experienced crucial change. With a sample size of 77, this results in a 75% failure rate among the family businesses.

The largest block of failures was caused by mergers or acquisitions (MorA), with 45 family businesses subject to MorA during the observation period, resulting in a share of 78% of all failures (see Table 5.13).

Table 5.13 Failures—Mergers or Acquisitions—Family Enterprises

Year of IPO	Family Enterprise	Survival time until MorA	Megers	Acqu.
1951	Kienzle Uhrenfabrik AG	11		✔
1960	G.M. Pfaff AG	25		✔
1961	Westag & Getalit AG	40		✔
1961	Pschorrbräu AG	8		✔

(continued)

Table 5.13 (continued)

Year of IPO	Family Enterprise	Survival time until MorA	Megers	Acqu.
1963	Neckarmann Versand KGaA	13		✔
1964	Pegulan-Werke AG	13		✔
1964	Braun AG	4		✔
1972	Dyckerhoff & Widmann AG	9		✔
1977	Leffers AG	20	✔	
1978	Progress-Werk Oberkirch AG	12		✔
1979	Mauser & Waldeck AG	7		✔
1981	Knürr Mechanik für die Elektronik AG	25		✔
1983	Joseph Vögele AG	6		✔
1983	Wella AG	20		✔
1983	Hagen Batterie AG	5		✔
1984	Zanders Feinpapiere AG	6		✔
1984	MCS modulare Comp. Und Software Syst. AG	10		✔
1984	YMOS AG Industrieprodukte	5		✔
1984	Hegener + Glaser AG	11		✔
1984	Nixdorf Computer AG	6		✔
1984	Garny AG	4		✔
1984	Scheu & Wirth AG	5		✔
1984	Nino AG	5		✔
1984	Sinn AG	4		✔
1984	ADV/ORGA F.A. Meyer AG	6		✔
1985	Peter Temming AG	1		✔
1985	König & Bauer AG	32		✔
1985	FAG Kugelfischer Georg Schäfer KGaA	7		✔
1985	Hugo Boss AG	4		✔

(continued)

Table 5.13 (continued)

Year of IPO	Family Enterprise	Survival time until MorA	Megers	Acqu.
1986	PUMA AG Rudolf Dassler Sport	3		✔
1986	Irmen & Richter Textil AG	2		✔
1986	Vogt Electronic AG	19		✔
1986	VDO Adolf Schindling AG	6		✔
1986	Oberland Glas AG	4		✔
1986	Kampa-Haus AG	21		✔
1986	Schneider Rundfunkwerke AG	12		✔
1987	Pegasus Beteiligungen AG	16		✔
1987	Hertel AG Werkzeuge & Hartstoffe	5		✔
1987	Glunz AG	11		✔
1987	Biotest AG	31		✔
1987	A. Moksel AG	5		✔
1988	Pietzsch AG	7		✔
1988	Computer 2000 AG	1		✔
1988	Macrotron AG für Datenerfassungssysteme	10		✔
1988	Oppermann Versand AG	1		✔

Moving on to the second largest block, bankruptcies comprise 17% of all failures. Ten family businesses experienced financial distress and filed for bankruptcy during the observation period (see Table 5.14). De-listings and firm dissolutions are negligible, due to a very low count in the low single digits.

In conclusion, the most prominent form of crucial change experienced by stock-listed family enterprises by far is acquisition.

Table 5.14 Failures—Bankruptcies, De-listings, Dissolutions—Family Enterprises

Year of IPO	Family Enterprise	Survival times	Bankr.	Delist.	Diss.
1961	WOLKO Schuhfabrik AG	9			✔
1977	ALTANA Industrie-Aktien und Anlagen AG	33		✔	
1977	Herlitz AG	25	✔		
1983	Treuwo Verwaltungs-AG	3	✔		
1983	GfC AG für Computersysteme in dr Medizin AG	5	✔		
1983	Gestra AG	14		✔	
1984	BCT Computer AG	1	✔		
1986	Traub AG	11	✔		
1986	Escada AG	23	✔		
1986	Technocell AG München	8	✔		
1987	BBS Kraftfahrzeugtechnik AG	20	✔		
1987	GMN Georg Müller Nürnberg AG	6	✔		
1988	Kunert AG	25	✔		

5.3.6 What makes Survivors Survivors?

So far, the data representing the sample of family businesses has been examined from various angles. Single sub-groups have been screened for remarkable features that may have an impact on the form of crucial change or on the overall survival time and have been cross-examined with other sub-groups or features for comparability. Finally, the primary focus is on the surviving family enterprises.

The successful family enterprises are featured in Table 5.15. The overview offers insight into all relevant features, such as turnover, family shareholding structure at the time of IPO, and degree of active ownership. The overwhelming domination of continuous AO is striking. Furthermore, 13 out of 19 firms were in very strong family control at the time of stock market flotation, with >75% of shares in family ownership. The combination of these features implies a strong family interest and involvement in the firm, independent of age. Some of these high involvement family firms were established in the 19th century, some in the 20th century. The age of the firm at IPO appears to have no effect on the degree of family involvement or, therefore, on the probability of AO success.

Table 5.15 The surviving Family Enterprises

Family Enterprise	Year of establishm.	Year of IPO	TO at IPO	Shareh. str. at IPO	Degree of AO	Number of reductions	Final state
Drägerwerk AG	1889	1979	100-499mio DM	>75%	continuous AO	0	FC
Dr. Ing. h.c.F. Porsche AG	1931	1984	>1bn DM	>50–75%	continuous AO	1	FC
Krones AG Hermann Kronseder Masch.fabrik	1951	1984	100-499mio DM	>75%	continuous AO	1	FC
Fuchs Petrolub AG	1931	1985	100-499mio DM	>50–75%	continuous AO	1	FC
Henkel KGaA	1876	1985	>1bn DM	>75%	.	2	FC
Axel Springer Verlag AG	1946	1985	>1bn DM	25–50%	continuous AO	0	FC
Euro-Kai KGaA	1961	1985	50-99mio DM	>75%	continuous AO	1	FC
Greiffenberger AG	1986	1986	<50mio DM	>50–75%	continuous AO	1	FO
Fresenius AG	1912	1986	100-499mio DM	>75%	at IPO	2	FO
Sixt AG	1912	1986	50-99mio DM	>75%	continuous AO	1	FC
Edding AG	1960	1986	50-99mio DM	>75%	continuous AO	0	FC
Adolf Ahlers AG	1919	1987	100-499mio DM	>75%	continuous AO	0	FC
Hans Einhell AG	1964	1987	100-499mio DM	>75%	continuous AO	0	FC
Hornbach AG	1877	1987	100-499mio DM	>75%	continuous AO	0	FC

(continued)

Table 5.15 (continued)

Family Enterprise	Year of establishm.	Year of IPO	TO at IPO	Shareh. str. at IPO	Degree of AO	Number of reductions	Final state
Bijou Brigitte modische Accessoires AG	1963	1988	<50mio DM	>50–75%	continuous AO	0	FC
Schwälbchen Molkerei Jakob Berz AG	1938	1988	100-499mio DM	>50–75%	continuous AO	0	FC
Marschollek, Lautenschläger und Partner AG	1971	1988	50-99mio DM	>75%	at IPO	4	FO
SAP AG	1976	1988	100-499mio DM	>75%	continuous AO	2	FO
Landshuter Kunstmühle AG	1898	1988		>75%	continuous AO	0	FC

Nearly all IPO's were launched in the 1980's. The oldest succeeding family enterprise is *Drägerwerk AG*, with an IPO in 1979 and a survival time until observation end of 39 years and ongoing. All firms with stock market flotation prior 1979 failed, even though one firm, *Westag & Getalit AG*, has documented a slightly longer ST of 40 years. This finding leaves space for speculation—do stock-listed family firms have a natural expiration date or end of life? Are forty years of stock market survival an approximate limit? Or is the lack of surviving early IPO firms possibly due to the aftershock of the historic events of two world wars and several heavy recessions? These intriguing questions are due for a follow-up analysis of the surviving firms and their development moving forward.

In conclusion, stock-listed family businesses with the following features appear to have a higher chance of survival—age at IPO launch 25–100 years, TO at IPO launch >100-500mio DM, family shareholding quota at IPO >50% (best >75%), few reductions in family shares, and a high degree of AO.

5.3.7 Long-term Survival vs. short-term Failure

Following the same structure of Table 5.15, the family businesses experiencing very short survival times of <10 years until crucial change occurred are represented in Table 5.16. This allows a direct comparison and identification of soft success factors. For instance, among the short-term failures, there are more very old family businesses than among the surviving family businesses. This supports previous observations. Furthermore, the family shareholder quotas are lower compared to the surviving firms. Merely 35% of all short-term failures had a family shareholding quota of >75%, compared to nearly 70% among the surviving family businesses. Regarding the number of reductions of family shares, the short-term failures have been identified with an average of 1.2 reductions, whereas the surviving family businesses reduced shares on average 0.8 times. The degree of AO also differs, with 55% of short-term failures experiencing a very high degree of AO (continuous AO) in contrast to 84% of surviving family businesses with continuous AO.

In conclusion, the observations resulting from the comparison of short-term failures to long-term survivors emphasize the identified soft success factors derived from Section 5.3.6.: Age, TO and family shareholding quota at IPO. Number of reductions and degree of AO also appear to have an impact on the chance of survival.

Table 5.16 Short-term Failures

Family Enterprise	Year of establishm.	Year of IPO	TO at IPO	Shareh. str. at IPO	Degree of AO	Number of reductions	Form of cr. change
WOLKO Schuhfabrik AG	1889	1961	<50mio DM	>75%	continuous AO	0	Dissolution
Pschorrbräu AG	1417	1961	<50mio DM	>75%	continuous AO	1	MorA/A
Dyckerhoff & Widmann AG	1865	1972	500-999mio DM	25–50%	continuous AO	1	MorA/A
Mauser Waldeck AG	1896	1979	50-99mio DM	25–50%	continuous AO	1	MorA/A
Joseph Vögele AG	1836	1983	50-99mio DM	>50–75%	continuous AO	1	MorA/A
GfC AG für Computersysteme in der Medizin	1973	1983	.	>50–75%	.	0	Bankruptcy
Hagen Batterie AG	1910	1983	100-499mio DM	>75%	continuous AO	1	MorA/A
Treuwo Verwaltungs-AG	1979	1983	.	>50–75%	.	0	Bankruptcy
Zanders Feinpapiere AG	1829	1984	500-999mio DM	>50–75%	continuous AO	2	MorA/A
BCT Computer AG	1976	1984	.	>75%	.	0	Bankruptcy

(continued)

Table 5.16 (continued)

Family Enterprise	Year of establishm.	Year of IPO	TO at IPO	Shareh. str. at IPO	Degree of AO	Number of reductions	Form of cr. change
YMOS AG Industrieprodukte	1926	1984	100-499mio DM	>75%	continuous AO	1	MorA/A
Nixdorf Computer AG	1952	1984	>1bn DM	>50–75%	continuous AO	2	MorA/A
Garny AG	1813	1984	<50mio DM	25–50%	continuous AO	2	MorA/A
Scheu & Wirth AG	1959	1984	50-99mio DM	>75%	continuous AO	2	MorA/A
Nino AG	1897	1984	500-999mio DM	>50–75%	no AO	1	MorA/A
Sinn AG	1850	1984	100-499mio DM	>50–75%	continuous AO	1	MorA/A
ADV/ORGA F.A. Meyer AG	1962	1984	50-99mio DM	>75%	at IPO	1	MorA/A
FAG Kugelfischer Georg Schäfer KGaA	1896	1985	>1bn DM	>50–75%	continuous AO	1	MorA/A
Peter Temming AG	1895	1985	100-499mio DM	25–50%	continuous AO	1	MorA/A
Hugo Boss AG	1924	1985	100-499mio DM	25–50%	continuous AO	2	MorA/A
VDO Adolf Schindling AG	1929	1986	>1bn DM	>75%	continuous AO	2	MorA/A

(continued)

Table 5.16 (continued)

Family Enterprise	Year of establishm.	Year of IPO	TO at IPO	Shareh. str. at IPO	Degree of AO	Number of reductions	Form of cr. change
Oberland Glas AG	1946	1986	100-499mio DM	>50–75%	continuous AO	2	MorA/A
Technocell AG München	1983	1986	100-499mio DM	>50–75%	at IPO	0	Bankruptcy
PUMA AG Rudolf Dassler Sport	1948	1986	500-999mio DM	>75%	at IPO	1	MorA/A
Irmen & Richter Rextil AG	1986	1986	50-99mio DM	>50–75%	continuous AO	1	MorA/A
Hertel AG Werkzeuge & Hartstoffe	1947	1987	100-499mio DM	>75%	continuous AO	2	MorA/A
GMN Georg Müller Nürnberg AG	1908	1987	100-499mio DM	>50–75%	continuous AO	1	Bankruptcy
A. Moksel AG	1948	1987	500-999mio DM	25–50%	continuous AO	2	MorA/A
Pietzsch AG	1965	1988	<50mio DM	25–50%	continuous AO	3	MorA/A
Computer 2000 AG	1983	1988	100-499mio DM	>50–75%	continuous AO	1	MorA/A
Oppermann Versand AG	1980	1988	100-499mio DM	>75%	continuous AO	1	MorA/A

5.3.8 Clusters, Patterns and Success Factors

In conclusion, there are certain features—referred to as soft features, due to the lack of empirical evidence for this narrative approach—that appear to influence the chance of family firm survival at the German Stock Exchange (see Table 5.17). Among the firm-specific influence factors, age at the time of IPO launch reveals certain clusters. Many of these firms were very old, especially among the acquisitions (MorA/A). Furthermore, the older firms are at lower risk of bankruptcy. Another clustering has been identified among the very large family businesses at IPO with a TO >1bn DM. Half of these firms survived as family-controlled, with a final family shareholding quota >50%.

Regarding family involvement, a high family involvement from beginning to end appears to have a positive impact on the chance of survival. Nearly 70% of all successful family enterprises have been identified with a family shareholding quota >75% at the time of stock market flotation. In addition, a high degree of AO has been identified for 85% of survivors. Hence, at least one family member has taken active measures in the form of an Executive or Supervisor, in order to maintain and ensure family influence. Still, as previously stated, continuous AO is necessary but not sufficient, since a high degree of AO has been identified among all groups.

The examination of the dilution process has also revealed certain findings. Surviving family businesses have also reduced shares through sale, although usually no more than in one to two reduction steps. In order to maintain family dominance through shares, the reductions must have been rather small. Furthermore, by selling small blocks of shares at a time, the time frame of reductions for the surviving family businesses has been identified as longer, compared to exit firms. This difference is a result of the tendency of exit-willing families to sell their major block in one or two steps within a short time frame. This finding is empirically supported by the quantitative analysis in Chapter 4.

With the observations in mind, the researcher would like to draw attention to the dissertation by Lantelme (2023). The study addresses the 250 largest German businesses, starting in 1958 with an observation end in the year 2018. Among these firms, 26 were stock-listed family businesses at the time. By 2018, merely two firms were still stock-listed family businesses (one was brought into a foundation in 2018). These findings support the observations of this study. Most stock-listed family businesses experience some form of crucial change. Only a few remain steady over decades. By addressing the success factors and clusters derived from this analysis, most survivors fulfill certain criteria. Very few do not meet the features to such an extent that have been identified as beneficial.

Hence, one may conclude that there are two types of surviving stock-listed family businesses—firstly, the survivors that fulfill the defined criteria of size, degree of family influence (shareholding quota at IPO), degree of family involvement (AO), etc. and can therefore resist the temptations or blows that come with being a publicly traded entity, or secondly, the family firms, that do not meet these criteria, but rather appear to be unattractive to potential acquirers due to industry, foundations, etc., and therefore exist unaffected.

Table 5.17 Summary of Soft Features for a prolonged Family Enterprise Survival

Firm-specific influence factors	Family involvement	Dilution process
Mature family businesses with a higher age at IPO have been found to suffer less of financial distress and therefore resulting bankruptcy.	A high family shareholding quota >75% at IPO appears to increase chance of survival	A low number of reductions, hence small reductions in family shares, should not be exceeded in order to maintain strong family influence.
Mature family businesses with a higher age at IPO appear to be desirable for acquiring firms.	Continuous AO appears to increase chance of survival	Resulting from small reductions, longer time frames of reductions increase survival time and the chance of survival, because most sales are ad hoc or by only two reductions.
Family businesses with a turnover at IPO >1bn appear to be at least risk of any form of crucial change, hence a higher chance of survival.		

5.4 Samples in Comparison

Although both samples are provided with certain features, which are unique to each sample, a certain comparability is possible through overlapping soft features. Nevertheless, comparability is reduced to the firm-specific features, since these are the only features the samples have in common. Table 5.18 displays the summary of soft features which have been derived for each sample on the basis of firm-specific traits. Furthermore, the table displays the overlap. *Maturity* has been identified as an enhancer for merger or acquisition after IPO, but this only applies to non-family businesses with a pre-IPO family background. The *size* (TO at IPO) of the firm, regardless of the existence of family influence, appears to reduce the chance of crucial change. These firms tend to remain steady throughout their stock market existence.

Table 5.18 Soft Features in Comparison—Family vs. Non-Family Enterprises

Firm-specific influence factors Family Firms	**Overlaps**	**Firm-specific influence factors Non-Family Firms**
Mature family businesses with a higher age at IPO have been found to suffer less of financial distress and therefore resulting bankruptcy.		Nearly all very old IPO-firms have been identified as former family-owned businesses (except for one missing value).
Mature family businesses with a higher age at IPO appear to be desirable to acquiring firms.	**Maturity:** Shorter survival times and MorA as crucial change for mature family firms and former family firms.	Mature firms with a higher age at IPO appear to be desirable to acquiring firms. Nearly all old-aged firms once had a family background.
Family businesses with a turnover >1bn appear to be at least risk of any form of crucial change, hence a higher chance of survival.	**Size:** Large family, as well as non-family businesses appear to be at lower risk of crucial change.	State-owned IPO-firms have been identified with the longest survival times, due to extended privatization phases into free float or until crucial change occurred.

References

Beck, S., Prügl, R. & Walter, K. (2020). Communicating the family firm brand: Antecedents and performance effects. *European Management Journal*, 38, 95–107.

Beck, S. & Prügl, R. (2018). Family firm reputation and humanization: Consumers and the trust advantage of family firms under different conditions of brand familiarity. *Family Business Review*, 31(4), 460–482.

Bundeszentrale für politische Bildung (2016). *Wirtschaftswunder*. Retrieved from https://www.bpb.de/nachschlagen/lexika/lexikon-der-wirtschaft/21146/wirtschaftswunder.

Bundeszentrale für politische Bildung (2002). *Gesellschaftliche Entwicklung*. Retrieved from https://www.bpb.de/izpb/10124/gesellschaftliche-entwicklung.

Capital (2019). *Der Untergang des Handelskonzerns Co op*. Retrieved from https://www.capital.de/wirtschaft-politik/der-untergang-des-handelskonzerns-co-op.

Fiedler, M. (2016). *Tagung zur Genossenschaftsgeschichte: Entstehung und Untergang der Coop AG*. Zentralverband Deutscher Konsumgenossenschaften. Retrieved from https://www.zdk-hamburg.de/blog/2016/08/tagung-zur-genossenschaftsgeschichte-entstehung-und-untergang-der-coop-ag/.

Frankfurter Allgemeine Zeitung (2010). *Rekordminus für die deutsche Wirtschaft*. Retrieved from https://www.faz.net/aktuell/wirtschaft/konjunktur/bruttoinlandsprodukt-deutsche-wirtschaft-schrumpft-2009-um-fuenf-prozent-1911421/infografik-konjunkturzyklen-1917647.html#fotobox_1_911421.

Frankfurter Allgemeine Zeitung (2018). *Deutsche Börsengeschichte—Hightech im Kaiserreich*. Retrieved from https://www.faz.net/aktuell/finanzen/finanzmarkt/wie-die-boerse-den-aufstieg-der-wirtschaft-finanziert-hat-15526462.html.

Freeman, J., Carroll, G.R. & Hannan, M.T. (1983). The Liability of Newness: Age Dependence in Organizational Death Rates. *American Sociological Research*, 48, 692–710.

Heilemann, U. (2019). Rezessionen in der Bundepublik Deutschland von 1966–2013. *Wirtschaftsdienst—Zeitschrift für Wirtschaftspolitik*, ed. 8, 546–551, retrieved from https://www.wirtschaftsdienst.eu/inhalt/jahr/2019/heft/8/beitrag/rezessionen-in-der-bundesrepublik-deutschland-von-1966-bis-2013.html.

Hewel, B. (1980). *Konjunktur und Wachstum—Theorie und Politik*. Wiesbaden: Gabler Verlag.

Lantelme, M. (2023). *The Continuity and Discontinuity of the 250 Largest Enterprises in Germany: A History-Based Analysis of Family Influence, Corporate Development and Ownership Transactions* (Doctoral Thesis). Zeppelin University, Friedrichshafen.

Lude, M. & Prügl, R. (2018). Why the family business brand matters: Brand authenticity and the family firm trust inference. *Journal of Business Research*, 89, 121–134.

Manager Magazin (2001). *Missmanagement bei Coop—Das fast perfekte Verbrechen*. Retrieved from https://www.manager-magazin.de/unternehmen/missmanagement/a-149040.html.

Parker, S.C. (2016). Family Firms and the "Willing Successor" Problem. *Entrepreneurship, Theory and Practice*, Nov. 2016, 1241–1259.

Peter, S. (2009). *Preussag: vom Staatskonzern zum Privateigentum*. Retrieved from https://www.ndr.de/geschichte/chronologie/Preussag-Vom-Staatskonzern-zum-Privateigentum,preussag100.html.

Rauschendorfer, N., Prügl, R. & Lude, M. (2021). Love is in the air. Consumers´ perception of products from firms signaling their family nature. *Psychology & Marketing*, 39(1), 239–249.

Wiklund, J., Nordquist, M., Hellerstedt, K. & Bird, M. (2013). Internal versus external ownership transition in family firms: An embeddedness perspective. *Entrepreneurship Theory and Practice*, 37, 1319–1340.

Zellweger, T.M., Kellermanns, F.W., Eddleston, K.A. & Memili, E. (2012). Building a family firm image: How family firms capitalize on their family ties. *Journal of Family Business Strategy*, 3(4), 239–250.

Zellweger, T.M., Eddleston, K.A. & Kellermanns, F.W. (2010). Exploring the concept of familiness: Introducing family firm identity. *Journal of Family Business Strategy*, 1(1), 54–63.

Conclusion 6

The final chapter of this dissertation is fully committed to the research questions. It concludes the results of prior chapters and lays the foundation for interpretation and derivation of practical implications. The chapter aims at tying up the relevant features which have been identified during the analyses and pointing out the constraints.

6.1 Chapter Overview

Initially, the limits of the study are introduced, along with concerns about the challenges the researcher was confronted with, how they were handled and where future research should latch on to further fill the research gap. By placing the limits in the front of the chapter, the researcher seeks to establish an awareness of the circumstances and allow the reader to fully grasp the concluding chapter in the right context. Before concerning itself with the research questions, this chapter summarizes and combines the findings from the quantitative and narrative analysis. By doing so, the essential findings are extracted and brought together. This allows the reader to recognize the identified success factors for stock-listed family firm longevity. From there, the chapter leads through the research questions and introduces the model that has been developed in connection to these. Based on the model, practical implications are presented, which aim at supporting stock-listed family firm longevity and providing family businesses that are considering going public with a basis for decision-making.

K. Stotmeister, *Publicly Traded Family Businesses*, Familienunternehmen und KMU, https://doi.org/10.1007/978-3-658-44303-0_6

6.2 Limits of the Study

Within the scope of this study, family firm longevity was at the center of examination. The aim of the study is to provide a foundation, which is based on former experience, for future family firm decision-makers considering a stock-market flotation. Based on historical data of family enterprises that have experienced failure or survival as a PIE, a model has been developed which reflects success factors for stock-listed family firm longevity.

As in the case of every study, the researcher faced certain challenges, which are worth mentioning at this point. Recollecting the data collection process, as described in Section 3.3., the study is based on historical data. Working with historical data always poses a challenge. Depending on how far back the data reaches, sources are limited. In this case, IPO data had to be fragmentally composed through various sources which were all paper-based at the time. There was no central data collection on stock market flotations after WWII. Furthermore, in parts, there were deviations in the data depending on the source. On some occasions there was even a complete lack of data. Hence, the researcher had to make decisions based on assumptions, if reasonable, or had to dismiss candidates because the data was too thin and unreliable. And as it is with historical data, it's limited to what's available—you can't make additional inquiries, because witnesses may not be alive anymore. Hence, the samples are not complete and data may differ slightly. Nevertheless, the data set is as clean as possible, due to the applied principle of reasonability.

Furthermore, due to lack of reliable data, several potential firms were excluded from the samples, which naturally led to smaller sample sizes. The sample of family businesses comprised 77, whereas the sample of non-family businesses comprised a total of 39.[1] Due to the small sample sizes as they are and the small number of founders' firms, the researcher decided to take founders and family firms into the same sample. Nevertheless, the complementary dissertation by Lantelme (2023) examines the 250 largest firms in Germany of the year 1958. Twenty-six of these firms were stock-listed family businesses at the time. By 2018, only two firms had survived. The development identified by Lantelme supports the findings of this study that longevity of post-IPO family businesses is limited, with few exceptional performers. Hence, by adding the twenty-six firms of the Lantelme study, the sample size *theoretically* grows to above 100. Future research may focus on expanding the sample.

---

[1] For further information, see Section 3.3.3. "Derivation of Final Sample Groups".

Moving along the study line, further limitations came to light in the process. For instance, within the quantitative analysis the distinction between weak and strong family firm survivors doesn't find full attention. The importance of the differences between weak and strong survivors doesn't come into focus until Section 6.3., "Combining the Findings". The combination of quantitative and narrative analysis uncovered these fine nuances. Hence, future research may pick up the surviving stock-listed family businesses with a stronger focus on weak and strong survivors.[2]

Furthermore, the time frame of observation ends in the year 2018. This cutoff was chosen due to the Covid-19 pandemic that forced the world economy into a deep crisis. As the dates were precisely selected to avoid economic irregularities and therefore allow for an equal base and *uninfluenced* development for all firms[3], the upper cutoff leaves right-censored survival durations. Hence, the survival spells of the surviving family businesses show a maximum of 39 years.[4] What happens beyond the upper cutoff is not addressed. The researcher strongly recommends a follow-up analysis with a focus on the further development of the surviving family businesses, and attention to distinguishing between weak and strong survivors. This would allow for the possibility of the most pressing questions this thesis has led to: whether stock-listed family businesses have a natural expiration date.

The sample of stock-listed family businesses was compared to the sample of stock-listed non-family businesses, due to the focus on the development as a PIE. Another aspect which may be interesting for future research is the comparison of development regarding longevity and family involvement of public and private family businesses. This would reveal findings on reasons for stock-listed family firm failures.

The challenges accompanying this study leave space for future research. The study is one-of-a-kind, with a focus on the German market, one of the most saturated markets of successful family businesses of old age. It contributes to the field of research by uncovering success factors for stock-listed family firm longevity and brings valuable insight into past developments of family businesses which have been at the same crossroads as future family firms considering going public. Future family firm decision-makers will have a foundation of experience and a model of success factors on which to base their decisions.

---

[2] For further information, see Section 2.5.1. "The Dilution Process".

[3] For further information, see Section 3.3.1. "Defining the Time Frame".

[4] For further information, see Section 4.3.2. "Survival Analysis" and Section 5.3.1. "Overview of the Sample".

6.3 Combining the Findings

The study followed a mixed methods approach. In a first step, a survival analysis was conducted by applying Cox PH models and Kaplan-Meier Estimators. This analysis revealed empirically significant findings, the most striking ones being a long time frame of share reductions and a low number of share reductions for increased survival times. In a second step, a narrative analysis was conducted in order to screen the data from a different angle. By clustering and cross-checking the data, conspicuous features became visible. Furthermore, by adding the narrative section, single cases were introduced which stood out through remarkable features. The addition of actual firm experiences underlines the findings by adding a vivid aspect, which makes it more tangible for the reader. The aim of the following subchapters is to demonstrate and visualize the differences between the surviving stock-listed family businesses and the ones, that experienced crucial change[5] and therefore lost their status as a stock-listed family enterprise.

In conclusion, the findings of both analyses are reduced to the essence, in order to establish a reliable model and thereby answer the research questions with precision.

6.3.1 Success Factors—Survivors vs. Failures

Initially, the findings of both analyses were combined into the graph shown in Figure 6.1. In total, six success factors were identified: long time frame of reductions, no or very few reductions in family held shares, a medium size at IPO with a turnover between 100 and 499 million €, continuous AO measures, a strong family shareholding quota at IPO of >75% and an optimal firm age at IPO between 20 and 100 years.

Long time frame of reductions: The surviving family businesses have been identified with remarkably longer time frames of share reductions compared to the failing family firms. On average, the time frames of reduction lie at 7.5 years with a maximum of 29 years.

[5] For a definition, see Section 2.5.2. "The Concept of Crucial Change".

Number of reductions: In close relation to the time frame of reductions is the number of reductions of family-held shares. Among the surviving family businesses, the number of reductions is small in comparison to the failures. A maximum of four reductions in shares was noted for one survivor. All other survivors were far lower.

Size at IPO: Nearly 50% of all survivors were among the medium-sized turnover group at IPO between 100 and 499mio €. The rest of the surviving firms tended to be larger, while the failing family businesses tended to be smaller.

Continuous Active Ownership: Nearly 85% of the survivors have implemented the highest degree of family involvement in the firm—continuous AO. Hence, in nearly all surviving businesses, family members maintained influence on the firm's development either by Executive or Supervisory means throughout the firm's PIE-life. This high degree of family involvement was the case among merely 63% of the failing family businesses.

Family shareholding quota >75%: In nearly 70% of all surviving cases the family/-ies held a shareholding block of >75%, in comparison to 50% among the failing businesses.

Age at IPO 20–100 years: Nearly 75% of the surviving businesses were within the optimal age range at the time of their IPO launch. The very young family businesses tended to be subject to bankruptcy, whereas the very old family businesses were sold shortly after their IPOs.[6]

The graph shows a clear advantage of the surviving family businesses in *all* aspects in comparison to the family firms that experienced crucial change.

[6] For further information, see Section 5.3.2.1. "Does the Age at IPO influence Longevity?".

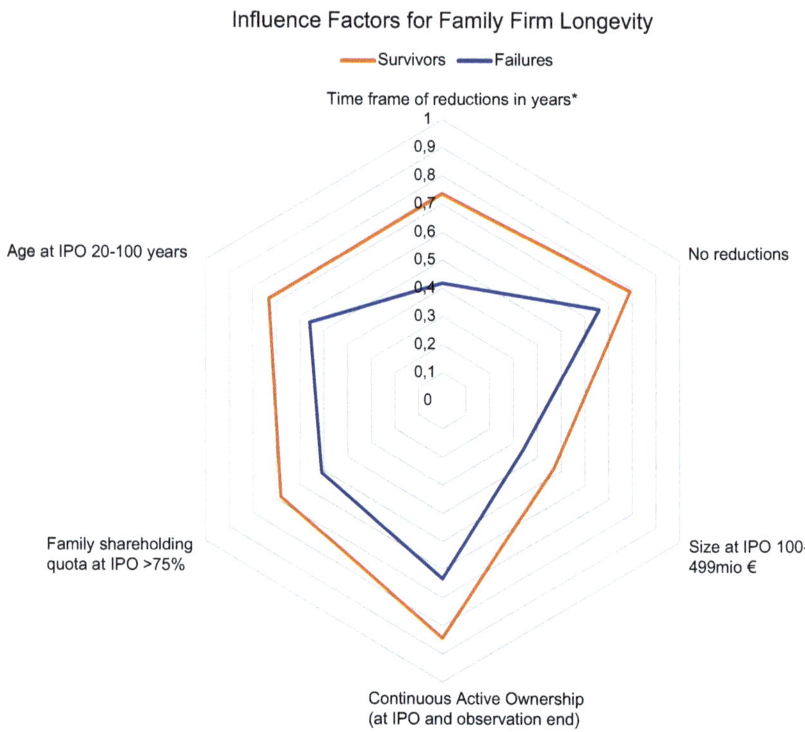

Figure 6.1 Success Factors—Survivors vs. Failures

6.3.2 Success Factors—weak vs. strong Survivors

Developing the graph in Figure 6.1 further, the surviving family businesses have been divided into weak survivors and strong survivors. This division is based on the categorization of family-controlled and family-owned businesses, as defined in the dilution process in Section 2.5.1. Figure 6.2 displays the identical graph, though applied to weak and strong survivors.

Long time frame of reductions: The weak survivors have been identified with very long time frames of share reductions in comparison to the strong survivors. On average, the weak survivors count nearly 20 years of reductions, whereas the strong survivors show an average time frame of reductions of just four years.[7] This stands in clear contrast to the findings provided in Figure 6.1.

Number of reductions: Based on the finding of short time frames of reductions among the strong survivors, this can best be explained by the number of reductions—the strong survivors show an average of 0.47 reductions in family held shares. Hence, most surviving family businesses have not reduced family shares at all throughout their entire PIE-life. If reductions were noted, these took place after a long survival span, shortly before the observation end in 2018. The weak survivors, on the other hand, have been identified with an average of 2.5 reductions and long time frames of reductions. In summary, the strong survivors have been identified with no reductions or one reduction after a long survival span, whereas the weak survivors have been identified with more reductions on average, beginning shortly after IPO. Even so, small reductions have not always led to complete family influence dilution.

Size at IPO: 50% of all weak survivors were within the optimal size range at the time of the IPO launch. Only 40% of the strong survivors have been found to meet this criterion, though the strong survivors tended to be even larger.

Continuous Active Ownership: Only 50% of the weak survivors have been identified with the highest degree of family involvement, though continuous AO is a clear success factor among the strong survivors. Continuous AO measures were practiced among 100% of the strong survivors.

Family shareholding quota >75%: The family shareholding quota >75% has been found to be applicable for 75% of all weak survivors, whereas it is merely applicable for 52% of the strong survivors.

Age at IPO of 20–100 years: Nearly 90% of the strong survivors were within the optimal range of age at IPO between 20 and 100 years. On the other hand, only 25% of the weal survivors were within this range.

The visualization in Figure 6.2 clearly displays differences between weak and strong survivors. Noteworthy strengths among the strong survivors (family-controlled with >75% shareholding quota at the time of the observation end) are short time frames of reductions due to no or late single reductions in family held

[7] Please note that some values in the graphs are scaled. The true values are mentioned in the description. The scaled values offer comparability.

shares, the medium turnover size as a minimum, the age at the IPO launch (maturity) and, most prominently, the decisive role of *continuous AO involvement*. The dominance of continuous AO measures among the strong survivors indicates the willingness of the family to remain involved as a reliable constant. The weak survivors, on the other hand, appear to enter the market with previously existent exit notions or tendencies.

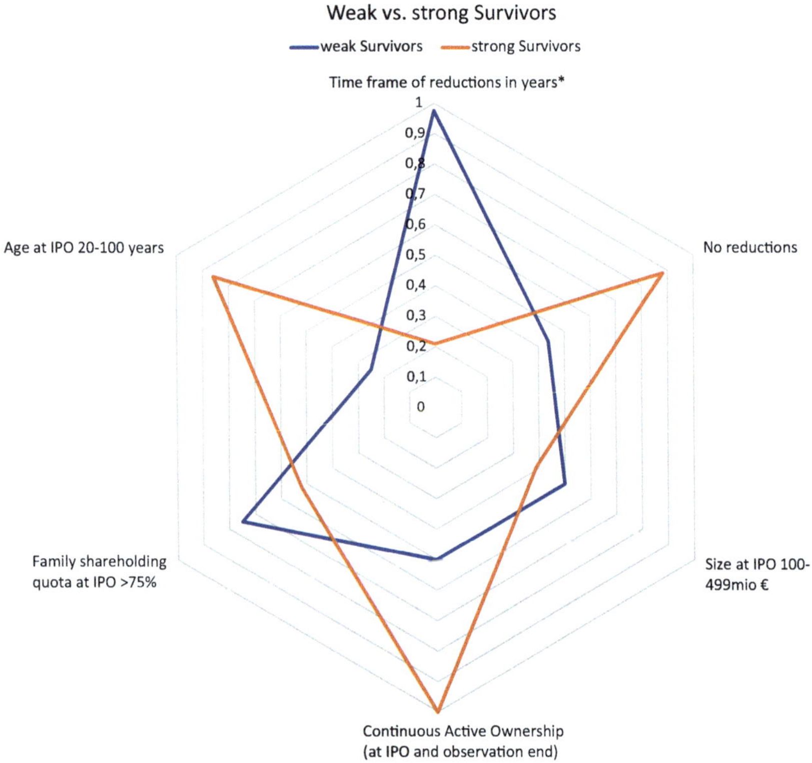

Figure 6.2 Success Factors—weak vs. strong Survivors

6.3.3 Success Factors—Strong Survivors vs. Failures

By bringing Figures 6.1 and 6.2 together, the strong survivors and the failures are to be compared in Figure 6.3. The weak survivors have been eliminated from the graph in order to show the essence of the success factors for stock-listed family business longevity.

Long time frame of reductions: The time frame of reductions is equal among the strong survivors and the failures.
Number of reductions: The strong surviving family businesses show an average of 0.47 reductions of family-held shares, whereas the failures have been identified with an average of 1.36.

Size at IPO: 46% of the strong survivors were within the optimal range of size by turnover, with a tendency towards being larger. Among the failures, 34% met this criterion.

Continuous Active Ownership: Continuous AO measures were practiced by 63% of the failures. The strong survivors show strength in this criterion with 100%.

Family shareholding quota >75%: The family shareholding quota >75% has been found to be applicable for 67% of all strong survivors and for 51% of the failures.

Age at IPO 20–100 years: Nearly 90% of the strong survivors were within the optimal maturity range at the time of IPO, compared to 56% among the failures.

In conclusion, after applying the graph to the different categories along the dilution line, five conspicuous success factors emerge, as displayed in Figure 6.3. Apart from the time frame of reductions, the strong survivors show strength in all the other features. They especially excel in the practice of continuous AO. Hence, this high degree of AO appears to play a crucial role in stock-listed family firm longevity. Furthermore, the graph suggests that a high degree of family shareholding and the age of the firm at the time of the IPO launch both enhance the probability of survival.

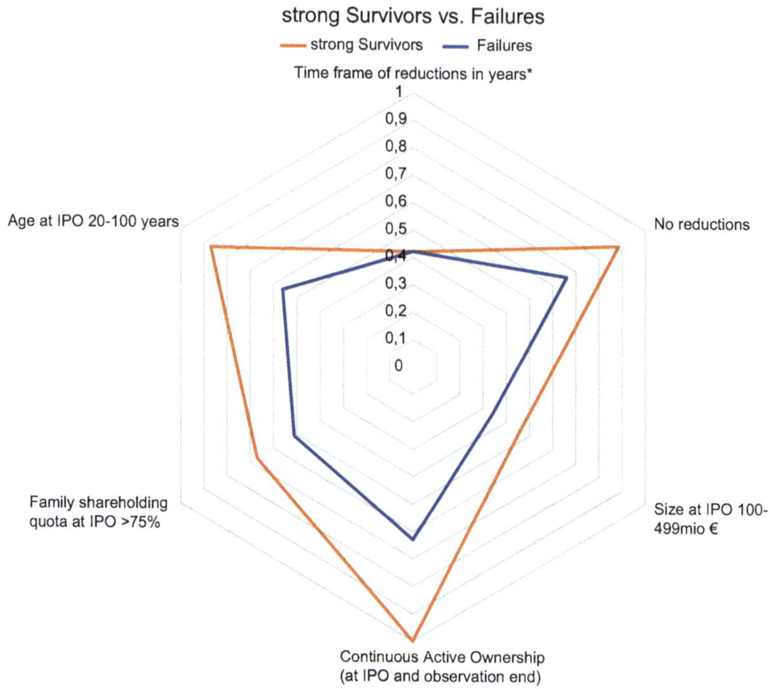

Figure 6.3 Success Factors—strong Survivors vs. Failures

6.4 Answering the Research Questions

The research questions will be discussed in the following. The main objective, however, is the model development. Each following subchapter is dedicated to answering one of the research questions. As introduced in Section 2.3. "Identifying Research Gaps and Formulating the Research Question", the research questions are as follows:

How did German stock-listed family firms develop after IPO, with a main focus on longevity and family involvement? – Development of a model based on the long-term analysis of historical data ranging from 1950–2018

- *How long do families of publicly traded family firms maintain their influence through shares after IPO?*

- *How does family influence (shareholding quota) develop after IPO?*
- *Which forms of crucial change led to failure (sale/family exit, delisting, bankruptcy, etc.)?*
- *Are there beneficial factors/success factors for family firm survival (industry, number of families involved, age of firm, etc.)?*

6.4.1 Survival Durations of Stock-Listed Family Enterprises

- *How long do families of publicly traded family firms maintain their influence through shares after IPO?*

The initial question is committed to the survival durations of family enterprises as PIE's. Family businesses have been identified with individually long survival durations. Nevertheless, the analyses have uncovered certain patterns. The Kaplan-Meier Survival Curves have revealed a critical threshold of 13 years. Most failures among stock-listed family enterprises took place within the first 13 years after IPO. After this critical threshold, the survival durations got remarkably longer and failures got fewer. Furthermore, family businesses that were very young at the time of stock market flotation have been observed with very short survival durations, mostly below 10 years, and mostly due to financial distress and bankruptcy. The very old family businesses at the time of the IPO launch (>100 years) have also been observed to have short survival durations. The surviving family businesses have been identified with a maximum survival time of 39 years and ongoing. This cutoff is due to the end of the observation period in 2018, hence these firms are right-censored and have undefined survival durations.

6.4.2 Development of Family Influence

- *How does family influence (shareholding quota) develop after IPO?*

Family influence has been measured by the family shareholding quota. The development of shareholding quota and the different stages are defined in the *dilution process.*[8]

[8] For a definition, see Section 2.5.1. "The Dilution Process".

Similar to the observations regarding the survival durations, the dilution process shows certain patterns. These two questions are interrelated, since the dilution of family held shares is connected to the survival durations of the firm. Nevertheless, the dilution process only comes into play among the family businesses that experienced MorA and among the survivors, since it is not of relevance for the firms experiencing any other form of crucial change, such as bankruptcy or delisting.[9]

Among the family businesses experiencing MorA, the dilution process and the time frame of dilution both vary. Patterns have nonetheless been identified in this field as well: The very old family businesses with >100 years at the time of the IPO launch have been identified with very short time frames of reductions. Hence, the dilution process was rapid. Naturally, there are exceptions, in which the family/ies have diluted shares over a longer period of time and through many reduction steps. This pattern has also been identified among the surviving family businesses, although here it also states the exception (weak survivors). The majority of the surviving family businesses have not diluted influence by selling shares or have only reduced shares once, but by very little. These firms are the strong survivors. They have remained steady in their shareholding quota throughout their PIE-life. Hence, there were no time frames of reductions, or if at all, very short ones, because the one and only dilution step was minor and at a very late point in time, shortly before the observation period ended.

6.4.3 Forms of Crucial Change

| *Which forms of crucial change led to failure (sale/family exit, delisting, bankruptcy, etc.)?*

The most prominent form of crucial change was MorA with 58% among the entire sample of family businesses. In total, 45 firms experienced either merger or acquisition, although one out of these firms experienced merger as cause for failure. Nearly half of the acquired firms (N = 20) were purchased by foreign firms and six were acquired by other family businesses. Bankruptcy was cause for failure among 13% of the entire sample of family businesses (N = 10). Minor forms of crucial change experienced among the sample were dissolution in one case (family exit) and two cases of de-listing.

---

[9] For a definition, see Section 2.5.2. "The Concept of Crucial Change".

6.4.4 Success Factors for Longevity

| *Are there beneficial factors/success factors for family firm survival (industry, number of families involved, age of firm, etc.)?*

In combination, the quantitative and narrative analysis have identified success factors for stock-listed family firm longevity. The Cox Survival Analysis has identified the *timeframe of reductions* and the number of *reductions total* of having a significant effect on the risk of failure. A long time frame of reduction has been identified with a risk-decreasing effect, whereas a high number of reductions has been identified with a risk-increasing effect on failure, thus reducing the survival time. A high number of reductions increases the risk of failure and therefore reduces the survival duration. A long time frame of reductions, on the other hand, has been found to prolong survival durations.

Furthermore, the narrative analysis has identified the size at the time of the IPO launch between 100–499mio €, continuous AO, a family shareholding quota >75%, and an age at the time of the IPO launch between 20 to 100 years to all have a beneficial effect on stock-listed family firm longevity. The surviving family businesses have been strongly clustered within these ranges. Section 6.3, "Combining the Findings," meticulously leads through these findings.

6.5 Model Development

Answering the research questions has led to insightful findings that paint a conclusive picture and allow for the development of theoretical statements. Hence, a model has been developed to combine the theoretical statements into a holistic display of relations (see Figure 6.4).

In the process of the model development, it became apparent that the above listed success factors need to be sorted into two categories. The first category comprises two variables which concern the business and are given for the acting shareholder group. These are *age* and *size*. The other three factors are fully influenced by the currently acting shareholder group. Hence, there are four success factors in total that have been identified as beneficial.

Family firms considering a stock market flotation should meet the four factors that are success relevant, already at the time of the IPO launch—size by turnover at least between 100–499mio €, a mature age of the firm between 20 and 100 years, a high degree of family influence with a controlling shareholding quota >50% (better yet >75%) and AO measures in place. Hence, the firm itself should meet the two requirements at the time of the IPO launch and the shareholding family itself has to meet the two requirements on their side. These success factors are called *preliminary success factors*, because they are success-relevant and given even before the firm is a PIE. Building upon these preliminary factors, the *sequent success factors* come into play from the point on of the IPO launch—maintaining continuous AO and controlling the share reductions of the family. Continuous Active Ownership measures have been identified among *all* strong survivors. It is of utmost relevance to maintain this high degree of family involvement in the firm's future development, either by positioning at least one family member in an operative leading role or in a supervisory role. Furthermore, the reductions in family shares must be held to a minimum in order to avoid dilution of family influence. If the family firm survives the critical failure phase of 13 years post-IPO, the odds appear to increase for long-term family firm survival.

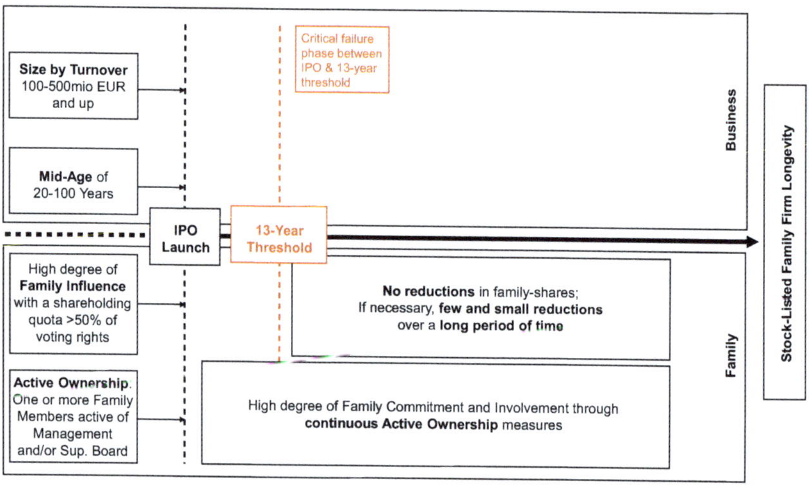

Figure 6.4 Stock-listed Family Firm Longevity

6.6 Practical Implications

The question whether to go public or not is of critical nature. It can be a starting point for a successful and thriving future, but it might just as easily be the beginning of the end. Family businesses and business families may see themselves at a crossroads, insecure about which path to choose. This study aims at latching on to this critical point of the IPO launch and exploring the outcome of those that have already taken this step.

Based on the theoretical model in Figure 6.4, measures of action have been developed and integrated into the model (see Figure 6.5). There are *three phases of active measures*—actions prior to IPO, actions prior and after IPO, and actions after IPO.[10]

Phase 1: Actions prior to IPO Four success factors have been identified and found to have an effect on stock-listed family firm longevity.[11] These success factors relate to the time of the IPO launch. Firms that have fulfilled these factors have been found to be more likely to survive as a public family enterprise. Hence, family businesses that are anticipating going public in the future and aim at maintaining family influence in the long run are advised to assess the firm for maturity of size regarding turnover, medium age between 20 and 100 years, a controlling family influence of >50%, and AO measures.

These four factors are referred to as beneficial factors prior to IPO. If a family firm meets these criteria at the time of the IPO launch, as displayed and described in Figure 6.5, the firm is expected to have a disproportionately increased chance of long-term survival. Turnover maturity has been identified as beneficial. In fact, the highly mature family businesses with a turnover >1bn€ have had the highest ratio of survivors.[12] Furthermore, a mature age between 20 and 100 years at IPO has been found to be beneficial for longevity. Among the very young family businesses bankruptcies were frequent and the very old businesses showed a high tendency towards MorA (willingness to exit?).[13] A controlling degree >50% of family influence regarding shareholding quota is recommendable, better yet >75% family shareholding quota. Initially, the beneficial limit was set at >75%.[14] As derived in Section 6.3.2. "Success Factors—Weak vs. Strong Survivors," the strong survivors showed a higher tendency towards >50%. As a result, for the practical implications, the level of beneficial family influence was adjusted. The fourth beneficial factor prior to IPO is the implementation of

[10] Recommendations described within the phases underlie the interpretation and speculation of the theoretical findings.

[11] See Sections 4.4.2. "Survival Analysis," 5.3.6. "What makes the Survivors Survivors?" 5.3.8. "Cluster, Patterns and Success Factors," 6.3. "Combining the Findings," and 6.5. "Model Development".

[12] For further information, see Section 5.3.2.2. "What about Size at IPO?".

[13] For further information, see Section 5.3.2.1. "Does Age at IPO Influence Longevity?".

[14] See Section 5.3.3.2. "Shareholder Structure at IPO".

AO measures. Recalling Section 5.3.3.3., continuous AO was identified among 84% of the surviving family businesses, and even among 100% of the strong survivors (Section 6.3.2.). Hence, in order to ensure continuous AO, measures must already have been implemented prior to the IPO launch.[15]

Phase 2: Actions prior to and after IPO The recommendations in this phase clearly concern the continuous Active Ownership. As displayed in Figure 6.2, *all* strong survivors ensured continuous AO measures throughout the observation period. Hence, this success factor deserves special attention. The overarching objective is to maintain family involvement. To ensure this, one must plan ahead. Recommended measures of action are to encourage next generation family members—not only a favored few, but the entire next generation shareholding group. The parent generation should take active measures to inform the next generation of shareholders. This may be possible by implementing annual next-generation meetings, where the future shareholders learn about obligations, responsibility, and family values. The goal is to create a next-generation shareholding group that has learned to trust each other, communicate with each other, and evaluate and make decisions together. Keep all next-generation shareholders equally informed, in order to decrease the risk of privileged treatment and its ensuing emotional disapproval. After a certain maturing phase of the next-generation shareholding group, future successors should be appointed. By integrating all next-generation shareholders into the appointment process and winning their approval, the risk of future resentment or appeal may be reduced. Furthermore, contractual specifications which define the qualifications of future successors, as well as keeping detailed records (preferably written by a legal counsel), of the shareholder meetings and the decisions made, may reduce the risk of future resentment and appeal as well. The parent generation may implement a professional Family Office that manages shareholder development, communication, and future inheritance planning. Families are a dynamic structure, and therefore the governance system needs constant reevaluation and even, at times, change to ensure continuous Active Ownership. A benefit of the present day, as opposed to what was available for the firms from the sample, is the state of research and knowledge on family ties. Today, business families can draw on a large pool of research findings and consultation on keeping family commitment afloat. Although even with these benefits, the task remains a challenge.

Phase 3: Actions after IPO The final phase of recommended active measures concerns itself with the family influence regarding the family shareholding quota.

---

[15] See Section 2.5.3. "The Concept of Active Ownership".

The analysis has revealed a 13-year threshold in which failures were remarkably more frequent. Hence, the recommendation clearly states a strict control of reductions in family-held shares within and beyond this period. Contractual specifications can manage unpredictable sales intentions by tying the shareholders to a mutual consent. Nevertheless, unpredictable situations, such as sudden inheritance or individual needs and wishes, may call for higher liquidity needs. Hence, separate financial reserves allow for shareholders to meet such sudden obligations without having to sell shares in the firm. A professional Family Office can set up a financial infrastructure which is individually tailored to the family's structure, needs, and wishes, and operates long-term wealth management. Family members may be very committed to the family and firm, but financial needs and wishes must be granted, in order to maintain the sympathetic commitment.

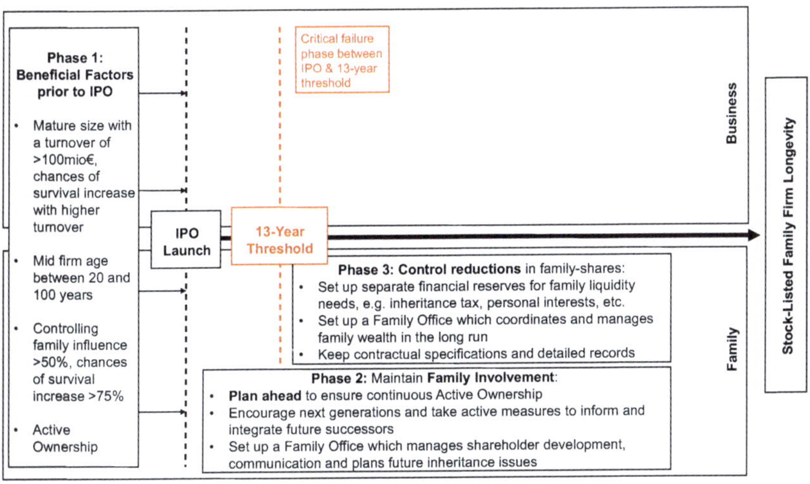

Figure 6.5 The Three Phases of Active Measures

The insightful findings of this study led to the development of the model of *Stock-Listed Family Firm Longevity* and subsequently to the *Three Phases of Active Measures*, offering recommendations that complement the research report on "Professionalizing the Business Family" by Binz Astrachan et al. (2020). They focus on how the business family can "professionalize" in order to provide a long-term constructive shareholding entity by channeling shareholder's values into the firm. Only by creating one joint force of family shareholders that act in concert can family firm longevity be ensured. As this study's findings show, such a joint force is even more important for stock-listed family firms.

With the recommendations on active measures for stock-listed family firm longevity, this dissertation comes to an end. Each family business is unique. And the family/ies behind the firm, even more so. The objective of this work was to examine the landscape of public family businesses and how they developed after IPO, in order to create a foundation of experience on which future decision-makers of family enterprises could base their decisions. By applying an explorative approach, the researcher was confronted with new insights along the line of the study. The approach called for attentiveness on behalf of the researcher in order to ensure the identification of these insights and thereby allow her to adapt the applied methods of analysis to cover all relevant angles of analysis. As a result, the combination of the quantitative survival analysis with the qualitative narrative approach came together to illuminate the data from various angles. By combining the findings, concrete results have been identified that contribute to theory-building on stock-listed firm longevity and allow for practical implications. Hence, by creating the model *Stock-Listed Family Firm Longevity* and the *Three Phases of Active Measures*, the researcher aspires to offer a glimpse of a yet unpredictable future.

References

Binz Astrachan, C., Waldkirch, M, Michiels, A., Pieper, T. & Bernhard, F. (2020). *Professionalizing the Business Family—The Five Pillars of Competent, Committed and Sustainable Ownership* (FFI Research Report). Retrieved from Family Firm Institute website: https://digital.ffi.org/pdf/ffi_professionalizing_the_business_family_v6.pdp.

Lantelme, M. (2023). *The Continuity and Discontinuity of the 250 Largest Enterprises in Germany: A History-Based Analysis of Family Influence, Corporate Development and Ownership Transactions* (Doctoral Thesis). Zeppelin University, Friedrichshafen.

Complete List of References

Achleitner, A.-K., Braun, R., Kaserer, C., Jarchow, S., Keppler, H. & Szewcyk, J. (2019). *Börsennotierte Familienunternehmen in Deutschland—Bedeutung, Merkmale, Performance.* München: Stiftung Familienunternehmen.

Ahmad, S., Omar, R. & Quoquab, F. (2020). Family firms´ sustainable longevity: the role of family involvement in business and innovation capability. *Journal of Family Business Management*, 11(1), 86–106.

Anderson, R.C. & Reeb, D.R. (2003). Founding family ownership and firm performance: evidence from the S&P 500. *The Journal of Finance*, 58(3), 1301–1328.

Andres, C. (2008). Large shareholders and firm performance—An empirical examination of founding-family ownership. *Journal of Corporate Finance*, 14, 431–445.

Anderson, J.A. (1984). Regression and Ordered Categorical Variables. *Journal of the Royal Statistical Society. Series B (Methodological)*, 46(1), 1–30.

Bauer, T. (2012). *Innovationen in Familienunternehmen—Eine empirische Studie.* Wiesbaden: Springer/Gabler.

Baus, K. (2013). *Die Familienstrategie—Wie Familien ihr Unternehmen über Generationen sichern (4. ed).* Wiesbaden: Springer-Gabler.

Basu, A. (2004). Entrepreneurial aspirations among family business owners: an analysis of ethnic business owners in the UK. *International Journal of Entrepreneurial Behavior and Research*, 10, 12–33.

Beck, S., Prügl, R. & Walter, K. (2020). Communicating the family firm brand: Antecedents and performance effects. *European Management Journal*, 38, 95–107.

Beck, S. & Prügl, R. (2018). Family firm reputation and humanization: Consumers and the trust advantage of family firms under different conditions of brand familiarity. *Family Business Review*, 31(4), 460–482.

Berghoff, H. & Köhler, I. (2020). *Verdienst und Vermächtnis—Familienunternehmen in Deutschland und den USA seit 1800.* Frankfurt: Campus.

Binz Astrachan, C., Waldkirch, M, Michiels, A., Pieper, T. & Bernhard, F. (2020). *Professionalizing the Business Family—The Five Pillars of Competent, Committed and Sustainable Ownership* (FFI Research Report). Retrieved from Family Firm Institute website: https://digital.ffi.org/pdf/ffi_professionalizing_the_business_family_v6.pdf.

Block, J.H. (2012). R&D investments in family and founder firms: An agency perspective. *Journal of Business Venturing*, 27, 248–265.

K. Stotmeister, *Publicly Traded Family Businesses*, Familienunternehmen und KMU, https://doi.org/10.1007/978-3-658-44303-0

Block, J.H. & Spiegel, F. (2013). Family firm density and regional innovation output: An exploratory analysis. *Journal of Family Business Strategy*, 4, 270–280.

Block, J. (2010). Family management, family ownership, and downsizing: Evidence from S&P 500 firms. *Family Business Review*, 23(2), 109–130.

Bremer, H. (1969). Grundzüge des deutschen und ausländischen Börsenrechts. In W. Kunkel, P. Lerche, W. Mieth & W. Vogt (Eds.), *Enzyklopädie der Rechts- und Staatswissenschaften*, pp. 1–205. Heidelberg: Springer.

Brown, J.M. (1970). Post-Offering Experience of Companies Going Public. *Journal of Business*, 3, 10–18.

Bundesgesetzblatt (1955). *Gesetz zur Bereinigung der auf Reichsmark lautenden Wertpapiere der Knversionskasse für deutsche Auslandsschulden (nr. 7)*. Bonn.

Bundeszentrale für politische Bildung (2016). *Wirtschaftswunder*. Retrieved from https://www.bpb.de/nachschlagen/lexika/lexikon-der-wirtschaft/21146/wirtschaftswunder.

Bundeszentrale für politische Bildung (2002). *Gesellschaftliche Entwicklung*. Retrieved from https://www.bpb.de/izpb/10124/gesellschaftliche-entwicklung.

Capital (2019). *Der Untergang des Handelskonzerns Co op*. Retrieved from https://www.capital.de/wirtschaft-politik/der-untergang-des-handelskonzerns-co-op.

Carpentier, C., L´Her, J.-F. & Suret, J.-M. (2008). Competition and Survival of Stock Exchanges: Lessons from Canada. *Review of Pacific Basin Financial Markets and Policies*, 11(2), 255–286.

Carpentier, C. & Suret, J.-M. (2011). The survival and success of Canadian penny stock IPOs. *Small Business Economics*, 36, 101–121.

Chancharat, N., Krishnamurti, C. & Tian, G. (2012). Board Structure and Survival of New Economy IPO Firms. *Corporate Governance: An International Review*, 20(2), 144–163.

Casillas, J.C., Moreno-Menéndez, A.M., Barbero, J.L. & Clinton, E. (2019). Retrenchment Strategies and Family Involvement: The Role of Survival Risk. *Family Business Review*, 32(1), 58–75.

Chirico, F., Gómez-Mejia, L.R., Hellerstedt, K., Withers, M. & Nordqvist, M. (2020). To Merge, Sell, or Liquidate? Socioemotional Wealth, Family Control, and the Choice of Business Exit. *Journal of Management*, 46(8), 1342–1379.

Cho, J., Miller, D. & Lee, J. (2018). Too much of a good thing: Family involvement and the survival of listed Korean firms. *Journal of Family Business Strategy*, 9, 223–237.

Churchill, G.A. & Brown, T.J. (2007). *Basic Marketing Research (6. Ed.)*. Mason, USA: South-Western College.

Cleves, M., Gould, W.W. & Marchenko, Y.V. (2016). *An Introduction to Survival Analysis Using Stata (3. ed)*. Texas: Stata Press.

Commerzbank (1954–2000). *Wer gehört zu wem—Mutter- und Tochtergesellschaften von A-Z (1.-20. ed.)*. Commerzbank Berlin. Hamburg: Hanseatische Druckanstalt.

Cox, D.R. (1972). Regression Models and Life-Tables. Read before the *Royal Statistical Society*, London, 187–202.

Cox, D.R. (1975). Partial Likelihood. *Biometrika*, 62 (2), 269–276.

Craig, J.B., Dibrell, C. & Garrett, R. (2014). Examining relationships among family influence, family culture, flexible planning systems, innovativeness and firm performance. *Journal of Family Business Strategy*, 5, 229–238.

Daepp, M.I.G., Hamilton, M.J., West, G.B. & Bettencourt, L.M.A. (2015). The mortality of companies. *The Royal Society Publishing*, 12, 1–8.

Deutsche Börse AG (2010). *1585—2010, Die Deutsche Börse feiert Jubiläum—eine Chronologie effizienter Märkte.* Düsseldorf: corps. Corporate Publishing Services GmbH. Retrieved from https://www.deutsche-boerse.com/resource/blob/321538/5d0c10548c7fe945fcff2a3d338d2856/data/jubilaeum425-1585_de.pdf.

Fiedler, M. (2016). *Tagung zur Genossenschaftsgeschichte: Entstehung und Untergang der Coop AG.* Zentralverband Deutscher Konsumgenossenschaften. Retrieved from https://www.zdk-hamburg.de/blog/2016/08/tagung-zur-genossenschaftsgeschichte-entstehung-und-untergang-der-coop-ag/.

Frankfurter Allgemeine Zeitung (2010). *Rekordminus für die deutsche Wirtschaft.* Retrieved from https://www.faz.net/aktuell/wirtschaft/konjunktur/bruttoinlandsprodukt-deutsche-wirtschaft-schrumpft-2009-um-fuenf-prozent-1911421/infografik-konjunkturzyklen-1917647.html#fotobox_1_911421.

Frankfurter Allgemeine Zeitung (2018). *Deutsche Börsengeschichte—Hightech im Kaiserreich.* Retrieved from https://www.faz.net/aktuell/finanzen/finanzmarkt/wie-die-boerse-den-aufstieg-der-wirtschaft-finanziert-hat-15526462.html.

Franks, J., Mayer, C. & Wagner, H.F. (2015). The Survival of the Weakest: Flourishing Family Firms in Germany. *Journal of Applied Corporate Finance*, 27(4), 27–35.

Fredebeul-Krein, T. (2012). *Koordinierter Einsatz von Direktmarketing und Verkaufsaussensdienst im B2B-Kontext - Grundlagen der explorativen Untersuchung*, pp. 65–92. Wiesbaden: Springer/Gabler.

Freeman, J., Carroll, G.R. & Hannan, M.T. (1983). The Liability of Newness: Age Dependence in Organizational Death Rates. *American Sociological Research*, 48, 692–710.

Frericks, S., Stotmeister, K. & Kormann, H. (in print, 2023). Extant Research and other Literature on Listed Family Enterprises. Fleischer, H. & Prigge, S. (Eds)., Listed family Companies. Hamburg Conference 2021: Law and Management of Family Firms.

Gagné, M., Sharma, P. & De Massis, A. (2014). The study of organizational behavior in family business. *European Journal of Work and Organizational Psychology*, 23, 643–656.

Gambatese, J.A. & Hallowell, M. (2011). Enabling and measuring innovation in the construction industry. *Construction Management and Economics*, 29, 553–567.

Glaser, B.G. & Strauss, A.L. (2010). *Grounded Theory—Strategien qualitativer Forschung (3. ed).* Bern: Huber.

Hair Jr., J.F., Celsi, M., Money, A., Samouel, P. & Page, M. (2016). *Essentials of Business Research Methods (3. Ed.).* New York: Routledge.

Hair Jr., J.F., Black, W.C., Babin, B.J. & Anderson, R.E. (2019). *Multivariate Data Analysis (8. Ed.).* Hampshire: Cengage.

Harhoff, D. & Wagner, S. (2009). The Duration of Patent Examination at the European Patent Office. *Management Science*, 55 (12), 1969–1984.

Heilemann, U. (2019). Rezessionen in der Bundepublik Deutschland von 1966–2013. *Wirtschaftsdienst—Zeitschrift für Wirtschaftspolitik*, ed. 8, 546–551, retrieved from https://www.wirtschaftsdienst.eu/inhalt/jahr/2019/heft/8/beitrag/rezessionen-in-der-bundesrepublik-deutschland-von-1966-bis-2013.html.

Hengstmann, W. (1935). *Die Familiengesellschaft. Dissertation der Rechts- und Staatswissenschaftliche Fakultät der Martin-Luther-Universität Halle-Wittenberg.* Berlin: Triltsch & Huther.

Hewel, B. (1980). *Konjunktur und Wachstum—Theorie und Politik.* Wiesbaden: Gabler Verlag.

Jain, B.A. & Kini, O. (2000). Does the Presence of Venture Capitalists Improve the Survival Profile of IPO Firms? *Journal of Business & Accounting*, 27(9), 1139–1176.

Jain, B.A. & Kini, O. (2008). The Impact of Strategic Investment Choices on Post-Issue Operating Performance and Survival of US IPO Firms. *Journal of Business Finance & Accounting*, 35(3), 259–490.

James, H.S. (1999). Owner as manager, extended horizons and the family firm. *International Journal of the Economics of Business*, 6(1), 41–55.

Khurshed, A. (2000). *Discussion of* Does the Presence of Venture Capitalists Improve the Survival Profile of IPO Firms? *Journal of Business Finance & Accounting*, 27(9), 1177–1183.

Kiefer, N. M. (1988). Economic Duration Data and Hazard Functions. *Journal of Economic Literature*, 16, 646–679.

Kim, Y. & Gao, F.Y. (2012). Does family involvement increase business performance? Family-longevity goals´ moderating role in Chinese family firms. *Journal of Business Research*, 66, 265–274.

Klasa, S. (2007). Why Do Controlling Families of Public Firms Sell Their Remaining Ownership Stake? *Journal of Financial and Quantitative Analysis*, 42(2), 339–368.

Klein, S.B. (2000). Family Businesses in Germany: Significance and Structure. *Family Business Review*, 13(3), 157–182.

Knur, A. (1941). *Die Familiengesellschaft. Eine vergleichende Untersuchung der Unternehmensformen.* München: Franz Vahlen.

Koch, W. & Wegmann, J. (2000). *Praktiker-Handbuch Börseneinführung—Ablauf des Börsengangs mittelständischer Unternehmen—mit Erfahrungsberichten vom Neuen Markt (3. ed.).* Stuttgart: Schäffer-Poeschel.

Kohler, U. & Kreuter, F. (2016). *Datenanalyse mit Stata—Allgemeine Konzepte der Datenanalyse und ihre praktische Anwendung.* Berlin: De Gruyter.

Kormann, H. & Wimmer, R. (2018). Vom Ursprung der Forschung zu Familienunternehmen. *Zeitschrift für Familienunternehmen und Strategie*, 05, 148–153.

Kormann, H. & Schlippe, A.v. (2017). Börsennotierung des Familienunternehmens—Ein Ansatz zur Überbrückung von Paradoxien und seine Erfolgsaussichten. *Zeitschrift für Familienunternehmen und Strategie*, 06, 200–205.

Kraiczy, N.D., Hack, A. & Kellermanns, F.W. (2014). New product portfolio performance in family firms. *Journal of Business Research*, 67, 1065–1073.

Lantelme, M. (2017). *The Rise and Downfall of Germany´s Largest Family and Non-Family Businesses—A Historical Study and Strategic Analysis from 1971 to 2011.* Wiesbaden: Springer Gabler.

Lantelme, M., Seibold, L.K.C. & Kormann, H. (2021). *German Family Enterprises—A Sourcebook of Structure, Growth, Downfall and Corporate Longevity* (2. ed.). Cham: Springer Nature.

Lantelme, M. (2023). *The Continuity and Discontinuity of the 250 Largest Enterprises in Germany: A History-Based Analysis of Family Influence, Corporate Development and Ownership Transactions* (Doctoral Thesis). Zeppelin University, Friedrichshafen.

Le Breton-Miller, I. & Miller, D. (2006). Why do some family businesses out-compete? Governance, long-term orientation, and sustainable capability. *Entrepreneurship Theory and Practice*, 30(6), 731–746.

Lindow. C.M., Stubner, S. & Wulf, T. (2010). Strategic fit within family firms: The role of family influence and the effect on performance. *Journal of Family Business Strategy*, 1, 167–178.

Löhde, A.S.K., Calabrò, A. & Torchia, M. (2020). Understanding the main drivers of family firm longevity: the role of business family learning. *International Studies of Management & Organization*, 50(2), 130–152.

Lude, M. & Prügl, R. (2018). Why the family business brand matters: Brand authenticity and the family firm trust inference. *Journal of Business Research*, 89, 121–134.

Lumpkin, G.T. & Dess, G.G. (1996). Clarifying the entrepreneurial orientation construct and linking it to performance. *Academy of Management Review*, 21 (1), 135–172.

Lumpkin, G.T., Brigham, K.H. & Moss, T.W. (2010). Long-term orientation: implications for the entrepreneurial orientation and performance of family businesses. *Entrepreneurship & Regional Development*, 22(3–4), 241–264.

Manager Magazin (2001). *Missmanagement bei Coop—Das fast perfekte Verbrechen.* Retrieved from https://www.manager-magazin.de/unternehmen/missmanagement/a-149040.html.

Mey, G. & Mruck, K. (2011). Grounded-Theory Methodologie: Entwicklung, Stand, Perspektiven. In G. Mey & K. Mruck (Eds.), *Grounded Theory Reader* (2nd ed.), pp. 11–48. Wiesbaden: VS Verlag für Sozialwissenschaften.

Moya, M.F., Pérez, P.F. & Lubinski, C. (2020). Standing the test of time: External factors influencing family firm longevity in Germany and Spain during the twentieth century. *Journal of Evolutionary Studies in Business*, 5(1), 221–264.

Naldi, L., Nordquist, M., Sjöberg, K. & Wiklund, J. (2007). Entrepreneurial Orientation, Risk Taking, and Performance in Family Firms. *Family Business Review*, 20(1), 33–47.

Niehm, L.S., Miller, N.J., Shelley II, M.C. & Fitzgerald, M.A. (2009). Small Family Business Survival: Strategies For Coping With Overlapping Family And Business Demands. *Journal of Developmental Entrepreneurship*, 14(3), 209–232.

Oakes, D. (2000). Survival Analysis. *Journal of the American Statistical Association*, 95(449), 282–285.

Parker, S.C. (2016). Family Firms and the "Willing Successor" Problem. *Entrepreneurship, Theory and Practice*, Nov. 2016, 1241–1259.

Peter, S. (2009). *Preussag: vom Staatskonzern zum Privateigentum.* Retrieved from https://www.ndr.de/geschichte/chronologie/Preussag-Vom-Staatskonzern-zum-Privateigentum,preussag100.html.

Pieper, T.M. (2010). Non solus: Toward a psychology of family business. *Journal of family Business Strategy*, 1, 26–39.

Pieper, T.M., Astrachan, J.H. & Manners, G.E. (2013). Conflict in Family Business: Common Metaphors and Suggestions for Intervention. *Family Relations*, 62, 490–500.

Presse- und Informationsamt der Bundesregierung (2015). *Deutsche Einheit—Regierungsdokumente und Erklärungen aus den Jahren 1989–1991.*. Retrieved from https://archiv.bundesregierung.de/resource/blob/975236/237440/63b9cde71a07804a8ee297d1561cd1ed/2009-11-16-regierungsdokumente-20-jahre-dt-einheit-data.pdf?download=1.

Rau, S. B. (2013). Emotions Preventing Survival of Family Firms: Comments on Exploring the Emotional Nexus in Cogent Family Business Archetypes: Towards a Predominant Business Model Inclusive of the Emotional Dimension. In *Special Issue—A New Business Model: The Emotional Dimension of* Organizations, 3(3), De Gruyter, 425–432.

Rauschendorfer, N., Prügl, R. & Lude, M. (2021). Love is in the air. Consumers´ perception of products from firms signaling their family nature. *Psychology & Marketing*, 39(1), 239–249.

Rost, J. (2003). Zeitgeist und Moden empirischer Analysemethoden. In *Von Generation zu Generation*, pp. 21–31. Retrieved from https://www.ssoar.info/ssoar/bitstream/handle/document/50712/ssoar-2002-rost-Zeitgeist_und_Moden_empirischer_Analysemethoden.pdf?sequence=1&isAllowed=y&lnkname=ssoar-2002-rost-Zeitgeist_und_Moden_empirischer_Analysemethoden.pdf

Rudolph, B. (1992). Die Entwicklung der Börse von 1945 bis in die heutige Zeit. *Börse als Informationsdrehscheibe und Handelsplatz*. 15. Symposium zur Bankengeschichte am 5. Juni 1992 in der Frankfurter Wertpapierbörse-IHK, Frankfurt.

Ruiz Jiménez, M.C., Vallejo Martos, M.C. & Martínez Jiménez, R. (2015). Organizational Harmony as a Value in Family Business and Its Influence on Performance. *Journal of Business Ethics*, 126, 259–272.

Rüsen, T.A., Kleve, H. & Schlippe, A.v. (2021). *Management der dynastischen Unternehmerfamilie—Zwischen Familie, Organisation und Netzwerk*. Heidelberg: Springer.

Sander, B. (2008). *Börsenerfolg Familienunternehmen—Höhere Rendite mit GEX-Werten.* München: FinanzBuch Verlag.

Santarelli, E. & Lotti, F. (2005). The Survival of Family Firms: The Importance of Control and Family Ties. *International Journal of the Economics of Business*, 12(2), 183–192.

Schlippe, A.v., Nischak, A. & El Hachimi, M. (2011). *Familienunternehmen verstehen—Gründer, Gesellschafter und Generationen* (2. ed.). Göttingen: Vandenhoeck & Ruprecht.

Schlippe, A.v., Groth, T. & Rüsen, T. (2018). *Die beiden Seiten der Unternehmerfamilie: Familienstrategie über Generationen* (2. ed.). Göttingen: V&R Verlag.

Schlittgen, R. (2012). *Angewandte Zeitreihenanalyse mit R (2. ed).* München: Oldenbourg.

Scholes, L. & Wilson, N. (2014). The Importance of Family Trust in Family Firm Governance. *Entrepreneurship Theory and Practice*, 38(6), 1285–1293.

Schürmann, W. (1980). *Familienunternehmen und Börse—Emittieren, warum und wie?.* Wiesbaden: Gabler.

Schürmann, W. & Körfgen, K. (1987). *Familienunternehmen auf dem Weg zur Börse* (2. ed.). München: Beck.

Schürmann, W. & Körfgen, K. (1997). *Familienunternehmen auf dem Weg zur Börse* (3. ed.). München: Beck.

Seibold, L.K.C. (2019). *Family Businesses´ Growth—Unpacking the Black Box.* Wiesbaden: Springer-Gabler Verlag.

Sreejesh, S., Mohapatra, S. & Anusree, M.R. (2014). *Business Research Methods—An Applied Orientation.* Switzerland: Springer International.

Stafford, K., Bhargava, V., Danes, S.M., Haynes, G. & Brewton, K.E. (2010). Factors Associated with Long-Term Survival of Family Businesses: Duration Analysis. *Journal offamily and Economic Issues*, 31, 442–457.

Stafford, K., Danes, S.M. & Haynes, G.W. (2013). Long-term firm survival and growth considering owning family adaptive capacity and federal disaster assistance receipt. *Journal of Family Business Strategy*, 4, 188–200.

Statistisches Bundesamt (2008a). *Klassifikation der Wirtschaftszweige—Gleiderung mit Erläuterung, Ausgabe 2008 (WZ 2008).* Wiesbaden, Germany. Retrieved from https://www.klassifikationsserver.de/klassService/jsp/common/url.jsf?variant=wz2008.

Statistisches Bundesamt (2008b). *Klassifikation der Wirtschaftszweige—mit Erläuterungen, Ausgabe 2008 (WZ 2008).* Wiesbaden, Germany. Retrieved from https://www.klassifikationsserver.de/klassService/jsp/common/url.jsf?variava=wz2008.

Statistisches Bundesamt (2008c). *German Classification of Economic Activities, Edition 2008 (WZ 2008).* Wiesbaden, Germany. Retrieved from https://www.destatis.de/DE/Methoden/Klassifikationen/Gueter-Wirtschaftsklassifikationen/Downloads/klassifikation-wz-2008-englisch.html.

Statistisches Bundesamt (2008d). *Kurzanleitung Wirtschaftszweigklassifikation.* Wiesbaden, Germany. Retrieved from https://www.bafa.de/SharedDocs/Downloads/DE/Wirtschafts_Mittelstandsfoerderung/unb_kurzanleitung_wirtschaftszweigklassifikation.html.

Steen, A. & Welch, L.S. (2006). Dancing With Giants: Acquisition and Survival of the Family Firm. *Family Business Review*, 19(4), 289–300.

Stiftung Familienunternehmen (2019). *Die volkswirtschaftliche Bedeutung der Familienunternehmen (5. ed.).* München: Stiftung Familienunternehmen.

Tellis, G.J., Prabhu, J.C. & Chandy, R.K. (2009). Radical Innovation across Nations: The Preeminence of Corporate Culture. *Journal of Marketing*, 73, 3–23.

Titscher, S., Meyer, M., Wodak, R. & Vetter, E. (2000). *Methods of Text and Disclosure Analysis—In Search of Meaning.* London: Sage.

Vallejo, M.C. (2008). Is the Culture of Family Firms Really Different? A Value-based Model for Its Survival through Generations. *Journal of Business Ethics*, 81, 261–279.

Villalonga, B. & Amit, R. (2006). How do family ownership, control and management affect firm value? *Journal of Financial Economics*, 80, 385–417.

Wilbon, A.D. (2002). Predicting survival of high-technology initial public offering firms. *Journal of High Technology Management Research*, 13, 127–141.

Williams Jr, R.I., Pieper, T.M., Kellermanns, F.W. & Astrachan, J.H. (2018). Family Firm Goals and their Effects on Strategy, Family and Organization Behavior: A Review and Research Agenda. *International Journal of management Reviews*, 20, 63–82.

Wiklund, J., Nordquist, M., Hellerstedt, K. & Bird, M. (2013). Internal versus external ownership transition in family firms: An embeddedness perspective. *Entrepreneurship Theory and Practice*, 37, 1319–1340.

Zellweger, T.M., Eddleston, K.A. & Kellermanns, F.W. (2010). Exploring the concept of familiness: Introducing family firm identity. *Journal of Family Business Strategy*, 1(1), 54–63.

Zellweger, T.M., Kellermanns, F.W., Eddleston, K.A. & Memili, E. (2012). Building a family firm image: How family firms capitalize on their family ties. *Journal of Family Business Strategy*, 3(4), 239–250.

Zellweger, T.M., Nason, R.S. & Nordquist, M. (2012). From longevity of Firms to Transgenerational Entrepreneurship of Families: Introducing Family Entrepreneurial Orientation. *Family Business Review*, 25(2), 136–155.

Ziegler, A., Lange, S. & Bender, R. (2004). Überlebenszeitanalyse: Die Cox-Regression. *Deutsche Medizinische Wochenschrift,* 129, T1–T3.

MIX
Papier aus verantwortungsvollen Quellen
Paper from responsible sources
FSC® C105338

If you have any concerns about our products,
you can contact us on
ProductSafety@springernature.com

In case Publisher is established outside the EU,
the EU authorized representative is:
Springer Nature Customer Service Center GmbH
Europaplatz 3, 69115 Heidelberg, Germany

Printed by Libri Plureos GmbH
in Hamburg, Germany